L. E. RU(

A
PERSONAL NARRATIVE
OF THE
SIEGE OF LUCKNOW
FROM ITS COMMENCEMENT TO ITS RELIEF
BY SIR COLIN CAMPBELL

Elibron Classics
www.elibron.com

Elibron Classics series.

© 2005 Adamant Media Corporation.

ISBN 1-4021-7315-6 (paperback)
ISBN 1-4021-0145-7 (hardcover)

This Elibron Classics Replica Edition is an unabridged facsimile of the edition published in 1858 by Longman, Brown, Green, Longmans, & Roberts, London.

Elibron and Elibron Classics are trademarks of Adamant Media Corporation. All rights reserved.

This book is an accurate reproduction of the original. Any marks, names, colophons, imprints, logos or other symbols or identifiers that appear on or in this book, except for those of Adamant Media Corporation and BookSurge, LLC, are used only for historical reference and accuracy and are not meant to designate origin or imply any sponsorship by or license from any third party.

A

PERSONAL NARRATIVE

OF THE

SIEGE OF LUCKNOW.

LONDON:
PRINTED BY SPOTTISWOODE AND CO.
NEW-STREET SQUARE.

Sir Henry Lawrence, K.C.B.
From a Photograph taken at Lucknow.

London Longman & Co.

A

PERSONAL NARRATIVE

OF THE

SIEGE OF LUCKNOW

FROM ITS COMMENCEMENT TO ITS RELIEF
BY SIR COLIN CAMPBELL.

BY

L. E. RUUTZ REES

ONE OF THE SURVIVING DEFENDERS.

WITH A PLAN OF LUCKNOW AND THE RESIDENCY
AND
A PORTRAIT OF SIR HENRY LAWRENCE.

SECOND EDITION.

LONDON:
LONGMAN, BROWN, GREEN, LONGMANS, & ROBERTS.
1858.

TO

DAVID INGLIS MONEY, ESQ., C.S.

My dear Mr. Money,

    It is with feelings of great pleasure that I avail myself of your kind permission to dedicate this volume to you; and independently of the satisfaction it affords me, I feel sure that it will be a gratification to you, to see recorded in my pages, however imperfectly, events in which your own Son, Mr. William Money, bore so prominent a part.

              I remain,

                    With great respect,

                          Yours sincerely,

                                L. E. R. REES.

London: *March* 1858.

PREFACE.

Those who read the following pages may wish to know who it is, that, with a pen so little skilled in authorship, and a hand still less accustomed to a sword, ventures to appear before them as an author and a soldier. The writer must indeed confess himself more surprised at his boldness in facing the public in type, than at his having faced the enemy in the trenches.

It will suffice to say that a Calcutta merchant, formerly attached to the Martinière College of Lucknow, unexpectedly found himself entangled in the meshes of the siege of that city, and having been by force of circumstances obliged to take his part in the defence, he recorded, from time to time, the events in which he was concerned, and those which passed before him.

Some friends in Calcutta, and among them Mr. David Money, to whom he had shown his Journal, were pleased to think that it might prove of interest to a wider circle of readers; and, encouraged by their friendly advice, he has ventured to let it see the light. His friend, Mr. John Lawrence, of the Uncovenanted Service, kindly placed at his disposal the notes which he had taken during the siege, and has thus enabled the author to enrich his Journal with much valuable information, apart from his own personal experiences.

In addition to this valuable aid, on his arrival in England, he is also indebted to the obliging permission to make use of the Journal kept by Lady Inglis, and the correspondence of Lieut. Farquhar, of the 7th B. L. C., which have respectively been printed for private use by their friends in this country.

A work of so little pretension requires no further preface. All that the writer feels impelled further to express, is his gratitude to that great and good man, Sir Henry Lawrence, to Brigadier Inglis, and to those noble soldiers who maintained the siege, as well as to Generals Havelock, Outram, and Sir Colin Campbell, by whose timely aid, under Providence, he feels unspeakably indebted for his own deliverance and that of others, from the torture and massacre, which, without their perseverance, courage, and skill, must inevitably have been his own fate and the common lot of all.

LONDON, 1858.

CONTENTS.

CHAPTER I.

THE FIRST DISTURBANCES IN LUCKNOW. — MAY.

My Journey to the North-west.— A pleasant travelling Companion. — Panic at Benares. — Allahabad. — Cawnpore. — Post to Lucknow. — Disturbed State of Oude. — Fate of Mr. and Mrs. White. — Sir Henry Lawrence's precautionary Measures. — Mutiny of the Seventh Oude Irregulars. — The Chief Commissioner's Levee and Address to the Sepoys. — Expedition towards Agra of Captain Hayes and Major Gall. — Murder of Captain Hayes, Mr. Fayrer, and Lieutenant Barber. — Escape to Cawnpore of Lieutenant Carey. — Major Gall's Fate. — Waking to a disagreeable Reality. — Mutiny of the 30th May. — Conversation with a Rebel. — A Game at Billiards interrupted. — Brigadier Handscombe's Death. — Murder of Lieutenant Grant. — Narrow Escape of Ladies in Cantonments. — Defeat and Pursuit of the Rebels. — Cornet Raleigh's tragic End. — Murder of Mr. Mendes   -   Page 1

CHAP. II.

LUCKNOW BEFORE THE SIEGE. — JUNE.

State of the Oude Districts. — The Native Police. — The City of Lucknow. — Martial Law. — Prisoners hanged. — Joy of the Acquitted. — News of Cawnpore. — Closure of Postal Communications. — Sir Hugh Wheeler. — Devotion of his Messenger. — Depreciation of Company's Paper.— Appearance of the Residency.— The Fort of Muchee Bhawn. — Discontent of the People of Lucknow. — Fanaticism of the Mussulman Population. — Anecdote.— Our Volunteer Cavalry. — Sir Henry Lawrence. — Policy of evacuating Oude. — Cholera. — Fatal Quarrel and Retribution. — Running a-muck. — Our State Prisoners - - Page 21

CHAP. III.

TRAGIC SCENES.

Major Marriott's Expedition. — Murder of Captain Burmester and Ensign Farquharson. — Death of Captain Staples. — Lieutenant Boulton's miraculous Escape. — Lieutenant Bax's Death. — Lieutenant J. Longueville Clarke's Gallantry and Capture of Fuzel Ally. — Death of himself and his Companions. — Uncertainty of the Fate of others in the Out-stations. — Wholesale Butchery of the Shahjehanpore Refugees. — Captain Patrick Orr and his Family saved. — Refugees from Duriabad, Secrora, and Seetapore. — Lieutenant Farquhar's Description of the State of the remaining Men of the Native Regiments. — Captain Adolphe Orr's perilous Position — Mutiny of the Military Cavalry Police. — Captain Weston's daring Act. — Mutiny of the Military Infantry Police. — Treason in our Camp. — Captain Adolphe Orr's miraculous Escape. — Anecdote. — Our Pursuit. — Mr. Thornhill wounded. — Retreat of the Mutineers. — Masonic Dinner on St. John's Day - - - - - - - 44

CHAP. IV.

THE BATTLE OF CHINHUTT.

Reconnoitring Party to Chinhutt. — Gallantry of Lieutenant Campbell and others. — Our Force moves from the Bailey-guard. — The Enemy's Acquaintance with our Plans. — The Kokrail Bridge. — Chinhutt. — Ishmaelpore. — Our Positions. — The Battle. — Colonel Case's Heroic Death. — Our Native Infantry. — The Enemy's

CONTENTS. xiii

Manœuvres. — Treachery of the Police Force and Native Gunners. — Our Retreat. — The Enemy's Cavalry cut up our Men.— Anecdote. — Our Artillery. — Europeans in the Enemy's Ranks. —Gallant Behaviour of our Volunteer Cavalry. — Incident of the Rebellion.—Noble Conduct of our Sepoys.—Lieutenant Farquhar swallows a Ball. — Sir Henry Lawrence in Action. — Defence of the Iron Bridge. — Beginning of the Siege.— Extracts from Lady Inglis's Interesting Journal. — Mr. John Lawrence's graphic Account of the Battle - - - - - - - Page 64

CHAP. V.

THE RESIDENCY ENTRENCHMENTS.

Panic in Lucknow. — The Hospital. —Kindness of the Women to the Wounded. — Remarkable Appearance of the City.— The Prisoners Escape. — Description of our Entrenchments. — Captain Anderson's House. — The Cawnpore Battery. — The School-houses. — The Brigade Mess. — The Sikh Square. — Gubbins's Battery. — The Bhoosa-guard. — The Residency. — The Hospital. — The Bailey-guard. — Dr. Fayrer's House. — The Post Office. — The Financial Outpost. — Sago's Outpost. — The Judicial Garrison. — The Jail. — The Begum's Kothy - 91

CHAP. VI.

LUCKNOW DURING THE FIRST TWO WEEKS OF THE SIEGE.

The Siege begins.—Barricades formed.— The Enemy's Artillery commanded by European Officers. — Lady Inglis's Journal. — Abandonment and Explosion of Fort Muchee Bhawn.— Anecdote. — Death of Sir Henry Lawrence. — Attack on the Bailey-guard Gate.—Johannes' House. — Cawnpore Battery.— Death of Mr. Ommaney and others. — Welcome Shower of Rain.—Deaths in the Garrison - - - - - - - - 114

CHAP. VII.

THE SECOND WEEK OF THE SIEGE.

My Journal. — Successful Sortie. — Death of Major Francis. — Another Sortie. — Daring Act of our Soldiers. — Interesting Missiles. — Beale. — Sad Reflections. — Death of Mr. Alexander Bryson. — Change of Garrison. — Expected Reinforcements. — An Attack. — Our Privations and Sufferings begin. — Captain Alexander wounded. — Attack on Gubbins's Battery. — Garrison Laws of Amputation. — The Enemy's warlike Shouts. — Despondency. — Our inside Annoyances. — My Luxuries diminish. P. 131

CHAP. VIII.

THE GRAND ATTACK OF THE TWENTIETH OF JULY.

"To Arms!" — Renegade Traitors. — Fierce Assault of the Rebels. — The Sick turn out. — Explosion of the Enemy's Mines and Attack on the Redan. — Lieutenant Loughnan's gallant Defence of Innes' Outpost. — Scaling Ladders. — Hardingham's Escape. — Erith Shot. — Conversation between Bailey and the Insurgents. — Anecdote. — The Enemy are beaten. — Attack on Sago's Financial, Judicial, and Anderson's Garrisons. — Defeat of the Insurgents at the Brigade Mess and Gubbins's Battery. — Lieutenant M'Farlane. — Loss of the Enemy. — After the Battle 143

CHAP. IX.

OUR TROUBLES INCREASE.

Constant cannonading. — Death of Major Banks. — Brigadier Inglis and Mr. Gubbins. — Mr. Polehampton, the Chaplain, dies. — Hospital Scenes. — Death and Disease. — Erith's Death. — Pigeon killed. — Friends in Hospital. — Mr. Thompson's Kindness to the Sick. — Dr. Scott. — Hospital Surgeons. — The Plague of "Flies." — The Martinière Pupils. — Rain. — News of coming Reinforcements. — The Enemy's Interruption to our Songs. — A sham

Attack.— "Hope deferred maketh the heart sick."— The Enemy's Mines.— Captain Fulton's Master-mind.— Our Casualties.— Dr. Brydon of Jellalabad and Lucknow - - Page 159

CHAP. X.

AUGUST.— THE MONTH OF MINES.

Our daily Food.— Captain Fulton's mining Operations.— Hely's Death.— Cholera.— Hope.— Disappointment.— Revelry of the Insurgents.— Their Taunts.— The Enemy's Mines discovered and blown up.— Attack of August 10th.— Explosion of their Mine at Sago's and miraculous Escape of two Soldiers.— Explosion and Attack on the Brigade Mess.— "Turk" as "Luchminia."— Blenman wounded.— Brice's Death.— Death of Major Anderson.— Anecdote.— Refractory Conduct of a Civilian.— Retribution - - - - - - 174

CHAP. XI.

AUGUST CONTINUED.— SORTIES.

Despair.— Captain Fulton's Successes.— War with Brickbats.— Our Artillery Officers.— Deaths.— An Episode of War.— Bitter Thoughts.— Hairbreadth Escapes.— Successful Explosion of the Enemy's Mine.— Orr's Miraculous Escape.— The Enemy repulsed. —Sortie.— "Bob the Nailer."— Sally out.— Other Sorties.— The Mohurrsun.— Desertion of Sergeant Jones and others.— Our Natives disheartened.— News from the outer world.— Character brought out by the Siege.— Our Casualties in August - 187

CHAP. XII.

THE SEPTEMBER MONTH.

Famine Prices.— Valuable Cigars.— Commotion among the Rebels. — On the Alert.— Mines and Countermines.— Attack of the 5th September.— Quiet Days.— Sudden Death.— Death of Captain Fulton.— His Eulogy.— Fatal Error.— Deprat's Death.—

CONTENTS.

The Protestant and Roman Catholic Clergymen. — Deprat's Military Experiences in Africa. — Offer of Service from the Nana. — Conversation with the Insurgents. — Characteristic Anecdote. — The only Effective Artillery Officer. — Casualties. — Suicide. — Continuation of my Journal. — Signs of Coming Reinforcements.
Page 205

CHAP. XIII.

HAVELOCK'S REINFORCEMENTS ARRIVE. — THE TWENTY-FIFTH OF SEPTEMBER.

Our Reinforcements arrive. — Street Fighting. — Providence. — Our Friends enthusiastically received. — The Cawnpore Massacre. — My Agent's Death. — News of the Indian Stations. — A Feast. — The Hornpipe. — Havelock's Victories. — The Nana. — A fit Retribution. — The Cawnpore Slaughter-house. — Havelock defeats the Enemy in every Engagement. — His Return to Cawnpore. — General Outram's characteristic Generosity. — Advance upon Lucknow. — The Volunteer Cavalry. — The Storming of the Alumbagh. — Reception of the Enemy's Cavalry. — The Battle of the Charbagh. — A Wily Foe. — Fire from the Kaiserbagh. — The Bagpipe a rare Instrument of Salvation. — Every House a Fort. — The "Forlorn Hope." — General Neill's Death - 222

CHAP. XIV.

THE TWENTY-SIXTH OF SEPTEMBER.

Horrible Fate of some of our Wounded. — Captain Arnold's frightful Situation. — Colonel Campbell's Position. — Colonel Napier and "Hell-fire Jack." — Attack of Colonel Purcell and the 32nd. — Noble Devotion of our Sepoys. — Honour to whom Honour is due. — Heroic Deaths. — Sir 'James Outram. — Wounded Officers. — Losses of the Volunteer Cavalry. — The 1st Madras Fusiliers and 78th Highlanders. — Sorrowful End of Lieutenant Jolie. — The 84th and 90th Regiments. — Havelock's heavy Sacrifice. — Our true Saviours. — Ruined Condition of our Entrenchments - - - - - - 239

CHAP. XV.

LUCKNOW AFTER HAVELOCK'S ARRIVAL.

Our extended Positions. — African Rifleman's Contempt of our Shells. — The Tehree Kothee. — The Order of the Day. — Embarras de Richesses. — Luxuries. — The Second Chapter of the Siege. — Sir Henry Lawrence's Foresight. — Purchase of Food. — Hunger imperative. — Kossids. — Position of our Men at the Alumbagh. — Our Colours and Band. — Indomitable Perseverance of our Foe. — Effect of our Shot and Shell upon the Enemy's Positions. — Picturesque Aspect of the City of Lucknow. — Meeting with old Friends. — Captain Alexander Orr. — Goldsworthy. — Berrill. — The Intelligence Department. — The Rebel King. — His Minister and Council. — The Commander-in-Chief of the Insurgents. — Danger of high Offices with the Mutineers. — The People of Lucknow. — Punishment for Adhesion to our Cause. — European Prisoners in the hands of the Enemy. — Rajah Man Sing of Sultanpore. — A Friend turned Foe. — The Rebels offer to treat with Sir James Outram. — An insolent Proposal. — Mutual Threats. — Fate of the Native Prisoners with the Insurgents. — Native Gratitude - - - - - - Page 250

CHAP. XVI.

OUR SORTIES AND DEFENSIVE OPERATIONS.

Lieutenant Lowe's Sally. — Lieutenant Hughes and Mr. Sinclair wounded. — Major Stephenson's Sortie unsuccessful. — Lieutenant Hardinge's Gallantry and Success. — Sorties of the 29th September. — Major Apthorp. — Death of Mr. Lucas. — Captain M'Cabe falls while leading his fourth Sortie. — Captain Shute's Attack on Hill's House. — Anecdotes. — Colonel Napier's Attack on Phillips' Battery. — Repairs of our Entrenchments. — Our Engineering Operations. — Easy Capture of "the Mound." — Strengthening our Position. — Sergeant Purdell shot at my side. — Death of my Captain. — Our Losses. — Affecting Death-bed Scene. — Sorrow and Joy. — Scientific Construction of the Enemy's Batteries. — Captain Crommelin's Engineering Works. — The Enemy's Mines. — Successful Repulse of the Enemy's Attack. — Our Mining Operations - - - - - Page 270

CHAP. XVII.

CONTINUATION OF THE SIEGE.

Notes from my Journal. — News of the Fall of Delhi. — Position of Alumbagh. — Death of Mr. Thornhill. — Reward to the Uncovenanted. — Injustice to non-Government Volunteers. — Prize Jewels. — General Outram's Division Order. — Reward of our Sepoys. — Auctions in our Garrison. — Brigadier Inglis's Improvements within the old Entrenchments. — Dr. Scott's Hospital Arrangements. — Commissariat Reductions. — Our Treasure Exhumed. — Sanitary Measures. — Fortifying of our New Positions. — Successful Explosion of our Mines. — Loss of the Enemy. — Captain Brasyer's Sikhs and our other Troops. — News of Sir Colin Campbell's Approach. — Our Intelligence Department. — Telegraph Signals - - - - - 289

CHAP. XVIII.

KAVANAGH'S EXPLOIT. — OUR OFFENSIVE OPERATIONS.

Mr. Kavanagh volunteers to carry Despatches. — His interesting Narrative. — Mrs. Kavanagh. — Lieutenant Hutchinson's Mines. — Havelock's offensive Operations. — Explosion of our Mines. — Our Attacks upon the Hirukhana, Engine House, King's Stables, Captain Lockhart's Post. — Ardour of our Troops. — Havelock's Success. — Our Casualties - - - - 302

CHAP. XIX.

SIR COLIN CAMPBELL'S OPERATIONS.

Sir Colin Campbell advances upon Lucknow. — His Force. — Lieutenant Gough's brilliant Charge. — Capture of the Dilkusha. —

Attack upon the Martinière College.—Captain Bourchier repulses the Enemy.—Advance upon the Secundrabagh.—Brigadier Hope's Charge.—Storming of the Secundrabagh Buildings.—The Enemy's desperate Resistance.—Emulation between Europeans and Sikhs. — Immense Slaughter of the Rebels.— Brigadier-General Grant's and Captain Peel's Naval Brigade.— Assault on the Shah Nudguff.— Attack upon the Mess House.— Capture of the Observatory.— Enemy's Attack repulsed.— Meeting between Sir Colin Campbell and Generals Outram and Havelock.— Havelock's Harangue.— His wonderful Self-command.—Officers who distinguished themselves.— Mr. Kavanagh's and Lord Seymour's Services.—Sir Colin Campbell's Despatch.—Sir Colin's Losses.—List of Officers killed - - - Page 316

CHAP. XX.

THE RELIEF OF LUCKNOW.—EVACUATION OF THE RESIDENCY.

Lucknow relieved.—The Sweets of Liberty.— New Delights.— The Letter-bag.—Anxiety of my Friends.—Death of Mr. Cameron.— Mr. M'Rae.—Lieutenant Dashwood's sad End.— Brigadier Inglis.— Mr. Gubbins and Sir Colin Campbell.— Kindness of Mr. Gubbins to wounded Officers.—Mr. Gubbins at the Council of War.—Bursting of useless Guns.—Narrow Escape.— The Ladies, Children, and Wounded leave the Residency. — Mrs. Inglis's noble Act.—Her Description of the Ladies' Exodus. — Move upon the Kaiserbagh.—Strategic Manœuvre of Sir Colin Campbell.— Evacuation of Lucknow.— Freedom.— Manœuvres. — Services of the 9th Lancers.— The Commander-in-Chief's General Order.—His Acknowledgment of the Services of Non-military Men - - - - - - 335

CHAP. XXI.

CONCLUSION.

Civilian Guard on the State Prisoners.— Our Escort.— Sir James Outram's Column remains at Alumbagh.— Mournful Death of

General Havelock.— Gratitude and Sorrow of the British Nation. — Captain Havelock. — March from the Alumbagh. — A weary Journey.— Fatigue and Anxiety. — Wyndham's Defeat. — Sir Colin's opportune Arrival saves our Cawnpore Entrenchment. — The Gwalior Rebels occupy the Station of Cawnpore.— The late General Wheeler's Entrenchments. —Sad Mementos of Sufferings. — Recollections of Sir Hugh Wheeler.— Our Communications with the Town cut off. — Our Entrenchment on the Ganges. — A Friend's Escape from the Scenes of Rebellion. — The only Survivor of the Futtygurh Massacre. — Warm Reception at Allahabad. — My Arrival at Calcutta   -   -   Page 353

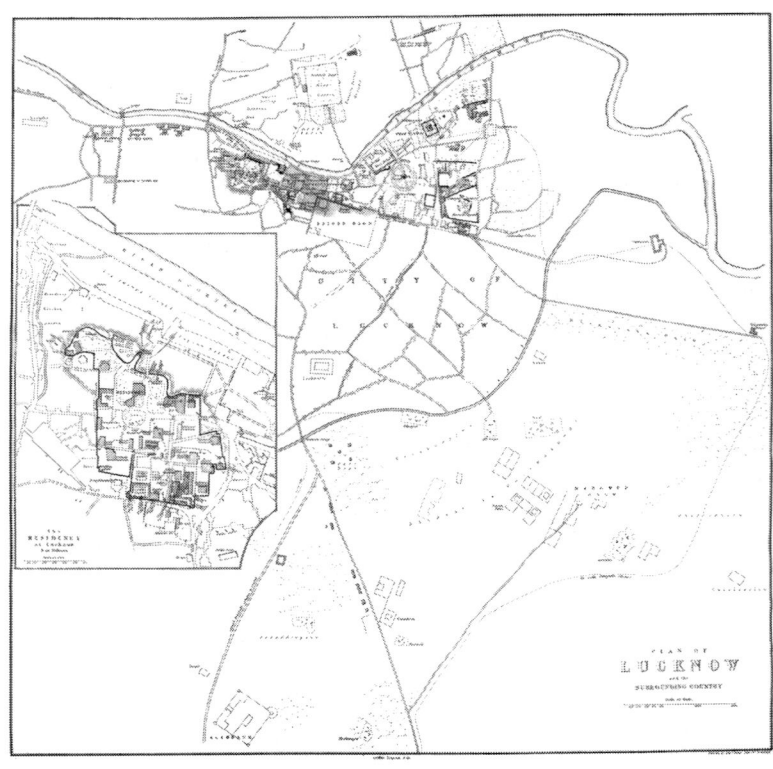

ERRATA.

Page 10, lines 7 and 8 from top, *for* " Cambridge " *read* " Oxford."
,, 242, line 15 from top, *for* " Loire " *read* " Lowe."
,, 270, ,, 3 from foot, *for* " Lieut." *read* " Captain."
,, 367, ,, 16 from top, *omit* " widow of Mr. Boileau, of the Civil Service."

PERSONAL NARRATIVE

OF THE

SIEGE OF LUCKNOW.

CHAPTER I.

THE FIRST DISTURBANCES IN LUCKNOW. — MAY.

My journey to the North-west.— A pleasant travelling Companion.—Panic at Benares.—Allahabad.—Cawnpore.—Post to Lucknow.— Disturbed State of Oude. — Fate of Mr. and Mrs. White. — Sir Henry Lawrence's precautionary Measures. — Mutiny of the Seventh Oude Irregulars.—The Chief Commissioner's Levee and Address to the Sepoys. — Expedition towards Agra of Captain Hayes and Major Gall. — Murder of Captain Hayes, Mr. Fayrer, and Lieutenant Barber. — Escape to Cawnpore of Lieutenant Carey.—Major Gall's Fate.—Waking to a disagreeable Reality.—Mutiny of the 30th May.—Conversation with a Rebel.—A Game at Billiards interrupted. — Brigadier Handscombe's Death. — Murder of Lieutenant Grant. — Narrow Escape of Ladies in Cantonments. — Defeat and Pursuit of the Rebels.—Cornet Raleigh's tragic End.— Murder of Mr. Mendes.

On the 10th of May, 1857, business called me to the Upper Provinces. My travelling companion was a native dependent of the King of Oude, possibly one of his emissaries, but in whom at that time I had every confidence. We had long conversations together on Indian politics; and unacquainted as I then was with native character, as it has since come out, I was not much shocked at the political opinions he at that time expressed. They were those of a man wishing to see his country free and his pockets full, and he spoke of the probability of becoming eventually a leader of banditti with the greatest *sang-froid* imaginable. He would live honestly as long as his means continued, but he could not work. He was a soldier (he had been a captain of cavalry), and he would not demean himself by either using the spade, wielding a pen, or keeping a shop. He seemed to take great interest in me, for he on one occasion drew his poniard and nearly stabbed a man for not being polite enough to me, and I had considerable difficulty in pacifying the police at Shergotty in consequence. But a few rupees distributed among these corrupt myrmidons of the law, who boldly asked for money, quieted the matter.

We proceeded on our journey, and with scarce another adventure arrived at Benares. There I first learned, to my horror and astonishment, of the barbarities committed at Meerut and Delhi, and of the probability of similar scenes being enacted in other parts of Upper India. I determined at once to push on to Allahabad, notwithstanding the alleged insecurity of the road. All my Benares friends had left the station, and, flying before an imaginary or real danger, had sought shelter in the Fort of Chunar. At Allahabad I found people in a fright about what appeared to me to be nothing. My agent there, Mr. Archer, who afterwards fell a victim to the mutiny which subsequently broke out, continually pooh-poohed all alarming reports, and I myself was in the highest spirits. There were patrols going the round, and precautionary measures were everywhere taken.

I remained above a week there, and formed one of a garrison where soldiering was enacted in a very pleasant mode. Capital dinners, first-rate wines, cheroots, songs, music, were the order of the day, with a little patrolling and keeping watch. So little, however, did I believe in anything serious being likely to occur, that I continued several business transactions, and wrote to Calcutta in the most hopeful strain respecting the state of things in the North-west. There were all manner of reports about bands of mutineers infesting the highway, and I must confess I at one time felt inclined to return to Calcutta; but, fearful of being looked upon as a needless alarmist by my friends, and at last convinced that, even in the event of an outbreak our Government would be in a position to crush it in the bud, I set out for Cawnpore in company with a friend, who with difficulty was persuaded to leave his wife behind. We met several ill-looking wretches, and one or two bands of whiskered and bearded armed men, who regarded us evidently with feelings of animosity; but nothing of consequence really took place, and we arrived at Cawnpore in safety. There I found people not quite at their ease.

I had purchased some linseed and rapeseed at Cawnpore, and my agent showed me the boats he had loaded and the goods still in the "godowns" he had hired for me. Urgent requests from my Lucknow correspondent to come over at once, made me lose no time in continuing my journey to that city. My friend accompanied me, and, keeping watch turn by turn with a brace of pistols and a double-barrelled rifle, we set out at night without encountering any other inconvenience than that caused by a wretched conveyance and still more wretched horses. On the way, early next morning, we met with great kindness from the toll-collector at Burmee, the son of Colonel Brown of the Bengal army, whose account of the state of the country of Oude was anything but reassuring. A large body of armed men had gathered at Mullapore, and several rajahs and landholders had unfurled the banner of rebellion. Mr. Lawrence, another friend, whom I afterwards met on the road, and who had also been obliged to leave his post in the district, owing to the threatening aspect of affairs there, confirmed what we had already heard. He too was proceeding to Lucknow; and thus reinforced, we arrived without accident on the 22nd of May.

I was greeted with a hearty welcome by my friend Deprat, who had everything prepared for my convenience and comfort in a handsome garden-house, which he possessed, half-way between the cantonment and the city, on the other side of the iron bridge. Poor Mr. White, my travelling companion, on the other hand, went to our friend Sinclair, whose firm he intended entering as a partner; but a fatality seemed to hurry him on to his doom. He left for Allahabad the same day on which he arrived, Sinclair accompanying him, reached that station, returned to Cawnpore with his wife, and, after vacillating for some time between Lucknow and Agra, both which routes were unsafe, it was said, he branched off to the latter town. He was never more heard of. He and his wife must have been murdered by the mutinous cavalry, who, on that very day, had despatched Captain Hayes and the officers belonging to the detachment which he had accompanied.

I remained several days at Lucknow before anything happened to make us think a general rising likely to take place. The people, however, looked sullen enough, and I perceived that Europeans were no longer treated with the respect which they had commanded before.

Sir Henry Lawrence's measures appeared to me excellent, and I believed, that, in the event of an insurrection, the guns of the fort of Muchee Bhawn, which we had taken possession of, and of which I shall afterwards speak more at length, would completely master the whole town. A possible attack on the Residency we did not believe in.

At this time our forces occupied various positions in Lucknow, as the policy evidently was to break up the regiments into companies, and not to allow the whole to be together. The Oude Irregular Force were at Moosabagh; the Military Police in the jail and Feradbuksh palaces; our European troops divided between the Residency, Muchee Bhawn, and cantonments, where also the 48th and 71st Native Infantry were stationed. The 7th Light Native Cavalry were

MUTINY OF THE 7TH OUDE IRREGULARS.

at Moodkipore. The Residency in Cantonments was the rendezvous; a few ladies were in the City Residency, but the bulk of the Europeans were at the Cantonment Residency along with the European artillery. The latter were then free to act, at the same time that they were close to the Native Infantry corps.

The mutiny of the 7th Oude Irregular Infantry had been the first startling event before my arrival at Lucknow. It had taken place at Moosabagh, a palace of one of the late king's wives, situated a short distance from the city, not very far from Hosseinabad and the Dowlatkhana, a mausoleum of one of the deceased kings of Oude, where the remaining Irregular Oude Force, under Brigadier Gray, were quartered. The Moosabagh mutiny placed the European officers of that regiment, Lieutenants Watson, Mecham, and Hadow, and the European sergeant, in the most imminent danger. Brigadier Gray, commanding the Oude Irregular Force, at once wrote to Major Gall, commanding the 4th Irregular Cavalry, requesting him to join immediately with every sabre at his command. That officer, who at once flew into his jackboots, was the first to arrive, and sent to take up a position in a grove of mango trees about a mile away from the mutineers. Meanwhile Sir Henry Lawrence had been collecting troops, and arrived with four guns, four companies of Her Majesty's 32nd Regiment, two Native Infantry corps and the 7th Light Native Cavalry.

The mutineers were frightened at these preparations, and, a few minutes before our troops had come up to attack them, broke up and fled at the sight of the port-fires which gleamed in the darkness of the evening. The 7th Light Cavalry sent some men after them, who succeeded in persuading a few to return without violence; others were made prisoners, and many came of their own accord and gave up their arms. That night our troops bivouacked close by: other arrangements were made next day, the prisoners tried, and the native officers and men discharged. The danger was over for the present.

Some days after Sir Henry Lawrence held a durbar in the Residency. The troops were drawn up, and the native officers were received on an open plain. Sir Henry Lawrence, in the midst of a brilliant European staff and the principal native noblemen of the city, invested with kheluts, or dresses of honour, two of the men who had proved their fidelity to our cause by denouncing some emissaries of the conspirators, and apprising the local government of the mutinous intentions of the 7th Oude Irregulars, previous to the outbreak. One of them, a havildar, or native sergeant, was promoted to the rank of a soubahdar, or native captain, and another, a private, advanced to the post of a jemadar, or native subaltern commissioned officer.

Sir Henry Lawrence took this opportunity of delivering to the troops a soul-stirring address in excellent Hindostanee, telling them that the British Government, ever anxious to reward loyalty, never missed an occasion of honouring its faithful servants; that some evil-disposed persons, seeing only a few Europeans here and there, imagined, by circulating false reports, they were able to overthrow the Government; but the power of England, which could send 50,000 Europeans to fight against Russia, could, in the space of three months, land twice that number in India; and much more to the same effect. If anything short of armed resistance could have averted rebellion, that speech of Sir Henry Lawrence would have had that effect. The city was tranquil for some weeks after; and the Chief Commissioner, well aware of the value of time, made the most of it in preparing for defence, in the event of insurrection.

About the 23rd of May two detachments of native cavalry were despatched towards Cawnpore, to clear the road between that station and Agra. One was under the command of Captain Fletcher Hayes, the military secretary, who, during the ex-king's reign, had held the very important office of Assistant Resident at his court, and whose capacities as a military officer, as a diplomatist, and as an able writer, had earned for him not only the confidence of Government, but a wide Indian reputation. At Cambridge he had obtained the degree of a Master of Arts, and his success as an Orientalist and an author had made him well known to the scientific world. That he should have volunteered to command an expedition, evidently of great danger, proved him a man of undoubted courage. Besides, he had the conviction, after having had the most hair-breadth escapes in the Gwalior war and the Sikh campaigns, that he should never meet with death by a bullet or a round shot. The sequel proved he was correct, though not in the way he interpreted it.

The other party was under the orders of Major Gall, the gallant officer who had played so prominent a part in the suppression of the mutiny of the 7th Oude Irregulars. At Cawnpore the two officers separated, and Captain Hayes, with his detachment, proceeded on towards Agra, but he was fated never to reach that town. Not far from Mynpoorie, one of the most tragic events occurred. Mr. Fayrer, a volunteer, the brother of the Residency Surgeon, was then between the advanced guard and the main body, commanded by Lieutenant Barber, who was ahead; Captain Hayes himself was in the rear of the main body, and Lieutenant Carey not far from him. Allowing Lieutenant Barber to proceed, Mr. Fayrer, arriving at a well, stopped his horse, and asked for water. It was handed to him, and, while in the act of drinking, one of his own men drew his sword and cut off his head. Captain Hayes now came up, and had scarcely time to draw his revolver, on seeing the dead body of his friend, before he received a spear wound in his back, and was immediately despatched by the other mutineers. Barber was still ahead when the scuffle in his rear attracted his attention. No sooner did he perceive his men had broken out into mutiny, than he turned round, drew his sword, and dashed into the midst of the cowardly rebels. They drew back, and two of them fell dead, struck by the bullets of his revolver; but the odds were too fearful for him to contend successfully against, and he was soon surrounded. Putting spurs to his horse, he turned the reins, and rode furiously away in the Agra direction, but he was pursued, fired at, overtaken, and cut to pieces. Carey, a splendid rider, a man of very light weight, and seated on a blood horse, swift as the wind, was more fortunate. He escaped to Cawnpore, having outridden all his pursuers, but reached that station only to fall in the general massacre, which subsequently overtook all our countrymen and countrywomen there.

Major Gall, on ascertaining that his own men were likewise tainted with the spirit of insurrection, very wisely returned, and thus escaped a calamity which would inevitably then have befallen him, but to which he afterwards fell a victim.*

On the night of the 30th May, I was tranquilly sleeping in my bed, when Deprat's servant woke me, and, with looks of horror and consternation, told me to get up at once, for the regiments in cantonments had broken out, and that not a minute was to be lost. I had scarcely time to jump up from my couch, when Deprat himself called out, "Le jeu a commencé. Dépêchez-vous!" I did not wait to dress, but hastily snatching up my clothes in one hand and my double-

---

* This occurred nearly three weeks afterwards. He was murdered in a village of Oude, while asleep in a seray or native inn, having gone out disguised as a native, with a party of his sowars. These villains, fearful of committing the deed themselves, betrayed him to the villagers, who were then sure of the aid of the traitors who should have protected him. He fell while carrying despatches to the Governor-General at Allahabad.

barrelled rifle in the other, I followed him to his magazine opposite his dwelling-house.

This he had fortified at his own expense and under the sanction of Sir Henry himself, who several times inspected his preparations. The Chief Commissioner availing himself of the services proffered to him by Deprat, whose military experiences in Africa rendered his co-operation valuable at so critical a time, had given him the command of a hundred native policemen, who were supposed to be faithful to our cause.

Deprat intended to defend his house to the best of his means, and, as it is situated not far from the iron bridge, he hoped, in the event of the mutineers marching to the city, to check their progress for some time, should they pass, as they naturally must have done, by his place. A couple of beds had already been brought up to the terrace; a sort of tent was pitched there; powder, ball, cartridges, supplied by Government, two small 3-pounder guns, spare muskets, provisions, and a supply of water had previously been conveyed there, so that in the event of our being attacked and our men proving faithful (twenty-five of them were Sikhs in whom we reposed the most implicit confidence), we could have held out for at least some days, though death in the end must assuredly have overtaken us. Fortunately, we had no occasion to put the strength of our fortifications to the test. Sir Henry Lawrence had beaten the rebels in cantonments.

Arrived on the terrace, by means of a movable ladder, we saw the sky towards the cantonments lurid with a blood-red glare. The bungalows had been set on fire; the sound of volleys of musketry was heard, and, still louder, the booming of cannon. Gradually the fire slackened. Horsemen were now galloping up and down; but we allowed no one to pass without a challenge. One scoundrel came riding furiously up from the cantonments. I cried "Halt!" and the man held in his horse. The following colloquy took place between us. "Who are you?" "A friend! I carry a message to the Residency." "What news, then?" "Good news." "Well, what good news?" "The bungalows are being burnt, and the Europeans are every where shot down." I fired my pistol, but the man had already galloped off. I had missed.

Deprat, meanwhile, had his mare saddled; and leaving me in charge of his party rode off to the cantonments. Many passed and repassed. The officers of the 48th, and some of the 13th, disguised in native costume, had been saved by a party of their own men, who escorted them to the Muchee Bhawn.

A portion of the 7th Light Cavalry, who had not joined in the mutiny, passed likewise. They were headed by their officers; and shortly after a wounded officer in Sir Henry's carriage followed.

In cantonments the mutiny first broke out in the lines of the 71st Native Infantry, and was quickly general throughout. Except the greater portion of the 7th Light Cavalry, a large number of the 13th, and a very few of the 48th and 71st, all our sepoys had turned against us. They first burnt the 13th mess house, and then fired into the 71st officers' mess. The gentlemen in the dining-room had lost no time in escaping when the fire once broke out; but fires having not been uncommon, even on previous nights, two of the officers, Lieutenant Thain, of the 13th, and Lieutenant Campbell, of the 71st, would not allow the mutineers to disturb them in their game of billiards, till a volley of musketry, too much for even their *sang-froid*, at last obliged them to conclude it.

My friend Campbell, as he passed a sentry, placed there by ourselves, was challenged by him. "Hookum durr," cried the man. The word "Friend," pronounced in good English and not with the Hindustanee accent, as "perhind," had no sooner escaped his lips, than a bullet whistled past his ears within half an inch of him. Brigadier Handscombe now advanced on the 71st lines, with a company of the 32nd regiment. It was dark as pitch, and nought could be seen but the flash of the rebels' muskets. The order to "fix bayonets" was given; and our Europeans could scarcely be restrained from charging without orders. They expected that word of command every instant; but it was never uttered. Colonel Handscombe, still wavering, said, " Do not fire. You might kill friends." Friends, indeed! He paid dearly for his confidence. Giving the order to halt, that fated officer advanced singly to the lines, with a view to address the mutineers, and bring them back to a sense of their duty. He was shot dead.

Our men, seeing their leader fall, advanced to the charge; but they found the lines deserted. They accordingly returned to the artillery ground, where Sir Henry and his staff were. The sepoys had advanced to the attack; but a few rounds of canister fired by Lewin soon made them retreat. Many rebels fell; but the grape, passing through the tent of Colonels Inglis and Case, killed also a number of the servants of those officers.

At another part of the cantonments poor Grant, of the 71st Native Infantry, fell a victim to the cruelty and cowardice of the mutineers. A friendly soubahdar had concealed him under a charpoy, or native bed, but he was dragged out and murdered. Lieutenant Chambers, the adjutant of the 13th Native Infantry, was wounded, and many others had most miraculous escapes.* One poor woman, Mrs. Y——y, came to us, with two of her children, next morning, with nothing but a shift on, while her husband was picturesquely attired in loose night-trousers, a sheet thrown over his shoulders as a toga, and a helmet-shaped pith hat on his head. In spite of their miserable plight I could not help bursting into laughter at the little man's ridiculous appearance. However, he had shown considerable pluck; for notwithstanding the numbers he had to oppose, he succeeded in saving his wife from a fate worse than death, and, availing himself with wonderful presence of mind of some interruption which diverted the attention of the ruffians for a time, managed to take his family into an adjoining field, where they lay all night shivering with cold and in the most agonising suspense. My friend Deprat at once provided them with apartments, clothes, and food.

Mrs. Bruère, who had also passed the night in

* Lieutenant Hardinge of the Oude, who, notwithstanding the heavy fire directed at all sides, patrolled the streets with some faithful Irregulars, was also wounded in the arm by a bayonet thrust.

cantonments, against orders, narrowly escaped being killed. Some of the faithful 13th saved her life by putting her through a hole in a wall at the back of the house, which they had made while the mutineers were calling for her. She and her poor children passed a dreadful night in a dry ditch. It is indeed wonderful what privations and sufferings ladies can endure.

Sir Henry having defeated the main body of the insurgents, now moved the guns upon the road leading to Lucknow. Their passage in that direction was consequently cut off. The city had been saved. At 2 o'clock the firing had almost entirely ceased. Our Europeans, and the officers who had been able to join the Chief Commissioner, laid themselves down on the ground and slept.

Next morning at early dawn the order for pursuit was given. The enemy had abandoned the cantonments, and were on their way into the districts. Our men followed and came up with them. Lieutenants Lewin and Macfarlane, opening grape and round shot on their ranks, killed a few more. By nine o'clock in the morning our Europeans were too exhausted by the heat of a May sun and the fatigue and watchings overnight to be able to pursue them further. At Moodkipore, about three miles away from the cantonments, where the lines of the 7th Light Cavalry were, they halted. The cavalry, who had not joined the rest of the mutineers overnight, now went over to the enemy, and cut up poor Cornet Raleigh, who had been ill and confined to his bed in his bungalow, on the day of the mutiny. Being asleep at the time, his regiment left for the cantonments without his being aware of it. No sooner, however, did he learn the fact than he got up and made a bed at the guard-house. He was already mounted on his horse, when he was met by a trumpeter, who shot him, and by other men, who afterwards hacked him almost to pieces. Our men found his body still warm, and the blood yet oozing from his wounds, when they came up to him. Poor fellow! what makes his end more sad is, that the unfortunate young officer — he was only seventeen — had joined his regiment but three days before. A lock of the hair of some young lady love, to whom perhaps he had plighted his faith, was found round his neck. One of his fingers, on which there had been a ring, was cut off.

Thanks to the excellent measures taken by Sir Henry, an insurrection in Lucknow itself had been prevented for the present. But the greatest excitement was apparent everywhere. Deprat and myself still continued to guard our isolated position, and

I was fortunate enough to make a prisoner of a native drummer of the 71st, laden with booty, which I brought up at once in company of the culprit, who was afterwards hanged, to the Cantonment Residency.

On Sunday, the 31st of May, a rather tragic event occurred at Mooshagunge in the city. Mr. Mendes, an uncovenanted clerk in the Chief Commissioner's office, had, in spite of the warnings of his friends, gone back to his own house in order to enjoy a quiet siesta. No sooner had his presence been made known to his neighbours, than, aided by the treacherous door-keeper in his employ, he was surprised and attacked by these fanatical Mussulmen, who had long owed him a grudge for having treated them with contempt on previous occasions. He must have retreated from room to room, for everywhere on the floor were bloody footprints visible. A hundred wounds in his body testified to the cruelty of his enemies. Two barrels of his revolver were found to be discharged, with what effect we could never learn.

CHAP. II.

LUCKNOW BEFORE THE SIEGE. — JUNE.

. State of the Oude Districts. — The Native Police. — The City of Lucknow. — Martial Law. — Prisoners hanged. — Joy of the Acquitted. — News of Cawnpore. — Closure of Postal Communications. — Sir Hugh Wheeler. — Devotion of his Messenger. — Depreciation of Company's Paper. — Appearance of the Residency. — The Fort of Muchee Bhawn. — Discontent of the People of Lucknow. — Fanaticism of the Mussulman Population. — Anecdote. — Our Volunteer Cavalry. — Sir Henry Lawrence. — Policy of evacuating Oude. — Cholera. — Fatal Quarrel and Retribution. — Running a-muck. — Our State Prisoners.

WE will now turn away from these unfortunate events, the horrors of which are further proofs, if proofs were required, how little natives are to be trusted, and with what consummate treachery they can veil their most diabolical purposes, and see what happened meanwhile at Lucknow.

With the exception of this city, the whole of Oude had passed out of our hands. The villages followed the examples of the towns of Fyzabad, Sultanpore, Duriabad, Salone, Purseedapore and other places, and sided with the insurgents, either from hatred to us, or fear of the mutineers. Some of the rajahs and landholders remained neutral, but none openly proclaimed themselves our friends. Many of them had retainers to the number of several thousands, and might, had they been so inclined, without great difficulty, have openly resisted the sepoys.

That the city people were well affected, every one doubted; yet, notwithstanding this general disbelief in the loyalty of the people of Lucknow, the daily reports sent in to us were most consolatory. The mahajuns (native bankers) and shopkeepers were, so it was said, determined to defend their property with their lives, should the insurgents ever march upon the city, a possibility held in some doubt. Their retainers would resist every attempt at coercion, and the native nawabs (noblemen and gentlemen) had engaged additional watchmen, and would have their property and families respected. Captain Carnegie's police were indefatigable, so it was stated, in repressing violence and disorder, and were, it was believed, firmly attached to us. Additional ammunition was served out to them and the Irregulars at the Hosseinabad buildings. The kotwal, a Punjabee, who had during the night of the 30th of May distinguished himself by his zeal and promptitude in taking measures to prevent an insurrection, was rewarded with a large sum of money and a valuable shawl dress of honour.

Meanwhile, there seemed to be visible a general discontent in the very air of Lucknow. It was considered unsafe for Europeans to visit the crowded parts of the city; yet Captain Carnegie, the magistrate, was never molested, and buggies and carriages, and perhaps one or two clerks walking to and fro the Hosseinabad buildings (where our Irregulars were), through one of the most frequented thoroughfares of Lucknow, never met with violence. Every evening I used to ride towards Muchee Bhawn, armed of course, without however meeting with any accident. On one occasion, my pistol dropped, and a man politely picked it up. Yet a lowering, sullen, obstinate look was discernible on almost every countenance. An order had been passed prohibiting the carrying of arms in the streets; but though this order was partially obeyed by the majority of passengers, now and then a man might be seen with matchlock and spear, or firelock and belt and pistols, whose bearing and firm step proclaimed him at once to be military. Nor were we, it was felt, strong enough to enforce obedience to our orders, and were therefore obliged not to appear to perceive an infraction of them.

Martial law had been proclaimed, and courts martial were being held daily upon such individuals as were either made prisoners at the time of the mutiny in cantonments, or who were suspected of having disseminated inflammatory addresses. The accused were at first all tried in the cantonments (of which we still occupied two or three houses, among them that of the Chief Commissioner), and then in the Residency in Lucknow. Several of them were pardoned — a mistaken leniency; — others were condemned to be hanged, much against the inclination of Sir Henry, whose kindliness of disposition was such, that it pained him to bear the responsibility of shedding the blood of even such wretches as the accused evidently were. But he also at last saw the necessity of adopting severe measures, and, with a sigh, I am certain, confirmed each death warrant.

Among those who were thus condemned was the soubahdar, who had been raised to that rank from a common native sergeant, and who had received from Sir Henry's own hands the sum of a thousand rupees and a dress of honour on the occasion of his address to the native troops in cantonment some weeks before the first outbreak. If any conciliatory measures could have averted the calamities which afterwards befel our Government, those adopted by the Chief Commissioner were certainly calculated to prevent them. But we had yet further to learn what deep treachery, what base ingratitude, and what Satanic atrocities natives are capable of. The horrors of Cawnpore were not yet known, and those of Shahjehanpore and Mithowly were only partially believed.

The number of criminals who were hanged amounted to about thirty-six, of whom eight or ten were executed of a morning, and four or five of an evening. Thousands and thousands of spectators assembled to witness the executions. Our guns were pointed at the populace from Fort Muchee Bhawn, to fire upon them in the event of an attempt being made to rescue the condemned. They were usually hanged on three gallows before one of the gates of the Fort. Only on one occasion an *émeute* might have occurred. A horse of one of the officers became restive, and the mob consequently moved onwards. The movement being communicated to others, the living mass advanced towards the gate, and nearly surrounded the European soldiers guarding the prisoners. The sentry at the gate, therefore, imagined an attack was meant, and called out "To arms!" and the artillerist at the gun was about to apply the portfire to the touch-hole, and shower grape and canister on the people, even at the risk of injuring our own men, when the masses again retreated, and the catastrophe was prevented in time.

Among the prisoners, on that or another occasion, were also four banniahs (native shopkeepers), who were proved to have been agents of the mutineers of Benares, and who had arrived here from that city in order to propagate rebellion at Lucknow. They belonged to a batch of eighteen others, who were also accused of the same crime, but of whom fourteen were released. The joy of the acquitted was something really ludicrous to behold. They rubbed their foreheads on the ground, danced and ran about like madmen, and could scarcely believe their own ears and eyes when their release was notified to them. They must have felt that if the case had been reversed, and we were in their hands as accused, we should have met with no mercy.

The news of the mutiny which had broken out at Cawnpore, and of the straits and sufferings which our beleaguered countrymen at that station had to endure, cast a gloom over the whole place. The besieged force there under Sir Hugh Wheeler, we at first heard, were still holding out against awful odds, but we learnt no particulars on which we could depend; and when at last all our hopes of their being relieved deserted us, and we heard dark reports of their capitulation and final massacre, we, in the midst of the indignation we felt, were yet thankful that we had not fared as badly as they. Though the dâks and all communications with other stations had been closed since the 5th of June, few of us expected that we should ever be besieged ourselves, and none imagined a siege could have been so protracted. Even Sir Henry himself did not think so; yet, to provide against all contingencies, like a wise and prudent general, he ordered immense supplies of wheat, corn, and all sorts of provisions into the Residency and Muchee Bhawn. This eventually saved our lives. But for his prescience, Lucknow would have been lost, and we should have been starved to death, or massacred long, long before this.

Sir Hugh Wheeler succeeded in sending two or three letters to Sir Henry, but his communications were so very scant, owing to the necessity of eluding the vigilance of his enemies, that the pieces of paper on which the few lines were scrawled naturally contained no details. One of these messengers, a bearer or valet of the unfortunate general, was shot in crossing the Ganges, and arrived with a fractured arm, with which he slunk about for three days in the jungles, avoiding the highways, and arrived here almost exhausted. His arm was amputated, and I believe he still lives. One of these letters contained news of the fall of Delhi, or at least was said to have contained such intelligence, for it is not now even known whether Sir Henry caused a salute to be fired for our supposed success before the walls of the Imperial City, from a belief of the truth of the report or from a *ruse de guerre*, to restore confidence in the midst of the city people. The natives are generally the first to obtain correct intelligence of public events, and they, therefore, doubted this. But they still believed that there might be something true about our success; and the Company's paper, which had gradually gone down from 20 per cent. discount (the rate at which the mahajuns had purchased it before the mutiny in cantonments) to 60 to 75 per cent. discount, rose to 40 and 50 per cent. discount, in consequence of the twenty-one reports of our cannon.

Long before this the mahajuns, and even the bank, had ceased to transact business. No drafts could be cashed or obtained, no loans were granted, no credit was given by natives to Europeans, and no purchases were made by merchants. The cantonments and the city were no longer inhabited by Europeans; and even Constantia House and the Martinière, upon which buildings a great deal of money had been expended for fortifications, were at the eleventh hour abandoned, with the sanction of Sir Henry Lawrence. From the anxious manner in which the natives desired to part with the Company's paper, it was evident that they at least put no faith in the stability of our rule.

The city was still apparently perfectly tranquil; and though, owing to our large purchases, provisions were getting rather dear, yet everything could be had, and in almost any quantity too. Few people, however, laid in large stores, for no one contemplated the events that subsequently happened, and we were too sanguine in our expectations of reinforcements from Calcutta.

The Residency itself was crowded with ladies, women and children, and every house and outhouse was occupied. Preparations for defence were continued, and thousands of coolies were employed at the batteries, stockades, and trenches, which we were everywhere completing. We buried the treasure and ammunition, of which fortunately we had a large supply, and brought together as many guns as we could collect. The Residency and Muchee Bhawn presented most animated scenes. There were soldiers, sepoys, prisoners in irons, men, women, and children, hundreds of servants, respectable natives in their carriages, coolies carrying weights, heavy cannons, field-pieces, carts, elephants, camels, bullocks, horses, all moving about hither and thither, and continual bustle and noise were kept up from morning to night. Tents were pitched; and in fact there was scarcely a corner which was not in some way occupied and turned to account.

Our engineer officers were also blasting buildings, and endeavouring to level as many houses as possible round about us. Unfortunately, the Chinhutt affair overtook us so suddenly that we could not complete these most important measures, and we wasted besides much valuable time and labour upon similar undertakings round about Muchee Bhawn, which we afterwards abandoned.

Muchee Bhawn * was surrounded by high walls, which, towards the side overlooking the river, presented the appearance of an ancient castle. The

---

* The buildings of Muchee Bhawn (muchee, "fish"—from the device over the gateway, and bhawn, Sanscrit for "house") had belonged to Nawab Yah Ally Khan, and were purchased by Sir H. L. for 50,000 rupees. They originally formed the castle of the ancient Sheikhs, who held it during the rule in Oude of the Viceroy Asoph ood Dowlah. Lucknow was then a village of little importance, but forming the head-quarters of the rebellious Sheikhs, who had become very troublesome, the Viceroy made an expedition in person to it, took their castle of Muchee Bhawn, and, liking the spot himself, removed his capital from Fyzabad to Lucknow, which he built.

buildings within, its towers, magazines, outhouses, and terraces, were so numerous and intricate, that a stranger might easily have lost his way among them. Towards the north, Muchee Bhawn commanded the iron and stone bridges; to the south and west, had been one of the most populous parts of the town, and which was now partially levelled, and continuing to be levelled; towards the east it was commanded by the Residency, and overlooked some very frequented thoroughfares, of which we were fast demolishing the houses. We strengthened the fortifications, planted cannon on the walls, and, where that could not be done, placed jingals (immense blunderbusses moving on pivots) on them. To all appearance the Muchee Bhawn Fort was a most formidable and secure stronghold, but in reality it could never have been long defended by us. Its old walls would have crumbled to dust by the continued reverberations of our own cannon, and it was besides not large enough to accommodate all the families that had found refuge in Lucknow, and we had not troops sufficient to garrison two places against a numerous and well disciplined enemy.

The question whether Muchee Bhawn was to be abandoned or not was several times mooted in the council chamber. Opinions were evidently fluctuating; for on one day it was determined to bring all the treasure, a great number of guns, a vast deal of ammunition, and all the provisions away from the fort. Again counter-orders were given, and some of the provisions and ammunition were actually sent back. Then again removals took place, and it was finally determined to hold Muchee Bhawn some time longer.

It was fortunate that the treasure was allowed to remain in the Residency. Mr. Deprat, who had been ordered to remove all his goods into the fort, was specially prohibited from taking them away, Government, so Sir Henry said, holding themselves responsible for any loss he might sustain. We occupied one of the rooms of the outhouses, and, during our residence there, lived as well as we could on Burgundy and hermetically sealed and other provisions. We seemed to have a presentiment of what privations we had afterwards to undergo, for we enjoyed ourselves as much as good living could effect. However, Deprat required at last my services in the Residency, whither he was removing all Mrs. Hayes's library, Mr. Jackson's furniture, and Lady Outram's property; and I removed to the house which he had obtained there.

The Muchee Bhawn, perhaps, notwithstanding its weakness, yet answered a political purpose. The natives entertained the highest opinion of its strength, and believed it almost impregnable. The place was commanded by Brevet-Major Francis, of the 13th Native Infantry, an excellent officer, who was ably seconded in his endeavours to arrange the interior economy of the place by the Fort Adjutant, Lieutenant Huxham, 48th Native Infantry. The strength of the fort consisted of two companies of Europeans, Captain Alexander's Horse Artillery battery, the mortar battery, and the gate guns. There were, besides, scores of large and small cannon, formerly belonging to the king, lying about the place without gun-carriages and useless. It is very probable that the fear of our guns playing upon the town from that fort prevented an insurrection of the city people after the mutiny in cantonments.

That the Lucknow people should rise against us was a very probable event, notwithstanding the false reports which we received of their universal contentment. We had done very little to deserve their love and much to merit their detestation. Thousands of nobles, gentlemen, and officials, who during the king's time had held lucrative appointments, and who were too idle to work, were now in penury and want, and their myriads of retainers and servants thrown out of employ of course. Then the innumerable vagabonds, bravos, and beggars, who under the native rule infested the city and found bread in it, were starving during our administration. The native merchants, shopkeepers, and bankers, who, while Wajid Ally was on the throne, made large profits from supplying the luxurious wants of the king, his courtiers, and the wealthy ladies of the thronged harems, found no sale for their goods; and the people in general, and especially the poor, were dissatisfied because they were taxed directly and indirectly in every way.

We had been so very anxious to show a large balance-sheet in our favour, that we were less careful to make the people happy than to make them fill our treasuries. There was a duty on stamps, on petitions, on food, on houses, on eatables, on ferries. There was an opium contractor, a contractor for supplying corn and provisions, a salt and spirit contractor, and in fact contracts were given for everything that in Paris would come under the name of *octroi*. Everything in the shape of food was consequently very dear; and the contractors, the most opulent of whom was one Shirf ood Dowlah, a renegade wretch, who under the king's rule even was infamous for his peculation and robbery, at a time when theft and plunder were openly committed, were making large fortunes, while the people suffered by their extortions.

The tax upon opium especially caused an immense discontent throughout the country, but particularly in the city. Opium was an article as extensively used in Lucknow as in China, and the sudden deprivation of this drug was most severe upon the poorer opium-eaters. Many who could not obtain it at the increased rates actually cut their own throats in desperation. Besides, our magistrates, though themselves anxious to be just, were too much hampered by regulations to which the people were yet strangers, to dispense equal justice, and were prevented by their sheristadars and native officials, whose corruption and venality were proverbial, from carrying out the dictates of their own consciences.

The kotwal of the city, who had shown himself so zealous in our cause, and who was attached to it, not from gratitude, but from the general detestation which he inspired, had no friends but our officials, who were ignorant of his real character and unfortunately placed too much reliance on his integrity. This man threatened any one, who he thought could pay him well, with an accusation, and, from the high position he held and the means at his command, he became a very formidable enemy to whoever was bold enough to oppose him or to laugh at his power. His debauched character, too, made him peculiarly obnoxious to fathers and husbands, whom, by means of his myrmidons, he could at any time deprive of a daughter or a wife. The natives were, besides, taught by our Mohammedan and Hindoo subordinates to look upon us as corrupt and unjust; for few of them took bribes without letting it be understood that the greater portion of them was appropriated by our magistrates and high officials, who, poor men, little knew how their characters for justice were maligned, and what fortunes their employees were making at the expense of their reputations.

Then there were fanatics in plenty in the city, who made use of religious enthusiasm to influence the minds of their co-religionists still more against us. Every true Mohammedan is at heart an enemy to the professors of Christianity, however much he may disguise his feelings for the time being, and no matter what amount of benefits and kindnesses he may receive at their hands. To slay or injure an infidel is with him a meritorious action. Lucknow was the seat of Mohammedan literature; and it need not, therefore, be a matter of wonder if the numerous preachers who started up against us, and cursed our rule, found large and sympathising congregations.

They easily persuaded their hearers that to rebel against us was acceptable in the sight of Heaven, and that Allah would bless with success any attempt at throwing off the odious yoke of the infidel foreigners, — the despoilers of their king, the revilers of their holy religion, the eaters of the unclean animal, and the consumers of the forbidden drink. And blending fanaticism with cunning, they added that the Hindoos, too, would have their religion disrespected, would be christianised, and would have to handle cow-fat and eat beef. Their hearers, already excited against us, were easily led to believe that the prisoners we were hanging were martyrs of a good and holy cause. One of these itinerant fakeers, who was caught in the act of preaching universal war against us, was condemned to receive a hundred lashes — a measure which cooled the ardour of his brethren for some time. Thousands of ill-looking wretches, however, might daily be seen passing under the gallows, registering vows of vengeance against us.

Of the real state of affairs, such as I have attempted to depict it, Sir Henry Lawrence was well aware. He had already put the Residency under garrison laws, and sentinels and patrols were everywhere posted. He had organised a body of volunteer cavalry, consisting of officers, clerks, and others, under the command of Captain Ratcliffe of the 7th Light Cavalry, with Captain Boileau of the Oude Irregulars for a second in command, and Mr. Alexander Bryson for sergeant. A body of infantry, consisting of civilians, were also drilled, and had to perform sentinel and other duties in the various houses and batteries to which they were posted, within the Residency compound.

Sir Henry Lawrence was indefatigable, and seemed almost never to sleep. Often would he sally out in disguise, and visit the most frequented parts of the native town, to make personal observations, and see how his orders were carried out. He several times had a thin bedding spread out near the guns at the Bailey-guard Gate, and retired there among the artillerists, not to sleep, but to plan and to meditate undisturbed. He appeared to be ubiquitous, and to be seen everywhere. All loved and respected the old gentleman, and indeed every one had cause, for none was too lowly for his notice, and no details were too uninteresting for him. Every one working under him, no matter how subordinate his position, knew that, if he performed his duties cheerfully and well, Sir Henry, who was a keen observer of persons, would not allow him to go unrewarded. The Uncovenanted, particularly, had a kind friend in him, and with the common soldier he was equally if not even more popular. On Sir Henry's removing the head-quarters of his office from cantonments into the Residency he was loudly cheered by the men. "Long life to Sir Henry; long live Sir Henry," resounded from all sides; and a long and loud "hurrah" continued as long as he was visible. One poor man vociferated so loudly that he burst a blood-vessel — a heavy price for a little enthusiasm.

Sir Henry seemed to all who saw him to be worn out with fatigue; and his immense responsibility at so critical a period appeared to bear particularly heavy on him.

Sir Henry Lawrence had received from Calcutta, some time before the siege, plenary powers to use his own discretion with regard to Oude. He might, so it was stated, either keep the country, or temporarily evacuate it. He unhesitatingly rejected the latter alternative; that we are still in possession of a position in Oude, and are in a fair way of retaking what we have lost, is entirely owing to Sir Henry. Though the loss our troops sustained during the siege and in the first relief by General Havelock's force was immense, some advantages at least were gained. Besides, had we abandoned Lucknow at that time, the moral effect would most probably have been still more ruinous to our Government, and would have entailed an incalculable loss of blood and treasure. And besides, the fact of our little garrison holding out so long against a far superior force of well-disciplined men, supplied with all the requirements of civilised warfare, must have not a little astonished the surrounding provinces, and made us rise in their estimation as much as we might have lost in prestige before. In a word, all who are intimately acquainted with the facts are of opinion that it would have been highly impolitic to evacuate Oude at a time when we had it in our power to do so with impunity; but after the 30th of May, when such a course might have been politic, it was no longer practicable.

The insurgents were said to be approaching Lucknow, but another foe was already in our camp quite as terrible as they. This was the cholera, which daily sent two or three men, principally from the fort of Muchee Bhawn, to their graves. It was heart-rending to see the hospital of that place constantly filled with the victims of this dire scourge.

Two sad occurrences took place shortly before the siege. One happened in the Residency. This was the murder of a European by a European, both brave and gallant soldiers, whom we could little spare at a time like the present. The wives of Riding-Master Eldrige and Sergeant-Major Keogh, both of the 7th Light Cavalry, had a quarrel, and the husbands, being appealed to by their better halves, took it up warmly; high words ensued, and on a term of abuse being made use of by the riding-master, Keogh drew his pistol, which he carried in his belt, and shot Eldrige dead. The sergeant-major was of course put under arrest, but he was not condemned to death, and on the commencement of the siege he was released and ordered to go to his duty. But a Power higher than any human tribunal did not allow him to go unpunished. A bullet from the enemy fractured his thigh; his leg was amputated, and he died from the effects of the operation.

At Muchee Bhawn, also, a more excusable crime was committed, for the murderer was a Sikh, labouring under the effects of some intoxicating drug or under temporary insanity. The man, apparently furiously mad, ran a-muck, killing or wounding with his sword whomsoever he saw. He succeeded in killing one Sikh and severely wounding two sepoys, before he could be secured. The poor fellow, who was put in irons, was deeply sorrowful at the murder he had committed, without cause, as well as without premeditation. The possibility of another and similar fit of madness on his part no doubt prevented his being released.

We had made several state prisoners, who were taken into custody as a precautionary measure, at the instigation, it was believed, of the kotwal, who no doubt imagined he should obtain charge of them, and could consequently squeeze a good deal of money out of them. But Captain Carnegie took them under his own care, and disappointed his expectations. Wuzeer Mirza, the nephew of the well-known Nawab Momtaz-ood-Dowlah, now siding with the insurgents, was subsequently set at liberty. The detention of these state prisoners, whatever the origin, was a wise and politic measure. It was feared, and justly so, that the enemy would force them, owing to their elevated rank, to take a prominent position in the coming revolution, and perhaps place one of them on the throne, and make the others ministers or sirdars.

One was Mustapha Ally Khan, the ex-king's elder brother, who by rights should have been placed on the throne, but who was excluded by the old king on pretence of being insane, — a charge perfectly ridiculous. Since then he never wore a turban or cap. "A crown only," he says, "shall encircle my brows."

Prince Rookun-ood-Dowlah, the son of Saad-ut-Ally, ruler of Oude, an old nobleman held in much esteem here, and Nawabs Mohammed Humayoon Khan, and Mirza Mohammed Shiko, nephew of the celebrated Solyman Shiko, of the royal families of Oude and Delhi, were the others. The young Rajah of Toolsepore, whose feuds with his father (whom it was believed he caused to be murdered) are so well known in India, completes the list. The rest of the prisoners were unimportant persons, merely attendants and servants on the others.

CHAP. III.

TRAGIC SCENES.

Major Marriott's Expedition. — Murder of Captain Burmester and Ensign Farquharson. — Death of Captain Staples. — Lieutenant Boulton's miraculous Escape. — Lieutenant Bax's Death. — Lieutenant J. Longueville Clarke's Gallantry and Capture of Fuzel Ally. — Death of himself and his Companions. — Uncertainty of the Fate of others in the Out-stations. — Wholesale Butchery of the Shahjehanpore Refugees. — Captain Patrick Orr and his Family saved.—Refugees from Duriabad, Secrora, and Seetapore. — Lieutenant Farquhar's Description of the State of the remaining Men of the Native Regiments. — Captain Adolphe Orr's perilous Position. — Mutiny of the Military Cavalry Police. — Captain Weston's daring Act. — Mutiny of the Military Infantry Police. — Treason in our Camp. — Captain Adolphe Orr's miraculous Escape. — Anecdote. — Our Pursuit. — Mr. Thornhill wounded. — Retreat of the Mutineers. — Masonic Dinner on St. John's Day.

MAJOR MARRIOTT, the Pension Paymaster, had, according to the policy then prevalent, been sent out into the district, ostensibly to pay the native pensioners, but really to try and restore our authority and to report on the state of the country. He was accompanied by two companies of the 48th Native Infantry, under Captain Burmester and Ensign Farquharson, of that regiment, and a body of the 7th Light Cavalry, officered by Captain Staples and Lieutenants Boulton and Martin. Encamping near a village in Oude, Major Marriott had become aware of the mutinous state of the native soldiery under his orders. Before sitting down to dinner, he apprised his brother officers of his intention to return to Lucknow, at the same time giving them permission, and strongly advising them to do the same. But Captain Burmester said that he had the most implicit confidence in his sepoys, and the other officers likewise remained.

Lieutenant Boulton had already made every preparation for escape, for he was less confident than his brother officers. His horse had been tied to a tree at a distance, and, accompanied by Captain Staples, whom he had persuaded to join him, he arrived safely at the tree, favoured by the darkness of the evening. Unfortunately they had but one horse, for Staples had only at the eleventh hour determined on quitting. They mounted the same animal, and galloped off. They were seen, fired at, and Staples, who was behind, was shot through the back and fell. The other officers were all killed while at dinner, but Boulton effected his escape. He was pursued by seven of his men, and a bullet sent after him wounded him in the wrist. He rode for six miles for his life, and, jumping a broad ditch, left his pursuers behind. He succeeded at last in reaching Cawnpore through the whole of the enemy's camp. Lieutenant Hutchinson, who had also been sent somewhere into the interior, was equally fortunate; he was pursued to the very Residency by a few of his rebellious cavalrymen. Lieutenant Bax, of the 48th, commanding an Oude Irregular corps in the district, also fell a victim to the treachery of his men.

The news from the districts, meanwhile, became every day more and more gloomy, and our intelligence every day more defective. I heard with sorrow and grief, from authentic news brought in by the native extra Assistant Commissioner who had accompanied him, that my sister's brother-in-law and friend, Lieutenant Joseph Longueville Clarke, second in command of the 7th Oude Irregular Infantry, had been murdered. He had earned for himself a distinguished reputation, and the thanks of Government, for the energy he displayed in tracking, and finally, after an incredibly long march, coming upon the camp of the famous robber chief and powerful feudal baron, the murderer of Mr. Boileau of the Civil Service,

Fuzel Ally. After a hand-to-hand struggle, in which he was wounded, he had succeeded in killing Fuzel Ally himself, his brother, and several followers. This success most probably retarded the rebellion for some months, and at all events deprived the insurgents of a chief who united indomitable courage with great skill and perseverance, and who had for many years held the king's and our own authority at defiance.

Longueville Clarke, and Mr. Cunliffe, and another, Mr. Jackson, I think, of the Civil Service, accompanied by the native extra Assistant Commissioner, who might have been a friend or a traitor for aught I know, had managed to reach the edge of the river Gaugra, at Byramghât, from Gonda. They either could not get boats to escape from their pursuers, or they arrived at the opposite bank, ran for a short distance, and were then killed in a village; or they were made prisoners after being wounded in a desperate resistance, tried by the rebels for the murder of Fuzel Ally, and shot; but at all events they fell victims to the cruelty of the insurgents. The reports of the manner of their death are various.

Poor Clarke had entrusted his sword and pistols to an old native dependent, with the request to forward them, in the event of his death, to a friend, with a view to have them transmitted to his father, Mr.

Longueville Clarke, the distinguished barrister, at Calcutta. This was faithfully executed.

Of my friend Captain Patrick Orr and his family I heard through his brother Adolphe, who showed me the letter, which contained the first intimation we had of the tragic fate of the Shahjehanpore refugees. These unfortunates having escaped the fate of Mr. Ricketts, the collector, and others, who were killed at church, arrived, to the number of twenty-eight, men, ladies, and children, in safety at Mohumdee, where Captain Orr was Deputy-Commissioner.

A party of the men who had served under Orr, when he commanded a King's Regiment during the native rule, forced themselves upon the party as an escort. Captain Orr, before allowing the sepoys to accompany them, as well as himself and his family, first made them swear on the head of a Brahmin jemadar, or native officer, the most sacred oath a Hindoo can take, that they would not touch a hair of their heads. They had scarcely set out a short distance, however, when the sepoys obliged the ladies and children to leave their carriages and to walk. The gentlemen, fourteen in number, were murdered one by one, near Mithowly, and the whole of the ladies and children, certain of their coming fate, assembling together in one body, were shot down while kneeling and singing a hymn.* Captain Orr, his wife and child, alone were saved. One of the sepoys interposed his body between them and the mutineers, seconded by other soldiers who had served under Orr before, and assisted in preventing their murder. They had to wander about for several days in the jungle, in constant dread of their lives, protected by a friendly Rajah, Lona Singh, and were joined by refugees from Seetapore and other stations. These were, Sir Mountstuart Jackson, the Misses Jackson, Lieutenant Burnes, little Miss Christian, Sergeant Norton, and one or two others.

Captain John Hearsey was not heard of. He was probably the European said to have been seen on an elephant with some ladies, made a prisoner, and shot.

Of Captain Bunbury, too, we knew nothing.

From Sultanpore we heard of the murder of Messrs. Stroyan, Block, and Colonel Fisher, and the escape of the ladies and the other gentlemen. Of the Fyzabad mutiny we learnt only inaccurate reports, and were

* The victims of this wholesale sepoy butchery were Lieutenant Scott, son of Major Scott, mother and sister; Captains Sneyd, Lysaght, and Salmon; Lieutenants Thompson, 25th Native Infantry, Pitt, Robertson, Rutherford, Key and wife; Ensigns Speus, Scott, White, and Johnstone; Mrs. Bowling and two children; Sergeant Reilley, wife and child; and the quarter-master-sergeant of the 25th, his wife and child.

therefore doubtful whether the inhabitants had really escaped or not. From Seetapore we had no news; and a party of the Volunteer Cavalry were therefore despatched by Sir Henry to escort the ladies of that station in. They met them — thirty officers and ladies — tired, weary, hungry, and sunburnt, and with blistered feet and hands, at a place called Bukshee Ka Talao, not far from cantonments which we were still keeping as a piquet. It was retained as such by two companies of infantry and a battery of horse artillery, that remained behind till the 29th of June, when they were ordered into Muchee Bhawn. There was another expedition of a detachment of Volunteers, who went towards Secrora, but who returned without effecting their object. A third reconnoitring party went to Nawabgunge, on the Cawnpore road; and a fourth, to Nawabgunge of Bara Bunky, on the Fyzabad road. Neither party saw an enemy. The latter only brought in a couple of sowars, evidently spies of the insurgents, who were pursued and captured.

Other refugees were, now and then, also coming in from other stations. Dr. Thompson, from Duriabad, was the first to come in from that station and give the news of the outbreak there; and Mr. Benson and family, and the other families, as well as Captain

Hawes of the 5th Oude Irregulars, followed. Several others escaped from Secrora; but by far the greatest number fell victims to the cruelty of the natives. Of this we had several tangible proofs. The body of an European woman, cut in quarters, was brought in; and the corpses of two or three others were seen lying on the roadside. Mrs. Dorin, wife of the officer commanding the 10th Oude Irregular Infantry, after having had the most wonderful escapes, arrived here in a miserable country cart, accompanied by Mr. Bickers, of the Uncovenanted Service, and his wife and children. The wife of a sergeant-major severely wounded likewise found her way in here.

I subjoin here an extract from Lieutenant Farquhar's interesting journal, which will show the exact position in which we were at this time:—" When we got to cantonments we were ordered to the Artillery parade-ground, where a camp was formed, and where we bivouacked for a fortnight with the eighty men who remained of our regiment (the 7th Light Cavalry). We were almost daily informed by spies that these eighty fellows intended to cut our throats. The 48th Native Infantry were encamped close to us; fifty of them stuck to their officers on the night of the mutiny, but, on the following day, 150 men, who returned, and merely expressed their sorrow for having deserted their officers, were taken back. These were pleasant companions to have close to one. The consequence was that the officers of each regiment had to sleep together, armed to the teeth, and two of us had to remain awake two hours each, to watch our own men. We kept these watches strictly, and by that means saved our lives. I used to sleep nightly—in my clothes of course—with my revolver under my pillow, a drawn sword on my bed, and a loaded double-barrelled gun near me. We remained in this disagreeable position for more than two weeks, and I can tell you I was far from sorry when an order came from Sir Henry Lawrence that we were to pay up our men and send them home on leave till the 15th of October, and then come down to the Residency."

The insurgents of the various stations in Oude were now said to have collected together, and to be approaching Lucknow in great numbers. A party of the Volunteer Cavalry was therefore sent out to Chinhutt, on the Secrora road, to the north of Lucknow, in order to reconnoitre. They left at one in the morning, and reached at three A.M., amidst showers of rain. They saw nothing; for the hostile troops had evidently not yet reached; and returned next day at two o'clock, cold, wet, and uncomfortable. Captain

Forbes at the same time reconnoitred towards the Nawabgunge direction.

The Oude military police, meanwhile, had for some days shown symptoms of being infected with the spirit of mutiny, which now had become general throughout the province. There were still a few native troops faithful to us, but we could of course not depend on the duration of their fidelity. The few sepoys of the 13th and other regiments that had not joined in the general mutiny in the cantonments, were those in whom alone we placed some sort of confidence. The native pensioners also, old men, that had fought for us in Cabul, and Burmah, and the Punjab, flocked around us to the Residency, and were likely to adhere to our cause, as it was obviously their interest to do so, unfitted as they were for plunder or long marches by their age. The artillerymen, on the contrary, were suspected to be tainted. One man was actually caught in the act of sending a seditious letter to one of the agents of the mutineer regiments in the country; —he was, I believe, subsequently hanged. Another was seen changing the elevation of our guns; a matter of little importance, truly, but still a proof of being ill-affected. Over each gun was placed a European artillerist, whose duty it was to watch narrowly the native gunners.

More than once, seditious conversation had been overheard between the men, by such as could understand the language. The native town-police were believed to be staunch, for, during the rising of the 30th of May in cantonments, they, as well as the Irregulars, under the command of Brigadier Gray in the Dowlatkhana and Hosseinabad, were strenuous in their exertions to preserve order.

Of the Military Police, Captain Weston, who commanded the whole force, of which there was then, however, at Lucknow only a regiment of cavalry, consisting of men under his immediate orders, and the 3rd Regiment under Captain Adolphe Orr, received constant intimation of the spread of disaffection among them. Notwithstanding this fact being well known at the Residency, Captain Orr had received orders from Mr. Ommaney, the Judicial Commissioner, to reside during the night at the jail, which was then guarded by the greater portion of his corps. Himself, Mr. Symes, his father-in-law, Watson, his sergeant-major, and young Maycock, his clerk and quarter-master-sergeant, shared the dangers to which he was thus every night exposed.

The jail was more than 2000 yards from the Residency, and in the event of a general rising, what could four Europeans have done in the midst of a rebellious soldiery and an infuriated set of scoundrels, should the mutineers, as was very likely, first set the prisoners at liberty. The sentinel might easily have killed his officer and allowed his comrades to despatch the rest, without hope of relief from the Residency. Captain Adolphe Orr and his companions, however, accepted their post of danger without a murmur, and slept nightly among the discontented police.

It was during the night of the 11th of June that the cavalry of the Military Police first broke out into open mutiny. Their barracks were situated on the new metalled road leading past the Motymahal palace, and the house lately occupied by the 32nd mess, to the Dilkusha and Constantia, a distance of about a mile and a half from the Residency. Intimation of this was soon conveyed to the authorities by one of the police spies. Captain Weston, on this occasion, proved himself to be a daring soldier and faithful servant of Government. Without hesitating an instant, and accompanied only by two native sowars, who might be traitors like the rest, he at once mounted his horse and galloped off to their barracks.

He found them drawn up on the plain in front of the building, and ready to start off; but his presence delayed them an instant, and they ceased shouting in order to listen to his speech. But all his efforts to induce them to return to a sense of their duty were of no avail. They drowned his voice by the uproar they renewed, and recommended him to start home, declaring that they had already too far committed themselves to hope for any favour from Government, and that they were unable to resist the torrent of the insurrection. No man, however, offered him the least violence, a proof of the respect and affection with which this officer inspired his men, even at a time when they showed themselves ingrates and rebels, and were in the act of throwing off the authority which they had hitherto acknowledged.

The infantry of the police were not long in following the example set them by the cavalry, and on the very next day broke out into rebellion. Captain Adolphe Orr, though he had removed his family into the Residency, still occupied his own house, about a thousand yards away from the bridge of boats, and not far from the Chutter Munzil palace. He and his father-in-law were about to take their customary siesta, when a havildar came rushing in, breathless with haste, and crying, "Sahib! Sahib! they have mutinied, and are coming: quick! quick! save yourself."

The two gentlemen immediately rushed to their stables, ordered their horses, and assisted in the saddling. They had just time to mount and to go out by one gate, when the men were seen coming in by the other, running and loading their muskets as they came. One or two shots were fired at them, but they were soon out of range, and galloped off for their lives to the Residency. They had had a narrow escape. The house, meanwhile, was plundered, and a thousand rupees of regimental money abstracted from the military chest.

The mutineers next directed their steps to the house lately occupied by the 32nd mess, robbing it of whatever they could take away, and destroying what they could not. They then advanced to Constantia, plundering the bazaars, which they found deserted as they went along.

Of the whole regiment only one soubahdar, one jemadar, six havildars, and twenty-six sepoys remained faithful to us. They continued to guard the prisoners at the jail who had not been released, and afterwards remained at their posts till they were relieved by a guard of the Irregulars.

As soon as this affair was known at the Residency, Sir Henry Lawrence called a council together, at which the course of action to be pursued was determined upon. The mutiny broke out at 11 A.M., and it was at 12 P.M. that the order for pursuit was given. No European cavalry had been organised at the time. Every one ran hither and thither, and whoever could seize a horse did so. Helter skelter, did we gallop on, keeping together as much as we could, and following close upon the field-pieces, on which, and the tumbrils, several volunteers had found seats. Our infantry could not be got ready in time, and our cavalry accordingly started without waiting for them, for time was valuable. They consisted of about fifty Europeans, officers, clerks, and others, and about sixty or seventy Sikhs.

The enemy, meanwhile, had taken up a position near the Martinière College at Constantia, piled arms there, and gone to rest, at first believing themselves secure from pursuit. They had afterwards, however, quite intimation enough of our intention, and before our artillery and cavalry could reach, formed square.

Constantia House, which at that time was garrisoned by a party of eight or ten volunteers, as many soldiers, and the masters and boys of the Martinière, was not molested by the mutineers. To its original strength, other fortifications had been added, so that on the whole, it presented rather a formidable appearance. One of the gentlemen attached to the College, had a most narrow escape. He had been to the city, and was returning in his buggy, at the very time when the mutineers were marching to Constantia. He came up with a few stragglers, who seized his buggy and questioned him rather narrowly. One of them asked another whether he ought not to be shot, considering he was a Feringhee; but they were evidently not inclined to be blood-thirsty. "He is only a schoolmaster," replied one contemptuously, and so they let him go his way.

The mutineers consisted of a complete regiment of native officers, non-commissioned officers, and nearly seven hundred men; together with two companies, one of the 2nd, and the other of the 3rd regiment of Military Police, that had joined the day previously. They retreated on the approach of our force, in excellent order; forming square and marching away without any hurry or confusion. They took the direction of the Dilkushar hunting park, and evidently purposed retiring on the Cawnpore route.

Our force now approached, commanded by Brigadier Inglis, of Her Majesty's 32nd Regiment. The artillery fired a few showers of grape at them, but the impromptu cavalry were not allowed to charge the main body. A few stragglers, who had been away from the head-quarters of the mutinous camp, and were surprised by our force, fell victims to the fury of our men, mostly of the Sikhs; ten or twelve were killed, and eleven taken prisoners.

Mr. Thornhill, of the Civil Service, displayed great courage on this occasion. He charged a party of two or three men, and in doing so was met with the bayonet of one and the sword and shield of another. Unfortunately, his horse became restive and unmanageable; and, before he had time to strike, he received a bayonet wound in his thigh. Nothing daunted, he wheeled about, and had just succeeded in hitting his antagonist on the head, when his horse again reared, and thus enabled his enemy to give him another thrust of the bayonet in the arm. The unfortunate gentleman, covered with blood, was then rescued by a party of Sikhs, who galloped up. Mr. Thornhill's opponent was seized by the hair, and with one swoop had his head severed from his body. The other stragglers escaped in one of the numerous little ravines which intersect the Dilkushar estate.

The main body, meanwhile, marched on through the park, halting every now and then to give us a volley of musketry. On this occasion, Captain Weston gave another proof of devotion and courage. He rode up, alone, and entering into parley with them, asked permission to address them. This they said he could not be allowed to do, without the sanction of the chief they had elected. This man, mounted on horseback, who directed all their movements, and who every now and then waved his sword at us and animated his men, however, refused to sanction his speaking to the sepoys, a proof that he feared that officer's remonstrance might lead some of the men to return to their duty. One fellow levelled his musket at Captain Weston. Bravery, even with such barbarous scoundrels as the sepoys had proved themselves to be, always ensures respect. A dozen arms were at once thrust forward to strike down the musket of the would-be murderer. "Who," said they, "who would kill such a brave man as this!" Captain Weston rode back to our force unmolested.

The enemy were from 600 to 800 strong; we, on the other hand, had only about 120, of whom the greater part were Europeans, and all mounted; but this force had never been beaten, and the moral prestige was with us. We had not yet been defeated at Chinhutt, and were all anxious to be allowed to have a brush with the enemy. But Colonel Inglis wisely judged it was possible we might be repulsed. That the enemy would have been obliged, in self-defence, to fight desperately, — for even cowards, when they cannot help themselves, can act like brave men, — was but natural to suppose, and our force was for the most part undisciplined, though, I doubt not, courageous enough. The ground was broken, and our artillery horses had the greatest difficulty in pushing over it; the enemy, besides, had the advantage of a capital position, and were in some measure secured by a copse of trees. Notwithstanding these disadvantages, our guns and cavalry pursued them for about a couple of miles away from the Martinière, the enemy still retreating in tolerable order, occasionally giving us the benefit of a volley of musketry. Unfortunately, our infantry could not come up in time. The 100 men of the 32nd at last arrived, but too late to be of service, for we were already returning. On their return, a party of town insurgents attempted to intercept our body, should they, as was hoped by the rebels, be led into the ambuscade, into which they were to be led by our treacherous guides. Brigadier Inglis, however, by making a detour at the corner of the Huzrutgunge Bazaar, and passing by the old 32nd Barracks, through the Motymahal plain, avoided this danger.

Before I conclude this chapter, I must not omit the mention of several dinners which were given as a relief, as it were, from the harassing thoughts of the day, and an agreeable mode of assembling, and discussing the news and expectations of the times. One of them was given at the post office by the Freemasons, on St. John's day. We sat down about twenty, the worshipful master, M'Grennan, presiding, and his senior warden, Bryson, acting as croupier. Seeing every one happy and delighted with the present, all philosophically forgetful of the future and the past, the thought suddenly came over me, "How many of us, now enjoying the champagne and claret which is profusely passing round, will be alive three months hence?" It was an ominous thought. Before the beginning of October, nine of our party were killed, and three lying grievously wounded in hospital. There were no songs sung, but speeches were delivered without number. The healths of the Royal family, of Sir Henry Lawrence, of Sir Hugh Wheeler and his gallant band of heroes, who were then still holding out, of Captain Alexander and the Artillery, of Colonel Inglis and the 32nd, and of almost every one present, were drunk; and appropriate speeches, of course, made thereon, especially by Mr. M'Grennan. If good wishes would have preserved life and given prosperity, what calamities would have been averted!

CHAP. IV.

THE BATTLE OF CHINHUTT.

Reconnoitring Party to Chinhutt. — Gallantry of Lieutenant Campbell and others.—Our Force moves from the Bailey-guard. — The Enemy's Acquaintance with our Plans. — The Kokrail Bridge. — Chinhutt.—Ishmaelpore.—Our Positions.—The Battle.— Colonel Case's Heroic Death. — Our Native Infantry. — The Enemy's Manœuvres. — Treachery of the Police Force and Native Gunners. — Our Retreat. — The Enemy's Cavalry cut up our Men. — Anecdote. — Our Artillery. — Europeans in the Enemy's Ranks. — Gallant Behaviour of our Volunteer Cavalry. — Incident of the Rebellion.—Noble Conduct of our Sepoys.—Lieutenant Farquhar swallows a Ball. — Sir Henry Lawrence in Action. — Defence of the Iron Bridge.— Beginning of the Siege. — Extracts from Lady Inglis's Interesting Journal. — Mr. John Lawrence's graphic Account of the Battle.

THE insurgents now, as stated by our spies, had really arrived within ten or twelve miles of Lucknow, and their intention was said to be to occupy the city. Sir Henry Lawrence therefore ordered another reconnoitring party to Chinhutt. The Volunteer Cavalry accordingly left this on the 29th of June. There was no doubt of the enemy's presence, for they had thrown out piquets to a considerable distance from the village. These our men drove in, but they could not pursue them with any degree of safety, and Chinhutt itself was evidently occupied by the enemy.

Five of the Volunteer Cavalry, Lieut. C. W. Campbell (Bengal Native Infantry), Mr. Bryson, Private Sampson, formerly of the 32nd, and two native officers of the 7th Light Cavalry, seeing a body of about eighteen troopers break from a wood, could not restrain their ardour, and, gallantly dashing at them as hard as they could, pursued them about five or six hundred yards. Our men then returned to Lucknow, without having accomplished the chief object of their expedition, viz., to ascertain what the number of the enemy really was.

Had the battle of Chinhutt taken place on the 29th instead of the 30th, there is every probability this small force would have beaten the rebels. On the night of the 29th, however, their advance guard was joined by the whole strength of the mutinous army, —a fact of which our spies said nothing. And it was upon this information that poor Sir Henry Lawrence was persuaded to plan and carry out the expedition which proved subsequently so disastrous. He, I suppose, thought, and thought rightly, that from five to six hundred British troops, Europeans and natives, commanded by English officers, would be quite sufficient to cope with three or four times that number of rebels.

Our force consisted of 300 Europeans of the 32nd Regiment, about 150 of the 13th Native Infantry, and a small number of the 71st and 48th (scarcely 100 men), 125 troopers belonging to the Oude Irregular Cavalry, mostly Sikhs, and 30 of our Volunteer Cavalry. The artillery consisted of one large howitzer drawn by elephants, four European guns of the Horse Light Field Battery, and six native guns of the Oude Field Batteries.

This small force, amounting altogether to scarce 600 men, were under the immediate orders of Brigadier-General Sir Henry Lawrence. A part collected at the Tehree Kothee, in front of the Bailey-guard, and left Lucknow early at dark. Many of the Europeans had indulged the previous evening a little too freely in liquor; but though this fact must have been known, they received, before setting out, nothing in the shape of a stimulant to prevent a reaction of the system, and to invigorate them for the fatigues of the journey. They moved on confident of success, and without making any preparations for covering their retreat, should they meet with a reverse, a contingency of which neither Sir Henry, his counsellors, nor any European individual of the force ever contemplated the possibility.

There is every likelihood that the spies, who gave us the intelligence on which we acted, had entered into a previous understanding with the rebels, though it is also possible they were themselves deceived in taking an advanced guard of the enemy for the whole of the hostile army. Of one thing I am positive, that the insurgents were perfectly well acquainted with all our movements; and they must certainly have received correct intimation of the strength of the force that was advancing to dispute their entrance into Lucknow. A little bridge crosses a streamlet with very steep banks called the Kokrail, about six miles distant from the iron bridge. Here our troops halted, and Sir Henry, it appeared, felt at one time inclined to draw up his little army there, and to await the coming of the enemy. It would have been wise to have done so, but a fatality seemed to have pushed him forwards, and he unfortunately again listened to the advisers who wished him to advance. There were rum and water and biscuits with the baggage, but no refreshment was offered to the soldiers, who were already beat by the morning sun, which was striking right into their faces.

Our little army now approached the plain of Chinhutt, a large village situated on the banks of a very extensive jheel or lake, close to which is built a sporting castle of the former kings. Arrived here, the whole of the enemy's army was found drawn up right in front of the village,—not four or five thousand strong, as the spies had reported, but numbering at least fifteen or sixteen thousand men, with not merely two batteries of field-pieces, but six or seven, consisting of more than thirty-six cannon of various calibre.

To the left of Chinhutt was the camp of the mutineers, strongly entrenched. Not far from it was a little hamlet of seven or eight huts. To our left was the larger village of Ishmaelpore, at which place, in fact, the action was really fought. Our 8-inch howitzer was placed in the middle of the road, right in front of the enemy. Our guns were more to the right. The European guns, under the immediate command of Captain Simons, who at the time was in command of the whole of the artillery, were in advance; and of the native guns, under Lieutenants Macfarlane, Bryce, and Alexander, two were on the same side, but nearer to the road to the right, a few yards in the rear, and two others were placed to the left of the road.

Our infantry was skirmishing in front of the village of Ishmaelpore, the 32nd before it, and the native infantry extending themselves to the left. Our cavalry was placed to the right of the guns a little to the rear. A ravine was running from north to south, then to our right. In this were placed our 300 police, armed with firelocks, bayonets, swords, and pistols.

Such were our positions, when the action of Ishmaelpore or Chinhutt began by our commencing fire with the 8-inch howitzer, directed by Lieutenant Bonham. A shell thrown at a range of 1300 yards burst right over the heads of the enemy's main column, and the fire kept up by us soon made the rebels move off the road. We thought the day was ours, and Captain Wilson, the Deputy Assistant-Adjutant-General, who throughout the action had behaved with great coolness, and was always in the thickest of the fight, came riding up, crying, "That's it! there they go! keep it up!" But instead of retreating, the enemy had only changed the position of their main body and their guns towards our right, and thence continued to cannonade almost simultaneously with ours, while their skirmishers at the same time advanced to our left.

The village of Ishmaelpore was filled with the enemy's sharpshooters. Colonel Case, at the head of his 32nd men, gallantly led them up to it, but fell, struck by a bullet. Had he lived he would probably have succeeded in clearing the village; but the death of their brave and noble leader seemed suddenly to have disheartened his men, and they all lay down on the ground behind a very little undulating rise in the field, though firing at the enemy as fast as they could load. Captain Bassano, seeing the Colonel fall, went up to assist him. "Captain Bassano," was the noble speech of the wounded hero, "leave me to die here. Your place is at the head of your company. I have no need of assistance."

Meanwhile, Major Bruère, with his Native 13th, Colonel Palmer, commanding the 48th, and Lieutenant F. M. Birch, with the Sikhs of the 71st Native Infantry, occupied the right of our force, and answered the enemy's musketry fire with great spirit.

The enemy's positions and subsequent manœuvres were admirable, and displayed generalship worthy of a better cause. Had the leader commanding the rebel army been obeyed to the letter, and had he had under his command men of ordinary valour, instead of a cowardly mass of native soldiers, distrustful of their own powers, not one man of our little force would have reached Lucknow to tell the tale of our disaster.

TREACHERY OF THE POLICE FORCE.

The enemy, as soon as the action began, poured a stream of cavalry on to our right, out-flanking us on that side, and getting on the road to cut off our retreat. Their infantry at the same time fired volleys of musketry on ours, still lying down before Ishmaelpore, which was now completely occupied by the rebels, who continued to fire with perfect safety to themselves from behind loopholed walls. They at the same time threw out skirmishers towards our front and left, thus attempting to form a junction with their cavalry to our right, and to make a complete circle, with our force in the centre.

The whole of the Police Force, as soon as the first shot was fired, went at once over to the enemy, as if by a preconcerted arrangement, and commenced firing at us. At the same time, our native gunners, without firing a shot, cut the traces of the artillery horses, and escaped, some deserting to the rebels, others galloping off in the direction of Lucknow, whence they went on towards Cawnpore, to give the first news of their defection and our defeat. The other native gunners, seeing themselves hemmed in, and not able to desert to the opposite side, hurried away as fast as the horses could carry them. Several of the cavalry threatened to shoot the men if they did not halt, but the only effect of such menaces was to induce them to stop till the threateners were out of sight.

The large howitzer, which the men had christened "Turk," continued to play on the enemy, and was worked splendidly, tearing great gaps in the enemy's ranks with each shell thrown from it by our European artillerymen. The native drivers of the elephants that had been yoked in it had, however, also escaped, and our position was now anything but comfortable.

The main body of the insurgent army now moved as if on a parade ground, the infantry in open columns of companies, artillery and cavalry at intervals, large masses of the latter gaining the road to cut off our retreat, and infantry skirmishers on the other side continuing to advance. The latter, however, were held in check by our sepoys, who, throughout that day's fight, behaved in a most gallant and noble manner.

The order for retreat was now given, but the 32nd still kept up a brisk and murderous fire, many men firing more than a hundred rounds of ammunition. Poor gallant Lieutenant-Colonel Case was still seen on the roadside, lying with eyes wide open, with his sword firmly grasped, in the midst of the corpses of his own brave companions in arms. Lieutenant Brackenbury was shot next, and Thompson, the adjutant, was mortally wounded. Captain Bassano was likewise wounded in the leg, but succeeded in arriving safe in the Residency, through the intrepidity of a sepoy of the 13th Native Infantry, who carried him for a considerable distance on his back. The men were now panic-struck, and retreated towards Lucknow as fast as they could go. Many poor fellows, desperately wounded and unable to rise, whom no one could or would assist, were seen fighting like bull-dogs held at bay, till they at last fell dead. Parched with thirst, and weak from exertion and fatigue, under the intense heat of a June sun, numbers fell down exhausted, and were cut up by the enemy's cavalry. Others fell, struck by apoplexy.

Captain Stevens was one out of very many who fell on that disastrous day. He was wounded in the leg, and managed to limp on for five miles afterwards; but the insurgents pressed on him closer and closer, till he too shared the death which had overtaken so many others. None asked for mercy, for none expected it. Dr. Darby in vain called out to the men to stop for God's sake, and to remember Waterloo and Vimiera. None heeded him; and Lieutenant Webb, his face black with gunpowder and the peak of his cap shot off, made himself hoarse with shouting to the men to halt. The officers of the 32nd

Regiment spared no exertions to retrieve the day; but with a few hundred men against myriads, what chance had they, even if the soldiers had not been half dead with exhaustion? The Sikh Cavalry, notwithstanding the heroic bearing and tact of their officer, Lieutenant Hardinge, had been the first to fly and to communicate the panic to our infantry. They had dashed at the enemy's cavalry, and cut their way through where the enemy, opening their flanks, did not render that necessary, and fled with all possible speed to Lucknow.

The European Artillery, meanwhile, had also been ordered to retreat, and all their guns, with the exception of the 8-inch howitzer, were put into movement and galloped off. Of the native guns, two were saved; the rest fell into the hands of the enemy. Sergeant Miller was sent off to bring back the elephants to drag the large cannon off, but unsuccessfully. Seeing the enemy's cavalry approach the howitzer, Lieutenant Bonham called out to Captain Ratcliffe to protect it. Four men accordingly fell out, of whom I can only remember the name of Mr. John Lawrence, and were thus exposed to a raking fire. They came in time to disperse four of the enemy's cavalry, who were riding up to the very muzzle of the gun. One of them fired his carbine

HEROISM OF PRIVATE JOHNSON.

at Lieutenant Bonham, and wounded him in the arm. That officer determined to spike the gun, since there was no chance of yoking the elephants again by the drag-ropes. Unfortunately there was no spike at hand. Sergeant Suttle, who was there, accordingly broke off the priming wire in the touch-hole, and abandoned it. A man named Johnson, of the cavalry, previously a private in the 32nd, performed a deed of daring which saved us one of the guns. Seeing it abandoned, he galloped up to it, the enemy as usual retiring on his approach, dismounted, and making over his horse to a brother soldier, mounted one of the artillery horses, and safely brought the gun in. He was recommended for the Victoria Cross.

Masses of the enemy's cavalry had gained the road between our men retreating and the little bridge. They were apparently commanded by some European, who was seen waving his sword, and attempting to make his men follow him and dash at ours. He was a handsome-looking man, well-built, fair, about twenty-five years of age, with light mustachios, and wearing the undress uniform of a European cavalry officer, with a blue and gold-laced cap on his head. Whether he was a Russian—one suspected to be such had been seized by the authorities, confined, and then released,—or, what is more likely, one of the renegade

Christians who had changed their religion and adopted the native habits, manners, and costume, I cannot tell.

Our Volunteer Cavalry, consisting of not more than twenty-five or thirty men, were now ordered to charge the enemy, who had actually occupied the road. Though these mustered about four hundred sabres, the Volunteers—though few of them had ever seen a shot fired—obeyed their order right gallantly. They charged; but the enemy never waited for their approach, flying, as they advanced, to what was then our right, and coming upon their own infantry skirmishers, who were still held in check by our native soldiers under the command of the gallant Major Bruère and Colonel Palmer, who were retreating, but halting every now and then to pour a volley into them.

Our men pursued the enemy nearly a mile off the field; and, on coming up with the insurgent infantry, sabred a few of them. The 13ths added not a little to swell the number of killed and wounded on the enemy's side. The 32nd men retreating had also succeeded in keeping off the stream of cavalry hovering on their left. The Volunteers had now lost one man in killed—poor Mr. M'Auliffe, the head clerk of the Deputy Commissioner's Office, who had but lately arrived at Lucknow to join his appointment—and two wounded. Mr. May, of the Engineers' Office, had his horse shot under him, and, spraining his ancle, found, like other wounded men, a seat on a gun-carriage. He had been so fortunate as to save the life of an officer who, during the siege, subsequently greatly distinguished himself—Ensign Birch, of the 71st Native Infantry. The Volunteers having succeeded in giving time for, and covering the retreat of our infantry and guns, returned to the rear, to prevent the enemy following up too closely.

On this retreat a striking incident occurred, which marked the distressing results arising from the insurrection. While the guns were galloping back, the musket of a sepoy of the 13th, running beside one of them, accidentally went off, and slightly wounded a gunner. Immediately suspecting it to be done intentionally, he drew his pistol, and shot the man dead.

When near the Kokrail Bridge, the guns were unlimbered, to give the enemy a few rounds of grape, as their masses had advanced very close; but not one round of ammunition remained,—our native gunners having evidently succeeded in treacherously making away with the greater part. The simple unlimbering of the guns, however, had the effect of causing the whole rebel army to halt. The retreat then went on again.

The sepoys on our side, though retreating, did so in order. They behaved for the greater part in the kindest manner to the wounded Europeans, taking up great numbers of them, and leaving their own wounded uncared for on the battle-field. They had been suspected of being also tainted with the general disaffection, and were therefore anxious to regain the esteem and confidence of their European officers. They gave indeed the most striking proofs of their fidelity and loyalty on that day, showering volleys of musketry, and, native-like, of abuse, on their assailants, and calling them all the most injurious epithets in their vocabulary. Major Bruère, who was wounded, was assisted by them to a place of comparative safety, and reached the Residency, only, however, to meet his death some months after.

The 32nd, less accustomed to the heat, and suffering from many more disadvantages than their native companions in arms, were many of them assisted by the artillery and cavalry, whenever practicable. Young Sequera, who was afterwards shot during the siege, dismounted from his horse, and, giving it to one of the wounded, arrived on foot; and in fact almost every other cavalry volunteer was encumbered with two, three, and even four foot soldiers,— one perhaps holding his hand, another laying fast hold on the crupper, the tail of the horse, or the stirrup, or on all together. Thus each of that noble body individually was the means of saving the life of more than one European comrade, and collectively they saved the whole force that escaped. No men could have behaved with greater coolness than they did; and nowhere was British gallantry more conspicuous than at that terrible retreat of Chinhutt. Besides Mr. M'Auliffe, the Volunteers lost Captain M'Lean, 71st Native Infantry, whose horse was killed by a round shot, and who was wounded in two places before the enemy cut him up. Private Sampson, of the 32nd, was knocked off his saddle by a musket shot in the head. Lieutenant C. W. Campbell, 71st Native Infantry, was very severely wounded in the left thigh. Captain Simons, commanding the Artillery, had in the very beginning of the fight been slightly wounded.

Lieutenant Farquhar, 7th Light Cavalry, received a bullet wound through the cheek; and two or three other volunteers, whose names I do not recollect, were slightly wounded in various places. Lieutenant Farquhar, it was afterwards discovered, had without being aware of it swallowed the ball, which the doctors had puzzled their brains in vain in attempting to discover.*

* I subjoin an extract from Lieutenant Farquhar's own journal, in which this incident is graphically described: "As for myself,

There were no doolies (hospital litters) to be had for the wounded. At the very onset of the action one of the dooly bearers was killed, and the rest of the bearers fled in confusion, leaving the doolies in the hands of the enemy.

The cavalry every now and then faced right about, and then proceeded on, their sergeant, Mr. Byron, being at least twenty yards in their rear and coming on at a gentle trot only. Several of them took firelocks out of the hands of the 32nd, and discharged them at the enemy. Numbers continued to drop off and to lie down on the broken ground traversed by our men.

Sir Henry Lawrence was seen in the most exposed parts of the field, riding from one part of it to

when I got to the European hospital, I found Dr. Boyd, of the 32nd, and Dr. Fayrer (both of whom I knew very well), ready to attend on me. They put me to a great deal of pain in probing the wound and taking out pieces of the fractured jaw; but they could not make out what had become of the ball, and I was not wiser. The doctors believed at first that it was all up with me, thinking that the bullet had lodged in my head. Ten days afterwards, however, I discovered that I had swallowed and digested it;— my digestion must have been good at the time! The ball, on going through my jaw, must have taken the direction of my throat, and I must then have swallowed it, together with the blood collecting in my mouth. The ball, when it struck me, must have been getting spent. Otherwise it would probably have gone through both jaws, and come out on the opposite side."

SIR HENRY LAWRENCE IN ACTION.

another, amidst a terrific fire of grape, round shot, and musketry, which made us lose men at every step. When near the Kokrail bridge, he wrung his hands in the greatest agony of mind, and, forgetful of himself, thought only of his poor soldiers. "My God! my God!" he was heard to say, "and I brought them to this!" So confident must he have been of success, that he had ordered his carriage to meet him half-way. The horses were of course taken out to escape with, but the carriage was left sticking in the sand. Captain James, the Assistant-Commissary-General, was shot through the thigh by his side.

When approaching the iron bridge, men, women, and children, rich and poor, crowded around the weary and thirsty men, and offered water, which was greedily swallowed. Nothing could exceed their kindness,—a proof that we yet had friends in the city, and found many sympathisers among the natives.

The enemy was close on our heels, but we now kept them at bay for more than half an hour. Our guns, with a sufficiency of ammunition, which had been brought from the Residency, and a fresh company of European infantry, effectually succeeded in keeping the enemy from crossing the iron bridge, and enabled us to make good the escape of the remaining fugitives. There was, however, not much time to lose, as numbers of the enemy's cavalry were fording the river below the bridge. Crossing near Motymahal, they rode up to the Khas bazaar, and occupied the whole of the south and east parts of the city. The guns of Muchee Bhawn, which, in default of artillery officers, were worked by Major Francis and Lieutenant Huxham, did great execution, and kept off the enemy from the stone bridge higher up, and commanded the north and west side of Lucknow. The officers of the 5th and 7th Oude Irregular Infantry had therefore time to effect their escape into Muchee Bhawn.

From that time, eleven o'clock of Tuesday, the 30th of June, the siege of Lucknow, which but for the unfortunate expedition of Chinhutt would perhaps never have occurred, or would at least not have been so protracted, may be said to have begun. We had lost 118 European officers and men, in killed, and 182 natives, killed and missing. No hope could of course be entertained of Europeans missing, though it is possible that some few of our native sepoys either went over to the enemy's side or escaped for their lives away from our entrenchments. Fifty-four Europeans, and only eleven natives, returned to the Residency wounded.

I cannot refrain from here adding the very interesting description, by Mrs. (now Lady) Inglis, of the condition of the ladies in the Residency previous to the battle of Chinhutt, and a brief notice of that action: —

"Every day news arrived from the district of mutinies and murders, and at the same time letters from Sir Hugh Wheeler, earnestly craving help, which, alas! it was not in our power to give. The enemy had broken the bridge over the river which ran between us; and to have got even a large force over without boats, which had also been taken away, would have been a most perilous undertaking indeed. The engineers pronounced it impracticable; but even had it been feasible, a European could hardly be spared from our garrison, when we were daily expecting to hear of a large army marching against us, and our force was a very small one. Still, it was very sad to reflect upon the situation of our poor countrymen, exposed, as we knew they were, to the greatest hardships and miseries, and surrounded by a band of the most cruel, bloodthirsty wretches that this world has ever produced. We continued in this state of suspense and anxiety, sometimes receiving reports that Delhi had fallen and troops arrived at Cawnpore, but never obtaining any reliable information. We ladies were prisoners, never being able to go beyond the Residency gates; but we used to spend our evenings at the top of the house, and the children were allowed to play in the gardens. Cholera was beginning to show itself in the place, and also small-pox. Numbers of guns were found buried in different parts of the city and brought into the

Residency. Officers and men were hard at work night and day, and exposed continually to the broiling sun;— there was so much to be done to put our position in a defensible condition, so few hands to work, and we never knew the day when we might be attacked. Many people were determined that not a shot would be fired, and made no preparations for a siege. John always said we should be attacked, and should have a hard struggle, our position being a bad one. On the 24th I was taken ill with fever, and was laid up until the 28th, when some suspicious marks showed themselves upon me, and the doctors pronounced my disease small-pox. This was not very pleasant news; but I was said to have it very mildly, though my face was covered. I immediately begged to be removed, to prevent the infection spreading, and John had a hut comfortably arranged for me, into which I was to have moved on the 28th, but news arrived that the enemy were close upon us; and as, in the event of our being attacked, the house we were in was not safe, it was thought better for me to wait, so as not to be obliged to move twice, as the hut would, of course, have to be abandoned. On the 29th the enemy were reported to be within a few miles of us; and it was thought advisable to bring in the force from the cantonments. Accordingly they marched in that evening; part came to the Residency, and the remainder were ordered to the fort. Colonel Case being in command there, he came in the evening to pay his wife a visit. Poor man, he little thought it was the last hour they would spend on earth together. The next morning we were awoke by a noise outside our windows, and found out a force of cavalry, infantry, and artillery were on the point of moving from the Residency. We had heard of no intended expedition, but immediately fancied they must be going out to meet the enemy. I was feeling very unwell, and dozed for some hours, and awoke, saying, 'Oh, I have dreamed our troops have been signally defeated.' My dream proved but too true. An officer was soon afterwards brought in wounded; and he brought the disastrous intelligence that the native troops with us had proved unfaithful. At the same time the report came in that our force was returning, and it was very doubtful whether they would be able to save their guns. You may imagine our feelings of anxiety and consternation. I posted myself at the window — for remaining in bed was out of the question — and watched the poor men coming in; a melancholy spectacle, indeed; no order; one after the other; some riding; some wounded, supported by their comrades; some on guns; some fell down and died from exhaustion, not half a mile from our position. The enemy followed them to the bridge close to the Residency, which was defended by a company of the 32nd, under Mr. Edmonstone, a gallant young officer. I could see the smoke of the musketry, and plainly discerned the enemy on the opposite bank of the river. Soon after John returned, and my heart felt overflowing with joy and thankfulness; but, to my very great sorrow, he turned to Mrs. Case, and told her her poor husband was killed. The shock was a fearful one, for she had just been assured by her servants of his safety. Poor thing! the luxury of quiet sorrow was not granted her; the enemy were firing heavily upon our position, and we were obliged in all haste to leave our room, and descend to the lower part of the house, where we were comparatively safe; we spent a miserable day, in a hot close room almost underground; and at dusk, when the fire had a little slackened, John moved us over into a room he had prepared for us in a court, surrounded by high walls, and which has been our abode from that time to the present, Wonderful to say, although the disease was just at its height with me, I did not suffer at all from the knocking about and fatigue and excitement of that wretched day. It was not for some time that we learnt the real account of this disastrous affair."

By the kind permission of my companion in arms, Mr. John Lawrence, I am enabled to conclude this chapter with a graphic account of the battle of Chinhutt, written two or three days after its occurrence: —

"30*th June, Tuesday.*—At four A.M. this morning a force consisting of 250 of the 32nd Queen's; the Sikh Cavalry, some 100 sabres; Volunteer Horse, some thirty-five; some of the 13th Native Infantry, and a batch of Carnegie's *gallant* Burkundauzes, were ordered to Chinhutt: we had also one 8-inch howitzer, drawn by elephants, and some ten field-guns, native gunners, and drivers. The morning was very close and suffocating when we set out. The big gun was rather an inconvenience, for the elephants literally crawled along the road. We got up to the village of Ishmaelgunge, on the Chinhutt road, about nine A.M. Here we drew up in battle array: the 32nd lay in the hollow of the road, to the left, under the village, with some of the 13th Native Infantry as skirmishers: in the centre of the road was the 8-inch, to the right the light field-guns, Sikhs and ourselves to the extreme right of all. We opened fire; and the sound of the 9-pounder yet rang in our ears when the artillery of the rebels opened with beautiful precision: every shot flew slap into us. Our guns hammered away manfully for an hour; and as for the Europeans working the howitzer, their conduct was beyond praise. The fire was awful; the enemy's cavalry now commenced pouring at us in one unceasing tide towards our right in the Lucknow direction, evidently outflanking us.

"After an hour's cannonade, the opposite artillery ceased its fire: in a few minutes rolling volleys of musketry from the village of Ishmaelgunge showed that Jack Sepoy was there. The Volunteer Cavalry was ordered to move further to the right, and then, for the first time, I got a view of the plain between Ishmaelgunge and Chinhutt. It was one moving mass of men: regiment after regiment of the insurgents poured steadily towards us, the flanks covered with a foam of skirmishers, the light puffs of smoke from their muskets floating from every ravine and bunch of grass in our front. As to the mass of the troops, they came on in quarter-distance columns, the standards waving in their places, and everything performed as steadily as possible. A field day on parade could not have been better; and what was to hinder the enemy from doing just as they pleased? Our artillery ceased its fire, but beyond might be heard the crashing roll of musketry in Ishmaelgunge, where the 32nd, outnumbered by myriads, still maintained a struggle. Our side was perfectly passive; Carnegie's *invincibles* had deserted; and while I was looking about for them, a bustle in my rear attracted my attention: the rascally gunners were cutting their traces, and were galloping away; the elephants for the howitzer gone, the Sikh Cavalry flying at full speed on the Lucknow road. A few European gunners, the Volunteer Cavalry, and the 32nd, remained; but now the enemy pressed on more closely, — he unlimbered his guns, and swept us with grape and canister; the deadly *mitraille* of musketry poured in one leaden shower from the swarming skirmishers. And now the valiant few of the 32nd are beaten near the village, and come upon the road; their gallant colonel (Case) falls dead as he approaches; some of our guns are spiked and abandoned (the howitzer among them), four are limbered, and the gun-carriages, covered with wounded men, gallop towards Lucknow. The 32nd also retreat; mixed up with them are some of the braves of the 13th Native Infantry, — noble fellows, who were seen carrying wounded soldiers to the gun-carriages, abandoning their own wounded comrades on the ground. The Volunteer Cavalry form upon the left of the road; the rest of the handful of England's army is in retreat. A cloud of insurgent cavalry is gathering on the far rear to the left of our retreating column. Do they mean to charge down among those staggering, half-dead heroes, who can scarcely walk along? The red and blue flags thicken among them; when the tremendous voice of our leader (Captain Radcliffe of the 7th Light Cavalry), is heard, — 'Three's right!' 'Trot!' and we sweep out of the trees, and off the road, and we are within a quarter of a mile of our opponents. Their '*gole*' still forms heavy and dark, and now two light guns open on us; but the 9-pounder scarce whistled over head when the stentorian '*Charge!*' was heard; the notes of our trumpet sounded sharp above the din of the fight, and we rode straight at them: the cowards never bided the shock; they galloped like furies from the spot. Five hundred cavalry and two guns to be hunted by thirty-five sabres; it was a miserable fact! The guns got under the shelter of a regiment of the line, which we dared not charge, for the first volley they gave us emptied two saddles; so, *sabring* up the scattered skirmishers, we wheeled and galloped to the rear of our slowly moving columns.

"The battle of Chinhutt was done; the line of our retreat was marked by the bodies of the 32nd, their arms, their accoutrements; men were falling untouched by ball; the heat of a June sun was killing more than the enemy. Hard upon our heels they followed; and as we got into the Residency so did the round shot of the pursuing foe whistle in the air. The siege then virtually commenced; how to end, the Lord alone can tell. In one fatal day the 32nd have left 3 officers and 116 men to tell the tale of British heroism; but, alas! also of British failure."

CHAP. V.

THE RESIDENCY ENTRENCHMENTS.

Panic in Lucknow. — The Hospital. — Kindness of the Women to the Wounded. — Remarkable Appearance of the City. — The Prisoners Escape. — Description of our Entrenchments. — Captain Anderson's House. — The Cawnpore Battery. — The School-houses. — The Brigade Mess. — The Sikh Square. — Gubbins's Battery. — The Bhoosa-guard. — The Residency. — The Hospital. — The Bailey-guard. — Dr. Fayrer's House. — The Post Office. — The Financial Outpost. — Sago's Outpost. — The Judicial Garrison. — The Jail. — The Begum's Kothy.

THE enemy now at our door, as it were, the crowded streets began to be entirely deserted. People were flying in all directions up the streets as far away from the Residency as possible. Horses without riders galloped up and down; elephants and camels were hurried away by their drivers; and the boats on the river shoved off far away from the English encampment and the iron bridge. Soon not a living man was seen. All outside our entrenchments was as quiet and still as if it were a city of the dead.

The Residency was one scene of confusion. Women and children were flying to the Resident's house from all the outposts, leaving their property unprotected. Every one thought of his life only; men were seen running to the trenches with arms in their hands. The hospital presented one of the most heart-rending sights imaginable, the more horrifying as it was quite new and unexpected. All felt the deepest compassion for the poor wounded, who were conveyed in long lines to the banqueting hall, now converted into a hospital. The women flocked around them, and gave them ice-water,—for up to this day we continued to be supplied with ice,—fanned them, supplied temporary bandages, and showed as much solicitude for them as if they had been their own relatives, which was probably the case with many of them.

It would have been well for the unfortunate sick and wounded if the same kindness had been shown to them throughout the siege by those whose professional duties did not oblige them to attend to the hospital; but unfortunately such scenes became so common that scarcely a thought was afterwards bestowed on the poor sufferers. People grew callous from a continued sight of pain, in the same way as they become accustomed to danger. Men covered with blood, some with mangled limbs, their muscles contracted with agony, their faces pale, their bodies almost cold, some with the death-rattle in their throats, others groaning and turning about restlessly, taken from the gun-carriage at the bridge and brought here in doolies, were lying in rows in the hospital. The surgeons and apothecaries were to be seen busy enough, cutting, probing the wounds, amputating, and bandaging. All the horrors of war were at once laid bare.

Meanwhile the batteries and works of defence, which had scarcely in many places been completed, began to be deserted; the coolies all making their escape. Many of our servants also decamped, and left us without food, without clothes, without attendance. The greater portion of them deserted during the first week; and for gentlemen, ladies, and children accustomed to all the luxuries and comforts of an Indian life to be thus suddenly thrown upon their own resources, and gradually to be deprived of all conveniences and attendance, was very hard indeed. Many, less fortunate than others, who had been able to retain at least some of their servants, were afterwards obliged to sweep their own rooms, to draw water themselves from the well, to wash their own clothes, to cook their own food, and to perform all the menial duties of a household. Besides this, some of us were cramped up into a little outhouse, or stable, that on former occasions few would have considered good enough for a bearer. Many were huddled into a large room in common with dozens of other families. All privacy was destroyed, and the houses within the Residency compound resembled small barrack rooms rather than the apartments of respectable families.

But I am anticipating. I said that Lucknow, shortly after the Chinhutt affair, was suddenly changed into a city as it were of the dead, and that its hum and bustle were instantaneously hushed into the most ominous and uncomfortable stillness imaginable. But we soon had proofs of its being peopled: for the whizzing of numberless bullets made every position one of danger. Many of us went on the terraces of our houses or garrisons, and with telescope in hand surveyed the hordes of the enemy still crossing the Goomtee, at a considerable distance below, and then galloping up the streets. The iron bridge was almost deserted: for the Redan, one of our batteries, had opened fire upon it, and swept a number of the enemy off it. The prison nearly opposite the Bailey-guard Gate of the Residency might now be seen full of life. The liberated prisoners, who that very morning and the day before had perhaps worked at our batteries, carrying beams and baskets of mud for us, were now seen making their escape, holding on by ropes, which they let down the high walls and barred windows. But it soon became too hot for us to remain. Ping, pang, whizz, bang, went the bullets, touching the very hair of our whiskers, and flying about in and from all directions. By the evening, the place in which I was,—one of the most exposed in the whole garrison, the house next to the Cawnpore battery,—was covered with as many bullet marks as there are stars in the heavens. They were countless.

At the head of the street leading to Cawnpore we saw numbers of curious natives, most of them unarmed, others armed, crossing from one side to the other. We were still novices in war, and killed and wounded only a few of them with our rifles and muskets, our officers at first preventing us from firing at them and the liberated jailbirds, while our guns which commanded the road did not open out upon them, as they should and might have done. Occasionally a cannon shot was fired at us, but these were rare on the first day. They had not had time yet to place their cannons in position, and accordingly did not give us so full a benefit of them on that day as subsequently.

Our entrenchments were in the form of an irregular pentagon. To the corner of the south and east side was the house of Captain Anderson, of the 25th Native Infantry, who commanded the garrison; a wall surrounded its compound. To the south, it faced the Cawnpore road; to the east, a road leading to it in one direction, and to the Baily-guard Gate in another. Within the compound was a trench towards the two tolerably deep roads with palisades within them. The house itself was defended by barricades, and, like every other place within the garrison, loopholed in all directions. It was two-storied, and had two large verandahs facing the east and west. There was then no battery near it, but yet it was one of the most strongly fortified places against an assault by storm.

Next to Captain Anderson's house, and communicating by a hole in a wall, was the Cawnpore battery, not, as it is now, sunk, but raised, and in a level with Deprat's house, which was standing to the right of it. The battery had then three guns, an 8-pounder facing the Cawnpore road, and a 9-pounder commanding Johannes' house, which was right opposite Deprat's. A third 9-pounder was intended to sweep the road leading to the right towards Golagunge, past the King's Hospital. Before the platform on which the large gun was placed, protected without by a stockade, and within by sand-bags, was a trench leading past Captain Anderson's compound wall.

Deprat's house, where I lived, had had a verandah overlooking Johannes' wall; but this was now walled up about six feet high, with mud about two and a half feet thick, but appearing from the street, owing to the platform on which it was erected, at least ten or twelve feet high. A sloping roof covered the verandah, which, besides the two feet of clear space between it and the mud wall, had, in a number of loopholes, other means of sight to fire from.

The mud wall was continued outside of the house, leading in a straight line to the wall of the next house. This continuation of a wall was about nine feet high, and a very cutcha* affair it was. Captain Anderson, of the engineers, had not had time to complete it as he desired. But the wall, as it was, protected very imperfectly a little yard with a well almost in the centre. No stockade was in front of it, and we all felt this to be a considerably weak point. Deprat's house itself was.

---

* There are no words in the English language expressing so forcibly the meaning of the Hindostanee terms, "*cutchâ*" and "*pukka*." The latter has reference to masonry, or any solid brickwork, the former to earthen or imperfect work. *Pukka* might be rendered as "made of bricks," "perfect," "well built," "strong," "clever." Cutcha is the opposite.

a lower-storied one, with three large rooms in it. Below it was a tyekhana, or cellar, having the same number of rooms as above, besides the one under the verandah. These, at the beginning of the siege, were stocked with liquors of all sorts, and goods, and the furniture of Lady Outram, Mr. Jackson, mine and his own.

Next to us was one of the houses of the mahajuns, Shah Beharee Loll and Rugbar Dial, but now occupied as a school-house by the Martiniere. The massive brick-wall of the house itself needed no other protection, but it yet had a stockade of high beams before it, and was loopholed of course. The house was a corner house, being separated from the King's Hospital, opposite its north side, by a fine road leading to the Residency, past its own entrance and those leading to the Sikcha jail and post office on the right. Facing it was the gate of the Begum's Kothee, leading past the left to a little road abutting in the financial commissioner's house; on its left was the judicial commissioner's house, and on its right the Residency Jailkhana, where formerly a guard of Captain Weston's police were over the prisoners within. The former road was then blocked up by a stockade consisting of huge beams, and extending past the school-houses to near the wall of Deprat's courtyard. Down this road, and between the two walls forming it, before arriving at the post office, was a barricade formed of a mud wall and a trench in front of it.

Continuing our line in a southerly direction, the Daroo Shuffa, or King's Hospital, came next. It was a very high and convenient building, now converted into the mess of the officers of the Oudh force and Native Infantry regiments, and from its lofty and well protected terrace, overtopping both Johannes' house and the buildings on the Golagunge roads, commanded capital positions for rifle-shooting and musketry. It was then known as the Brigade Mess, and had in its rear a parallelogram, bounded by tolerably convenient outhouses, occupied by officers and other families, and divided by another range of low pukka buildings into two large and commodious squares.

Next in order, and almost in a direct line with the Brigade Mess, were low pukka buildings, then known as the Sikh Square. A sort of scaffolding was made within to enable the Sikh guard and native Christians that garrisoned the place to fire from a more elevated position. Behind it, in another square or rather parallelogram, were the artillery bullocks, and further in, another square, the horses of the 7th Light, and of the Sikh Cavalry.

A narrow lane separated the latter outpost from Gubbins's battery, for it was not then barricaded at its entrance. The only defence to the approach of the enemy up the lane was a barricade of earth hastily thrown up and strewed with a few brambles. The garden, in the centre of which was the house of Mr. Gubbins the Financial Commissioner, was bounded to the south by the Golagunge road and by the walls of a house known as Young Johannes. These were commanded by outhouses belonging to Mr. Gubbins's yard, those to the left being guarded by our Sikhs, from whose roofs a low earth wall covered with sand-bags enabled them to fire. Those to the right, and separated by a high wall from the former, which they otherwise resembled, had in them a passage leading to a half-moon battery erected by Mr. Gubbins at his own expense, but for the cost of which he was about to be remunerated.

This battery had at first only a 9-pounder, which, however, could play in three different points: one commanding the road between Johannes' house to that leading low down to Hill's shop in the direction of the iron bridge; another, the Golagunge Bazaar; and a third, numerous little buildings to the west. Gubbins's outpost advanced out of a straight line towards the west, projecting considerably in that direction. Another battery of one gun, also a 9-pounder, faced a low garden, originally belonging to Mr. Gubbins's house, and surrounded by a low wall, behind which the enemy was afterwards wont to fire at us. The gun was next to a range of outhouses, the roofs and interior of which were occupied by our sentries. Another very narrow lane, to the west, used to lead to a thickly peopled part of the town, which had then been mostly knocked down, but not sufficiently to prevent the enemy's occupying the ruins, and peppering at us thence, and erecting batteries against us in front. Gubbins's garrison was commanded by Major Apthorp.

Next to Gubbins's west side were what were called the Bhoosa entrenchments, commanding a musketry fire through the loopholes all along the outhouses and walls surrounding them. In front of them were the ruins of a number of houses occupied by the enemy, in several of which they subsequently erected batteries of guns. Included in the Bhoosa entrenchments were the bullock-sheds, the butcher-yard, the slaughter-house, and a guard-house of Europeans. Behind these was the Bhoosa store (cut chaff), in what was formerly the Ball Alley (or racket court), facing a low terrace, which also commanded the west side. Still further to the rear was Ommaney's house, protected towards the Bhoosa entrenchments, in the event of their being taken by the enemy, by a deep ditch and a hedge of cactus, and fortified, should Gubbins's outpost be carried by the rebels, by a couple of guns, intended to sweep the road leading to it and to the Sikh Square.

Between the Bhoosa entrenchments and the Bherykhana, or sheep-pen, which adjoins the former, there was an uncompleted battery, since finished, and then supplied with mortars. There was only a very weak native guard there, as the ground facing it had been in a great measure levelled, and consisted of only low ruins, and was, besides, commanded by the Bhoosa entrenchments and Gubbins's battery on one side, and the Church garrison and Innes' outpost on the other. Captain Boileau commanded these outposts.

The churchyard was contiguous to the sheep-pen. In its centre was the church, a Gothic building, with twenty low steeples, then converted into a store-room for grain and guarded by a dozen Europeans. At the gate to the east was a mortar battery, destined to shell the whole of the western and northern buildings as far as the iron and stone bridges. The victims of the former insurrection at cantonments were the first who were buried here. It had not before been used as a place of interment, but it was soon destined to be filled with heaps of the corpses of the gallant defenders of the Lucknow garrison.

Innes' outpost, so called from having been previously to the siege the residence of Lieutenant M'Leod Innes of the engineers, was separated from the churchyard by a low mud wall, and faced to the west several very large houses, subsequently strongly fortified and filled with insurgent rifle- and matchlockmen. The house, a long, commodious lower-roomed building, had a verandah to the east, covered by a sloping pukka roof, and another to the north.

It consisted of four large and several small rooms fronting the verandahs, and as many opposite them; in a centre room of which was a little staircase leading to the roof, and commanding through a hole in the wall a position to the west. Next there was a sort of courtyard leading to a bath-room, which projected considerably beyond the walls of the main building, in this respect resembling Gubbins's battery. From the outside, the bath-room buildings looked considerably steep. To the left or south of them were several large houses, in front of which was a pond of stagnant water surrounded by reeds and long grass. To the right was a Mohammedan cemetery, on a very considerable elevation of natural formation, and commanding the outpost from the enemy's side. In front of the house, and in rear of the buildings already alluded to as possessed by the enemy, was an extensive low garden, then even covered with high long grass, plantain trees, and prickly brambles. A stockade protected a portion of the west side of our ground from that which we tacitly allowed to be that of the enemy. To the north an earthen wall separated the compound of Innes' house from the enemy's positions, which consisted of the mound already mentioned, a number of mud huts, and two or three pukka buildings scarcely six yards off, and overtopped by a mosque opposite, but further commanded by several high buildings across the river.

Still further on were a garden and the ruins of what had formerly been Shirf ood Dowlah (Jaggernath's) house and the office of the Central India Horse Company's posts, both which buildings had very wisely been levelled by our engineers. The whole of the north side of these positions was situated on the road leading along the river from the Residency water-gate to the iron bridge, in a direction from east to west. Where our mud wall was broken through, two stockades of beams stopped the gaps. At the end of one of these stockades was a mud shed with a flight of stairs leading to an upper room, known as the cock-loft, and commanding a capital position of the iron bridge, which was scarcely five hundred yards off. A little mosque, which I afterwards made my residence, was in the centre of the compound of this outpost and two or three low sheds or out-offices; a continuation of our earth wall, with stockaded gaps at intervals, formed the only separations from what the enemy could easily have traversed. It was considered a sort of neutral ground.

Fortunately, this part was completely commanded by the Redan, the best, most strongly fortified, and most complete battery of the whole garrison, erected by Captain Fulton, one of our very best engineer officers, who deserved the greatest praise for the scientific manner in which he constructed it. The whole of the river side, and the buildings on the opposite banks, could be played on with our cannon from here; and in the event of an attack, both the north and east as well as the west sides could be swept with our grape from the two 18-pounders and 9-pounder on it. It was in the form of more than three-quarters of a circle, and was elevated considerably above the street below.

Along the Redan to the north, in an irregular line, extending as far as the hospital, was a wall of fascines, and of earth-work, above which, and through whose loopholes formed by sand-bags, our men were able to fire with certain effect. A low trench ran within the Residency compound so as to give greater shelter to the men. From without, the wall had, however, a much more formidable appearance. This line of earth-work having a battery of two guns—9-pounders—at the entrance called the Water Gate, but now blocked up by a stockade, was known as No. 1 Battery. Along the Redan, past the Residency and the hospital, and as far as the Bailey-guard, was a clear space, formerly used as a garden, and bounded by a brick wall to the east, and the buildings known as the Captain's bazaar to the north, a fine road leading past these boundaries from the Bailey-guard Gate towards the iron bridge. This space, at least a thousand yards long by four hundred wide, being exceedingly low, and gradually becoming lower at the entrance opposite the upper Water Gate, formed a glacis for the entrenchments above.

The Residency itself was a very extensive and beautiful brick building, with lofty rooms, fine verandahs, and splendid porticoes. Besides having a ground-floor and two upper stories, it had a tyekhana, or cellar of splendid apartments, as lofty and well arranged as any in the house. These were built to shelter the residents at the Court of Lucknow during summer from the extreme heat of the day. Skylights and cellar-windows gave an excellent light to them. The commodiousness of the whole house offered accommodation to very numerous families, about eight hundred to a thousand souls, officers, men, ladies, and women and children, all finding place in it.

There were little turrets leading up to a fine terrace, whence a most beautiful view of the whole city could be obtained, the more so, as the Residency ground was of a much higher elevation than that of the houses surrounding it. A flagstaff and signal-post to communicate with Muchee Bhawn were on the top.

The hospital was another extensive building, resembling the Residency *par excellence*, but having besides the ground-floor only one upper story, and no tyekhana below. The front rooms of the ground-floor were made use of for the officers, the interior for the men, and the back part for a dispensary. It was formerly the banqueting hall of the Residents, the lower apartments having been made use of for an office. A battery of three guns, an 18-pounder, a 13-inch howitzer, and a 9-pounder, were placed between the Water Gate and hospital. The right wing of the hospital served as a laboratory for making fusees and cartridges, and fronting it was placed a battery of three mortars.

The Bailey-guard was a continuation of the hospital, but built on ground to which one had to descend considerably. A portion of it was used as a store-room, another as the treasury, a part as an office, and the remainder as the barracks of the native soldiers who guarded this place, commanded by Lieutenant Aitkins. Having on its left only the brick wall surrounding the neutral space of the Residency garden, already spoken of, it was by no means a strong position. To the right of these buildings was the Bailey-guard, *par malheur*, the guard-room of the sepoys formerly guarding the Residency, but, being without our boundaries, unapproachable by either ourselves or the enemy. The gateway to the right was lofty, and a fine piece of architecture. The gate was, however, to be blocked up with earth, and in the event of an entrance being forced, two 9-pounders and an 8-inch howitzer between them could shower grape and canister into the assailants.

Dr. Fayrer's house, like the Bailey-guard, facing the east, was also commanded by the clock-tower of the Firadbuksh palace, and the out-offices of the Tehree Koty and Nakarkhana. It was a fine and commodious lower-roomed house, raised on a considerable elevation, with a terrace, whence there was excellent rifle shooting. It was commanded by Captain Weston and Dr. Fayrer, who is a first-rate shot, and has sent many a sepoy to answer for his sins in another world. A 9-pounder loaded with grape was placed in a north-eastern direction, to command the Baileyguard gateway, if possible.

Coming out of Dr. Fayrer's house, and down the road to the left, was the civil dispensary, which being situated between Dr. Fayrer's, the post office, the Begum Kothee, and the jail, was one of the safest places in the whole garrison. It had previously been a portion of the post office.

The post office, during the siege, was one of the most important positions we had, commanding as well as being commanded by the Havilath jail and a mosque to the right, and the clock-tower and out-offices of the Tehree Kothee to the left. It was made the barrack-room of a great portion of our soldiers, and contained two 18's and a 9-pounder pointed in different directions, and protecting in some measure the Financial Office and Sago's garrisons below. Besides these, there were three mortars playing into the Cawnpore road, the Motymahal palaces, and the buildings round about the new palace and the old jail. There was also a workshop attached to it for the manufacture of tools and the preparation of shells and fusees. It was the head-quarters of the engineers, whose office and residence it was made, and besides offered accommodation to several families.

The wall bounding the south side communicated by breaches made in it with the jail, native hospital, school-houses, and the Cawnpore battery, as well as with the Judicial and Anderson's garrison.

The Financial Office outpost, a large two-storied house, was, like Sago's garrison, at first not intended to be within the line of our defences, and was only retained on account of the positions being most probably untenable by the enemy, since they did not command any part of the Residency houses, which overtop them, at the same time that they were useful in repelling advances made from the positions of the rebels on a level with it. It was barricaded on all sides with furniture and boxes within, but the out-offices and gateway were apparently very weak. The house itself was large and extensive, and had two verandahs, both well barricaded. It communicated with the Residency through the post office, and was directly below Dr. Fayrer's house. Captain Sanders, of the 13th, commanded this outpost with great ability and courage.

Sago's outpost, a lower-roomed and comparatively

ther small building, was contiguous, being only separated by a wall from it. Both these outposts, during the siege up to the arrival of the first reinforcements, were particularly dangerous, and their gallant garrison deserved particular praise for the brave defence they made. Previous to the siege it was the residence of Mrs. Sago, the mistress of a charity school. Both this and the Financial Office garrison were commanded, not only by those opposite the post office and Fayrer's battery, but also by a large building known as Azimoollah's Kothee, and a small brick building formerly used as a gambling house by the Lucknow shodas.*

A narrow passage, which during the siege proved fatal to many a poor fellow, led up to the Judicial Office, an extensive upper-roomed house, commanded by Captain Germon, 13th Native Infantry, situated between Anderson's and the post office garrisons, and also a very important position, greatly exposed to the enemy's fire from the east, and from a high turret of Johannes' house to the south. It had in the king's time been the residence of the late well-known Mr. George Beechey. A wall of fascines and earth protected it from the road-side.

The jail, a very fine airy and lofty quadrangular

* Bad characters.

building, divided into four equal-sized compartments, with barred doors and four openings, was surrounded by a fine square of comfortable out-offices, and situated between the Cawnpore battery to the south, the post office to the north, the Judicial Office to the right or east, and the school-houses and Native Hospital to the west. It was used as a barrack-room.

The native hospital, a square of low out-offices, was situated between the school-houses, the brigade mess, the post office and civil dispensary, and the jail. It was a tolerably safe place.

The Begum's Kothee*, so called from having previously been the dwelling-place of the grand-daughter of Buksh Ally, and whose mother had been Miss Walters, was one of the most extensive buildings within the whole line of our entrenchments. A lofty gateway nearly fronting the road leading to Johannes' house served as an entrance. A double range of out-offices formed a square within a square, one side of which consisted of a fine emambarah, or place of Mohammedan worship. Some of these buildings contained fine and lofty apartments, afterwards made use of by officers' families; others were lower-roomed cook houses, but having very deep foundations, and appearing from the road leading

* Lady's house.

past the post office to Dr. Fayrer's to be considerably high. A fine upper-roomed house, painted green and yellow, served as the commissariat store-rooms. A mosque, which at the desire of the Begum was not made use of, was within this Kothee. The male inhabitants of the place were required, as the Begum Kothee was supposed to be pretty safe, to garrison the Bhoosa entrenchments, being in the very centre of our defences.

Mr. Sequera's house, and the stabling next to it, then used as a canteen and liquor store-room, were, together with the main guard-house behind, considered as forming part of the Begum Kothee, and were connected with it by a breach in a wall and several narrow passages.

Having given as good a description of our entrenchments as I am able, I now return to the state of affairs at Lucknow during the first week of the siege. My readers will, however, already have an idea that our defences were by no means strong, and that our chief ones rather consisted in the number of our guns and the quantity of our ammunition, than the strength of our earth-works and batteries.

CHAP. VI.

LUCKNOW DURING THE FIRST TWO WEEKS OF THE SIEGE.

The Siege begins.—Barricades formed.—The Enemy's Artillery commanded by European Officers.—Lady Inglis's Journal.—Abandonment and Explosion of Fort Muchee Bhawn.—Anecdote.—Death of Sir Henry Lawrence. — Attack on the Bailey-guard Gate. — Johannes' House.— Cawnpore Battery.— Death of Mr. Ommaney and others.—Welcome Shower of Rain.—Deaths in the Garrison.

THE siege had fairly begun, and in the midst of plenty (for we were rich in luxuries the first days) we suffered the inconvenience of not being able to use them. Deprat's house, near the Cawnpore battery, was swarming with men,— the Europeans firing wherever they saw an object moving or suspected it to be moving, and the Sikhs, who behaved so shamefully at Chinhutt, sulkily sitting down, doing nothing, or sneering at our efforts. I ofttimes felt a great inclination to pitch into the rascals, but to do so would have been bad policy. Deprat, with his usual generosity, gave away *saucissons aux truffes*, hermetically sealed provisions, cigars and wine, and brandy to whoever wanted any. Many took away large supplies of provisions, &c., and only signed, or did not sign at all, for what they took away. The consequence was that poor D. had soon nothing left for himself; and the thousand and one cannon-balls and musket-bullets which afterwards penetrated the house, and in the end converted it into a heap of ruins, smashed to atoms whatever was not taken away. The splendid library of Captain Hayes, consisting of priceless Oriental manuscripts, and the standard literary and scientific works of every nation of Europe, and dictionaries of every language spoken on earth, from the patois of Bretagne down to Cingalese, Malay, and ancient Egyptian, were for the nonce converted into barricades. Mahogany tables, valuable pieces of furniture, carriages, and carts, were everywhere within our entrenchments taken possession of for the same purpose. The records of the offices, in large boxes, chests of stationery, and whatever else could be laid hold of, were made use of to serve as a cover from the enemy's fire, which now constantly increased.

Sir Henry, throughout this trying time, was seen everywhere. He visited every post, however exposed its position, however hot the fire directed against it; and it must be confessed that the enemy's artillerists, taught by ourselves, were excellent marksmen. With incredible rapidity, with remarkable ingenuity, and with indomitable perseverance, they had, in the very first week, made batteries in positions where one would have fancied their erection impossible, — some having actually been moved to the tops of houses, and others placed most cleverly in places where our own batteries could not effectually open on them, and which were well protected from musketry fire.

It is also probable that their artillery was commanded by European officers, wretches for whom no punishment would be ignominious or severe enough. One of these was seen several times laying a gun and giving orders, apparently like one having authority.

A young man, whose name I do not wish to mention, on account of his family, was most probably the person who had commanded the enemy's cavalry at Chinhutt. Two of his cousins were fighting valiantly against the rebels in the Residency; another was massacred at Futtygurh, after combating for us; a fourth was wounded in action against the Agra rebels; and a fifth had accepted a military appointment under Government, and distinguished himself, as I afterwards learnt, in several engagements against the mutineers. The apostate himself had long been disowned by his relatives. But it is also likely that some Russian officers had entered the army of the insurgents.

A person had been seen in the lines of the 71st Regiment Native Infantry, and as orders had been issued previously that all suspicious characters should be arrested, the officer who had gone his rounds at once seized a man skulking away, dressed like a pauper European, and had him brought before him. The Sepoys, of whom he inquired about him, were rather anxious to screen the man, and this so increased his suspicions that he had him at once arrested. He at first had given himself out as a Siberian refugee, then contradicted himself on cross-examination, and at last wanted to make it appear he was a Portuguese. One of the officers on cross-examination spoke to him in that language, to which he was unable to reply. He then tried to make them believe he was a Jew, with equal want of success, and then that he belonged to some other nation. He was ordered to be imprisoned, but on the occurrence of the mutiny, he was either released or effected his escape.

Many of these batteries were not farther off than fifty to a hundred yards, and told tremendously on our buildings; indeed I have seen, for example, the enemy's cannon knock down pillar after pillar from Captain Anderson's house, till at last the verandah fell in. Mr. Capper, of the Civil Service, was buried beneath the ruins, but notwithstanding the shower of balls which rained upon the spot, was fortunately extricated by one or two soldiers of the 34th, directed and aided by Messrs. Jeoffroy and Barsotelli,—one a Frenchman and the other an Italian, both travellers who had been, like myself, overtaken by the times. The proximity of some of these batteries, which the enemy occasionally shifted to other places as soon as ours could be made to play on them, prevented our shells from having the effect which otherwise they would have had; though many of these missiles did great execution.

I here again avail myself of a quotation from Lady Inglis's Journal.

"The first few nights and days were very miserable. I was ill in bed, poor Mrs. Case in great grief, and we could not help feeling our position a most perilous one. You must remember that we well knew if the enemy succeeded in overpowering us and storming the place, death in its most horrible form awaited every member of the garrison. I never shall forget the first morning after the siege commenced. The enemy having stopped firing at night recommenced at daylight, and made an effort to storm the gate. Every man was at his post. We could gain no information as to what was going on, and to our inexperienced ears the cannonading and musketry sounded terrific. We all thought the place would be taken, and tremblingly listened to every sound, when Mrs. Case proposed reading the Litany, and the soothing effect of prayer was marvellous. We felt different beings, and, though still most anxious, could feel we were in the hands of our Heavenly Father, and cast our fears on Him. The enemy were completely repulsed that day and many others, when they made similar attacks; but we soon got accustomed to the firing, for it seldom ceased day or night, and settled ourselves down in our new abode — a small room, which, throughout the siege, has been our dining and sleeping apartment, except for a short time, when we had the use of a large room in the same court."

One of the first victims to the enemy's cannon was Miss Palmer, the daughter of the colonel commanding the 48th, — an accomplished young lady, who was, I heard, engaged to be married to a young officer. She was sitting in the upper story of the Residency, when a shell burst close to her, and a piece struck her. Her leg had to be amputated, and she died a few days after.

We still had a few hundred men in Muchee Bhawn; but it was evident that we could not, after the disaster of Chinhutt, hold that place also. Orders were accordingly sent by Sir Henry to blow up the place, and to come within the Residency. Captain Francis, aided by Lieutenant Huxham, his fort adjutant, managed this splendidly. They left in the dead of night, passing through the midst of the hostile piquets along the road, without a shot being fired at them, without losing a man. The enemy, never suspecting such a move on our part (for they had held the most extravagant ideas respecting the impregnability of that fort), were very weakly guarding the highroads.

The rebel garrisons of the houses near the iron bridge and at Ismaelgunge were so thunderstruck at seeing our men, that they dared not attack them when they heard the heavy tramp of our gallant soldiers and the rattling of our guns. I believe, however, that the shelling from the Residency aided not a little in keeping the road clear.

The last cannon had reached with the last man when a tremendous report shook the earth. The portfires had burnt down, and the Fort Muchee Bhawn was no more! All our ammunition, which we had not had time to remove, and about 250 barrels of gunpowder, and several millions of ball-cartridges, were destroyed, along with all the buildings and their contents. An immense black cloud enveloped even us in the Residency,—darkness covering a bright starry firmament. The shock resembled an earthquake.

Our accession of strength was very necessary. We had saved all but one man, who, having been intoxicated and concealed in some corner, could not be found when the muster roll was called. The French say, *Il y a un Dieu pour les ivrognes,* and the truth of the proverb was never better exemplified than in this man's case. He had been thrown into the air, had returned unhurt to mother earth, continued his drunken sleep again, had awoke next morning, found the fort to his surprise a mass of deserted ruins, and quietly walked back to the Residency without being molested by a soul; and even bringing with him a pair of bullocks attached to a cart of ammunition. It is very probable that the debris of these extensive buildings must have seriously injured the adjacent houses, and many of the rebel army, thus giving the fortunate man the means of escaping.*

On the 2nd of July an event occurred which a few days later cast a gloom over the whole garrison. The good and brave Sir Henry Lawrence, while

---

* Our men were not a little astonished when they heard him cry, "Arrah, by Jasus, open your gates." And they let him in, convulsed with laughter.

reclining on his bed in his room in the second story of the Residency, was struck by a piece of a shell which had burst between himself, Mr. Couper his secretary, and Captain Wilson, the deputy assistant adjutant-general, who was reading a memorandum to him at the time, and whom it slightly wounded. Only a short time before, another shell had fallen into the same apartment, but had injured neither Sir Henry nor any other occupant of the room. In spite of warnings, he had made no arrangement to leave the place for a better shelter from the enemy's fire. The rebels were apparently perfectly acquainted with all the different apartments, and their occupants and uses, and directed their fire accordingly, especially into the Residency and the various powder magazines.

Only a very few were made acquainted with the public misfortune which had befallen us. So serious a wound in an old man like Sir Henry, I was certain would end fatally. His leg had been amputated, and he died on the morning of the 4th of July, almost to the last fully possessed of his senses in the midst of the agonies he suffered. His nephew, Mr. G. H. Lawrence, was wounded on the same day.

Sir H. Lawrence had nominated Major Banks as his successor. It had not been generally known that our brave old general was dead, for even after he had been buried for some days, the report was circulated that he was getting better. At last, no doubt remained on the minds of any that Sir Henry was indeed no more, and the grief with which this news was received was universal. He had closed a long and noble career, and his death was worthy of his life. He fills the soldier's grave right worthily. No military honours marked our last acts to his corpse. The times were too stern for idle demonstrations of respect. A hurried prayer, amidst the booming of the enemy's cannon and the fire of their musketry, was read over his remains, and he was lowered into a pit with several other, though lowlier, companions of arms. We owe him a heavy debt of gratitude. Peace be to his soul!

Brigadier Inglis, in his report of the 26th September, pays a tribute to the memory of that good man in the following words, which I may safely aver express the thoughts of every one of the garrison:—

"The late lamented Sir H. Lawrence, knowing that his last hour was rapidly approaching, directed me to assume command of the troops, and appointed Major Banks to succeed him in the office of Chief Commissioner. He lingered in great agony till the morning of the 4th July, when he expired, and the Government was thereby deprived, if I may venture to say so, of the services of a distinguished statesman and a most gallant soldier. Few men have ever possessed to the same extent the power which he enjoyed of winning the hearts of all those with whom he came in contact, and thus ensuring the warmest and most zealous devotion for himself and for the Government which he served. The successful defence of the position has been, under Providence, solely attributable to the foresight which he evinced in the timely commencement of the necessary operations, and the great skill and untiring personal activity which he exhibited in carrying them into effect. All ranks possessed such confidence in his judgment and his fertility of resource, that the news of his fall was received throughout the garrison with feelings of consternation, only second to the grief which was inspired in the hearts of all by the loss of a public benefactor, and a warm personal friend. Feeling as keenly and as gratefully as I do the obligations that the whole of us are under to this great and good man, I trust the Government in India will pardon me for having attempted, however imperfectly, to portray them. In him, every good and deserving soldier lost a friend and a chief capable of discriminating, and ever on the alert to reward merit, no matter how humble the sphere in which it was exhibited."

On the 2nd, the same day on which Sir Henry was wounded, the enemy, who had perhaps become aware of the circumstance by one of their spies, attempted to make a partial rush at the Bailey-guard Gate, but they were so warmly received, that they soon discovered it to be a miserable failure. Fortunately, all days are not 30ths of June, and there were then no traitors in our ranks to join them. As a friend jestingly observed to me, after we had heard of their defeat at the gateway, "They will find it a tough nut to crack, taking the Bailey-guard" (the name by which the natives know the whole of our entrenchments). Lieutenant Graham received a bayonet wound in the groin by one of the assailants, who were bold enough to advance to the very wall of the Bailey-guard. At the Cawnpore battery, where I then was, they only showed themselves for a few minutes; quite long enough, though, to enable us to pick off a few men. Lieutenant Foster, of the 32nd, was slightly wounded on the same day, at the brigade mess, where the enemy's fire was very hot.

On the 3rd and 4th the cannon and musketry, if possible, increased. At the Cawnpore battery the bullets, which were at first aimed high, gradually came lower, and several of our poor fellows were on that day shot at that exposed post. Johannes' house, which is right across the road, was still unoccupied, as the natives evidently were afraid it was undermined, a rumour which had been circulated before the siege. It was a pity that it had not been previously demolished, as it was a few days afterwards taken possession of by the rebels, whose riflemen could command from its upper stories not only the Cawnpore battery, but Anderson's garrison, the jail barracks, the post office, and the entrance to the Begum Kothee. Ramsay, the assistant in charge of the telegraph, was shot at the Residency House, and died instantly.

On the 5th a heavy shower of rain fell, which swept away a good portion of the filth which had been allowed to accumulate, and had become most disgusting. The stench from dead horses and bullocks, and other animals killed by the enemy's fire, was worse than disagreeable, it was pestilential, and laid the seeds of the many diseases from which we afterwards suffered. The insurgents' great guns slackened, which led us to hope that their ammunition was failing them, but their musketry fire continued to be almost as brisk as before. Still they could not have had a great supply of ball-cartridges, for we saw several fellows, notwithstanding our own fire, engaged in picking up bullets. I shot one of them, and his body afterwards not a little affected our olfactory nerves.

We were at night several times called "to arms,"

but these alarms proved to be false ones. This was fortunate, for if the enemy had made an attack he would have found most of our men at the Cawnpore battery in the last stage of intoxication The men had found their way for some days, notwithstanding all precautions, into our cellar, and had of course diminished the large quantities of champagne and brandy stored up there. The claret and Haut Sauterne had not found many admirers, and remained untouched; but Deprat's chests, with valuables and gold and silver watches in them, had likewise been broken open and rifled. In the position in which we then were, no search could be instituted, nor could the culprits be punished. The only thing which could be done, and which the Brigadier did, was to get what remained removed to the school-houses, and have it sold by Mr. Schilling, the principal, to whatever gentleman desired any. Officers, of course, had the preference, and in the course of a couple of days nothing remained.

Mr. Ommaney, the Judicial Commissioner, was the next high official whom death reached. He was quietly sitting in his chair, when a cannon ball (passing over the body of Serjeant-Major Watson, of Captain Adolphe Orr's Corps of Police, who was lying down on his bed), hit him on the head, and scattered a portion of his brains. He died almost immediately after, and the Serjeant-Major expired also, though the ball had not touched him. Whether Mr. Watson's death was caused by suffocation, or the force with which the air was suddenly disturbed, or fear, I know not; but of the facts of his death, and of the round shot only passing but very closely over him, not the least doubt need be entertained.

On the 7th a very heavy shower of rain did us the greatest service in the world. Not only did it in a measure purify the air and remove a portion of the stench and filth from the place, but it kept the " babalog " * great guns quiet and saved us from one of the greatest dangers to which we were ever exposed. Indeed, but for this timely shower we might all have been hurled into the air, and by this time nothing but a few dry bones might have remained of us.

Before the hospital battery, a good deal of bhoosa (chopped straw for bullocks' fodder) had been allowed to remain in the open space to which I have already alluded. Notwithstanding our vigilance, one of the enemy had succeeded in coming close to it

* The "children," or "dear children," the term by which old officers used to address the loyal sepoys in whom they had such confidence.

and setting it on fire. We had been so suddenly overtaken by the Chinhutt affair that we had had no time to remove it. It was only a few yards distant from a large powder magazine buried under ground; and if the flames had heated the ground, it would have ignited, and of course blown us all up. The rain saved us, but the fire was not quite extinguished, and smouldered away for a whole week. Nor were we aware of the danger we had escaped till all was over.

It would have been impossible for us to put out the fire ourselves. The exposure, particularly at night, where the glare of the fire would have shown our forms even more distinctly than in the day, and afforded good cover to the enemy, was such, that every man who should have approached it would, without fail, have been killed by the enemy's sharpshooters. The rascal who had done this mischief succeeded in effecting his escape. He was fired at by Corporal Gately, but unsuccessfully.

A poor old merchant, who had a double-barrelled rifle in his hand, and who also missed his aim, and was not prompt enough in making it over to the soldier who had asked him for it, was in consequence for more than a month under the ban of public military opinion. The soldiers looked upon the inoffensive old gentleman as a spy, and accused him most unjustly of being in correspondence with the enemy. His friends therefore advised him to remain in his house. He fell ill afterwards; and when he had recovered, the men had become aware of their injustice, or had forgotten it.

Mr. Marshall, an old man of sixty, long a resident at Cawnpore, who had last year received the contract for the sale of opium from Government, was shot through the face, the ball passing through the right eye and coming out of the mouth. He suffered great agony for some days, and then expired.

Our deaths were very numerous up to this day. They averaged about fifteen to twenty daily, and were mostly caused by rifle and musket balls. Many owed their deaths to a rebel African, who, from Johannes' house, fired almost without ever missing his aim.

CHAP. VII.

THE SECOND WEEK OF THE SIEGE.

My Journal. — Successful Sortie. — Death of Major Francis. — Another Sortie. — Daring Act of our Soldiers. — Interesting Missiles. — Beale. — Sad Reflections. — Death of Mr. Alexander Bryson. — Change of Garrison. — Expected Reinforcements. — An Attack. — Our Privations and Sufferings begin. — Captain Alexander wounded. — Attack on Gubbins' Battery. — Garrison Laws of Amputation. — The Enemy's warlike Shouts. — Despondency. — Our inside Annoyances. — My Luxuries diminish.

I SHALL now continue my narrative in the form of a journal, taken from notes kept during the siege, but my readers will pardon me if I am guilty occasionally of an anachronism by anticipating events.

Wednesday, July 8th.—Notwithstanding the heavy rain which fell yesterday, a party of ours, and among them a promising young civilian, named Maycock, dashed out to-day, under the command of Captain Mansfield and Lieutenants Lawrence, Studdy and Green,—the former of Her Majesty's 32nd, the latter of the 13th, Native Infantry. The Brigadier knew too well the value of European life to wish to risk it.

Fortunately no life was lost, but two 32nd's and one Sikh were wounded. They spiked a gun, and paid off some forty of the rebels. A little more of this, and they will get disgusted. The city has been sacked. This we could imagine, from the wailing of women, and the cry of the men; the wealthy inhabitants, so some spies say, have bolted, and all that Jack Sepoy may now expect are hard knocks, an article he by no means seems to like.

Major R. B. Francis, the officer who had done such good service while commanding Muchee Bhawn, died to-day. He had been quietly sitting in his room, in the brigade mess, when a cannon ball, breaking through the wall, smashed his right leg to pieces, and broke his left leg at the same time. They were amputated, but he died shortly after. A number of native sepoys (Sikhs) deserted last evening.

Thursday, July 9th. — Cannon and musketry still have a monopoly of noise. Another batch of ours from Innes' garrison, consisting of a few Irish soldiers of the 32nd and three or four civilians, made another sortie to-day. They crept cautiously up to the enemy's battery, not far from the iron bridge, and, emerging suddenly upon the rebel guard, struck them with fear and surprise. They were evidently not very vigilant, and though it was only between twelve and two o'clock in the day, were found either asleep or eating their food, the sentries only being armed. They soon managed, however, to fly to their muskets, but had only resolution enough to fire when the terrible whitefaces were returning. One brave fellow, who has since been killed, and whose name is either O'Keen or Keogh, I forget which, took advantage of their astonishment and terror, and spiked their gun, while his comrade Smith bayoneted a couple of fellows after firing his piece. The remaining Volunteers acted as a covering party to these two brave men. After having effected their purpose, which was done more quickly than I can relate it, they succeeded in reaching their post, scarce a hundred yards distant, without the loss of a single man. Immediately after, however, volley after volley was poured into Innes' garrison from the discomfited foe. The enemy's guns quiet to-day, or nearly so.

Poor Bryson, one of my best friends here, shot dead through the head. His poor wife is distracted, and treasures up his last words. He had left her this morning gay and jovial, as he always was, and jestingly told her, when she begged of him not to expose himself too much, that the bullet had not yet been moulded that was to hit him. The fire constantly kept up on his (Sago's) garrison, and particularly on the narrow passage which leads up to the Judicial garrison, was so hot, that his body could not be removed for many hours, for the evening was bright with a clear moonlight. M'Grennan, a friend of ours, however, proposed that a party of volunteers should carry his body to the hospital, expressing his conviction that no bullet could hit us while engaged in such a good work. And so we carried him up the steep passage slowly and carefully, and bullets fell all around, but never touched us. Poor Bryson! he was a noble and gallant fellow, an excellent husband, a fond father, and a staunch friend. A practical philosopher, he was always gay and smiling, hospitable and kind to all. As sergeant of the Volunteer Cavalry, and every day during the siege, he behaved as a gallant and true-hearted volunteer soldier should.

July 10*th*. — Very heavy rain. A number of us had been working all night in putting tarpaulin over the *bhoora* (bullocks' fodder) in the racket-court, and were to-day engaged in burying dead animals and making better cover from the enemy's fire. The musketry is milder, and the enemy's ammunition is evidently running out. Though their great guns are going again pretty fast, it is not always round shot that they are sending us. They are now firing billets of wood, pieces of iron, copper coins, and even "*bullocks' horns.*" What interesting missiles! We hear that a number of the insurgents, disappointed at not yet having been able to take the Bailey-guard, have left with their loot. A great talk of speedy reinforcements coming, but I do not believe a word of it.

July 11*th.* — Working at the batteries, bringing sand-bags, using the spade, and carrying messages from one place to another. Poor Beale (overseer) wounded in the back from a rifle shot in Johannes' house. He had been most active, poor fellow, in constantly going to and fro in the midst of a very heavy fire. He died a week after. He had only a short time back lost his little daughter.

The same game. When shall we be relieved? They say troops are coming; but when? and where from? Cawnpore in the hands of the enemy; other parts of India have no doubt been also disturbed. I fear there can be nothing in the many reports they confidently give out as true, that we are to be soon relieved. Talk of reinforcements! Where from? Maybe the Cham of Tartary and the Grand Lama of Thibet, at the head of an army of " Cashmere goats!" No troops yet in Cawnpore, and they talk of them here.

I leave the Cawnpore battery, for there is no remaining any longer in it. Our property is being plundered before our eyes, and we can say nothing to it, and the house itself is almost roofless, and nearly in ruins. There is hardly a point in the wall which is not covered with bullet marks, and round shots are everywhere sticking in the walls or have made breaches in them. I do not exaggerate when I say that at least eighty of these would-be messengers of death have struck the house. The rooms, too, were crammed full of officers, soldiers, and others; and as our servants had all left, Deprat and I were obliged to make arrangements to live with some families, which we accordingly did, and to join other garrisons.

July 12*th.*— Talk of troops coming to our aid! It is time indeed, for our privations are beginning. I am, like every one else, in constant danger of being shot, and have to work like a slave. I had to stand in the rain all night doing sentinel's duties, and caught a cold in consequence. This too after having just come off heavy fatigue duties, burying putrid horses, and carrying commissariat stores! Lieutenant Charlton, of the 32nd, was severely wounded in the head to-day. This officer had particularly distinguished himself on several occasions.

July 13*th.* — Rain and shot, the former as usual,

the latter slightly more brisk. It is evident that the enemy have got a further supply of ammunition. We had to stand to arms to-night, but it proved a false alarm.

July 14*th.*— A grand attack to-day all round, that is, the enemy is shouting *ad infinitum*, and sounding the advance at the bugler's discretion. Great guns and musketry are loaded and fired as fast as they can be, but that is all. Every hostile battery, every house, vomits forth fire in some shape or other, but not a man appears. Jack Sepoy evidently will not come to the scratch. He is no doubt of Falstaff's way of thinking, that discretion is the better part of valour.

A poor clerk of the name of Wiltshire, who had effected his escape from the Duriabad mutineers, and had succeeded in reaching Lucknow in safety, but with the loss of all his property, and his clothes in rags, died of cholera to-day. Conductor Baxter, who was shot on the 11th, also died. Lieutenant Lester was killed. A number of other poor fellows went to their long homes.

July 15*th.*—The enemy plays the same game as yesterday. Unfortunately the shots tell; but they have of late been less numerous: still our European deaths now average about ten a-day. The natives we of course don't count. We feel their loss is nothing very great; but it pains us all to hear of a poor European being knocked over. We not only deplore his loss as a man, but we are selfish enough to regret that we have one less in our garrison, and anticipate the future with no enviable feelings. If we are not relieved in a month, we must become the prey of those ungrateful scoundrels around us.

My cold is worse. Grubbing about in wet holes making receptacles for dead bullocks and dead horses, does not conduce to its improvement. Pretty employment this for the educated youth of the nineteenth century! But necessity has no law; and we all, great or small, work hard at the spade as well as the musket, which, however, is now in no great requisition. We allow the enemy to fire away to his heart's content, and do not reply, except with our big guns and our mortars. It is useless to waste ammunition on pukka, brick walls, and well covered batteries. The enemy have hit upon a very clever trick to preserve themselves from our fire, making deep trenches before their guns, so that we can only see their hands while in the act of loading. They can command a hundred times more labour than we can; and one of our lives is more valuable, too, in the same proportion.

I am off to see my friend Sinclair, the merchant, who is lying wounded in hospital. A musket ball penetrated his thigh, while he was firing in Innes' outposts.

Captain Clare Alexander, an excellent man, and a first-rate artillery officer, was injured to-day while examining a mortar. The whole of his face was burnt with powder, and he looks a dreadful figure. black as ebony, and covered with blisters, which afterwards suppurated. Poor Bryce, also of the Artillery, who had succeeded in bringing in one of our guns from Chinhutt, was also wounded to-day in the thigh. Fortunately, it is only a slight wound.

July 16*th.* — The usual amount of firing. Very hot indeed. I mean the weather, not the fire; this has slackened. At night, however, an attack of the enemy on Gubbins' battery. The Sikhs and the Europeans, and among them my friend D., beat back the enemy, who had succeeded in coming close to the wall. Poor Lester, of the 32nd Native Infantry, had been shot there. He expired of his wounds next day. Lieutenant O'Brien, of the 84th, was also wounded in the arm, though not dangerously.

July 17*th.* — Musketry and great guns much as usual. Brown, of Sago's garrison, shot through the leg to-day. The following note from my journal proves correct: — "Brown shot — leg amputated: now he will die; he *shall* die; for it is a law in medical science, as practised by the garrison surgeons, that death follows amputation as sure as night follows day."

And so it is. Indeed, the law of garrison amputation and the famed law of the Medes and Persians have both the same characteristics. They never fail. Whether it be the want of proper care, or the heat of the weather, or the want of vegetable food, or the absence of proper restoratives, or from any other cause, or all these reasons together, it certainly is an undoubted fact, that every amputation has been succeeded by death. Every day eight or ten poor fellows are still carried to the grave-yard, which is rapidly being filled up.

July 18*th.* — The enemy's bugles sound, and they shout, "*Leea! leea! jalloo bahadour!*"—"It is taken (viz. the entrenchment)! it is taken! advance my braves!" as usual. However, they have not yet taken our little stronghold; "bahadour" will not "jallao" (advance).

Still, however, it is always "bang bang, bhom bhom, rattle rattle," unceasingly. The rascals have evidently received reinforcements, and another supply of ammunition. When will this end? for how much longer can we hold out? I do not fear their taking our place, at least before another month; but daily our force lessens, and when we have become only a handful of effective men, we must, in the end, fall an easy prey to even this cowardly, though savage, enemy. As for treating with the assassins of Cawnpore, the very thought must be banished. Our only consolation is, that we shall die fighting. The death of a brave man, and the death of a coward, is after all only death. We can expect no mercy. Our only hope lies in reinforcements from Delhi, for Calcutta is too distant, unless Sir H. Lawrence's requisition for more troops has been promptly responded to. Indeed, our hope is not great. God alone can save us.

July 19*th*.— The inside annoyances are dreadful. The stench from human ordure, from decaying horses, dogs, and men, assails the olfactory nerves most awfully, and little is done to mend matters. Before the siege commenced, there was a very smart sanitary commissioner appointed. The uncompromising zeal that he had displayed in having the chance deposit of a cock-sparrow cleaned up was then something magnificent to behold. Pity that it afterwards flagged! He could no longer, too, command the same labour as before. We Europeans were incessantly harassed, and our sweepers deserted daily.

Our luxuries are fast diminishing. I am afraid my friend D. and myself have been a little too liberal with our good things, and instead of, as usual, taking brandy and water *ad libitum* and smoking cheroots *ad infinitum*, we are obliged to content ourselves with one glass of brandy and water a day, and a glass of wine in the evening; and as for cigars, I can only afford one or two a day, and not even that; for many a poor devil, who has perhaps not had a smoke for days, looks so longingly that I, for one, can scarcely resist the satisfaction of occasionally giving away half, or even a whole cigar. Even the stump of a cheroot is looked upon as a luxury by many a poor uncovenanted volunteer now. I am quite proud of my riches, for I have at least a couple of hundred cigars left. Of pickled salmon and truffled sausages none remain now. Deprat has given away to his friends what little he had saved from being plundered. Our fare is not particularly good:—beef and chupattees, with a few extras. Still I fare better than many. I at least have enough.

Lieutenant Harmer, 32nd Regiment, was struck by a round shot, while sitting at table with his brother officers, none of whom it however injured.

CHAP. VIII.

THE GRAND ATTACK OF THE TWENTIETH OF JULY.

"To arms!" — Renegade Traitors. — Fierce Assault of the Rebels. — The Sick turn out. — Explosion of the Enemy's Mines and Attack on the Redan. — Lieutenant Loughnan's Gallant Defence of Innes' Outpost. — Scaling Ladders. — Hardingham's Escape. — Erith Shot. — Conversation between Bailey and the Insurgents. — Anecdote. — The Enemy are beaten. — Attacks on Sago's, Financial, Judicial, and Anderson's Garrisons. — Defeat of the Insurgents at the Brigade Mess and Gubbins' Battery. — Lieutenant M'Farlane. — Loss of the Enemy. — After the Battle.

I was cleaning my musket, and whistling a merry air, when the cry of "To arms," and the doubling of men past my little room, made me come to a dead halt. In runs a friend, and tells me that the rebels had been seen, assembling in large bodies towards the church side and across the river, and that I had better be off to my post. My preparations were quickly made, but I had scarcely time to put on my belt, when a loud report shook the earth. I at first imagined that one of our powder-magazines had been blown up, but I soon after learnt that a mine had been sprung by the enemy, near the Redan.

I hurried on to Dr. Fayrer's battery; but though that garrison was not a minute's walk from my place, I had scarcely reached half-way when the most hellish fire ever heard began in right good earnest. The enemy indeed seemed to have come this time to the resolution of taking the Bailey-guard by storm, and displayed in the attempt more courage than we had given them credit for.

They assaulted us from every point, and volley after volley of musketry was poured into us, shell after shell burst within our entrenchments, and their cannon roared unceasingly. The enemy's artillery was still evidently commanded by a practised officer, most probably a European, for we could plainly discern several in their ranks. How it is possible for white men to join black murderers, who make war like wild beasts, not like men, I cannot conceive. No punishment seems to me great enough for such miserable wretches, these haters of their own race. Wealth acquired in such a service must indeed be a bane. Besides, its very precarious nature can hardly make it worth while. This is not a war of the oppressed against the oppressor, of a nation rising against their rulers, of Hindostanees against Englishmen. No, it is a war of fanatic religionists against

Christians, of black against white, of natives against Europeans, of barbarism against civilisation. Had it been different, had patriotism prompted the rebellion, had the natives, as one nation, determined to shake off the yoke of the foreigner, and had they conducted their war against us like soldiers and brave men, instead of acting the part of cowards and assassins, then indeed might they have enlisted sympathy with their cause, not only among the nations of continental Europe, but even among the people of England themselves. Men of other European countries might have fought against us without dishonour and without reproach. Now, however, they are only to be branded as villains of the deepest dye, as traitors to their own cause, as murderers of their own white countrymen, and abettors of the assassination of women and children of their own race.

But to return from this digression. Our own guns were not long in replying. As the enemy approached, they were mowed down by our grape by scores; and as their leaders advanced, shouting and encouraging their men, they were picked off by our rifles and muskets. Captain Weston and Dr. Fayrer on this occasion did right good service. This tremendous fire of musketry and cannon, both from out and in, rendered our position one mass of sulphurous smoke, so that we could scarcely see. I must confess that for some minutes I felt the fear of death predominant within me. I was certain, and I think most of our little handful of men too, that this was our last day upon earth. I accordingly said a short prayer, committed myself to God's care, mentally bade adieu to those I loved best in this world, fired my musket, and with the firm resolution to die like a "soldier," prepared to meet the combat.

My selfish fear soon wore off. As the fire became more and more infernal, and as we saw their men boldly advancing, my fear gave place to a nervous excitement, and at last the desire to kill and to be revenged predominated over every other feeling. I did not stay long at Dr. Fayrer's battery, for my anxiety to know more of the injury the mine had done us made me desirous of proceeding towards the Redan. I accordingly left, showers of balls falling around me, none fortunately, however, touching me. I arrived at the Water Gate battery, where I saw the men still advancing, but evidently not so boldly as before. I picked off a few of them, and then a strange feeling of joy came over me. I no longer thought of myself, but only of the number I could kill. The fire now slackened, and I could talk to my companions in arms.

All of us were determined to sell our lives as dearly as possible. Even of the wounded and the sick many had left their couches, seized any musket they could lay hold of, and fired as often as their strength enabled them to do so. It was indeed heart-rending to see these poor fellows staggering along to the scenes of action, pale, trembling with weakness, and several of them bleeding from their wounds, which reopened by the exertions they made. One unfortunate wretch, with only one arm, was seen hanging to the parapet of the hospital entrenchments with his musket, but the momentary strength which the fear of being butchered in his bed and the desire of revenge had given him, was too much for him. He died in the course of the day. Every garrison was a separate field of battle, and I shall now attempt to notice the principal points of attack.

The Redan had not been injured by the explosion. Fortunately they had miscalculated the distance, and therefore their mine did no damage to us. They were ignorant, however, of this, and fancied they had made a breach, for, owing to the smoke caused by the mine and the fire of our guns and theirs, they could not see before them. They doubled up the glacis with bayonets fixed, covered by the musketry of a regiment or two stationed on the house opposite, and known as "Captain Fatty Ally's." The obstacles in the way, however, checked their advance, and whilst in this plight hundreds were shot down. Still they were unwilling to retreat; one of their leaders waving his sword, on the point of which he had placed his cap, shouted "Come on, my braves." Again they advanced, but again terrible gaps were made in their ranks by our grape, and one of our musket balls killed their leader. They now retreated in confusion, but not without others of their brethren being shot down in incredible numbers. Heaps of slain and wounded proved our victory on that side to be complete. The attack had lasted about an hour, but the fire of the enemy still continued, and still all the engines of war were at play with undiminished force.

My attention was now attracted to the Brigadier and his staff, who were at the Redan not far from me, at the Water Gate battery. They were clapping their hands, and every now and then shouting "Bravo! bravo!" while their eyes were turned towards the church side, to Innes' outpost. The enemy had made a most fierce assault there. The defences at that side were very weak; but the enemy approached cautiously, fearing that the place was undermined where there were no palisades. They therefore attacked only those points which were comparatively the strongest. The commandant, Lieutenant Loughnan of the 13th Native Infantry, had received orders that should he, as was feared, not be able to hold his post, to retire within the Residency; but not before he had done all in his power to repel the assailants. The force under his command consisted of only twenty-four European soldiers, twelve uncovenanted gentlemen, and about twenty-five sepoys.

At one time during the attack, our men, seeing the rebels come on swarming as thick as bees, and nothing but one sea of heads and glittering weapons before them, thought of retreat; but Mr. Loughnan and the civilians would not hear of it. "Give a shout, my boys!" cried Loughnan, "a loud one and a strong one." And shout they did, with right good will. "Hurrah! hurrah! hurrah!" resounded from all the different quarters where attacks were expected. The enemy were evidently checked in their advance by the cheering of our friends. They at once came to a dead halt, and not only imagined us stronger in number than we really were, but fancied (as we afterwards learnt) that we had received a reinforcement from the Residency. Their indecision did not last long; for again they advanced, and now came immediately beneath our walls, where our musketry could not touch them.

As other bodies, however, approached, they were shot down, one by one, by a party of volunteer gentlemen, who had taken a position in the house itself, upon a staircase leading to the terrace, where they could, under considerable shelter to themselves, do a good deal of mischief to the enemy advancing upon the front of the house. The rebels had made a very foolish move here. Instead of bringing scaling-ladders along with them, they moved ahead without them, and only on reaching the walls perceived their mistake. Then only they shouted, "*siree layou*," "bring the ladders." The ladders were accordingly brought, but the men who carried them could scarcely make a few paces, when our volunteers and soldiers shot them down. This happened several times, and each shot told and removed three of the number at the same time. For no sooner did one fall than two of his companions, only too glad of an excuse to escape from our well-aimed and murderous fire, carried the body off, and did not return.

A number of our muskets had been ready for the combat, and they were discharged so rapidly by one man, while another loaded, that the enemy fancied our force there to be pretty considerable. The large body of the enemy, meanwhile, who had stationed themselves beneath the east walls, and who were in vain waiting for the ladders, attempted to scale them. Several succeeded in reaching the top, but they were thrust down with the bayonet. Loughnan saw the danger, and was anxiously thinking of some other mode of defence. Hand-grenades he had none, and there was no means of firing, for no sooner was one bold enough to put his head over the wall, than a dozen bullets were at once fired at him.

Messrs. Erith and Alone, two of the volunteers, accordingly suggested bricks and mortar, and succeeded so well in dislodging the enemy with these and other missiles of a very impure nature, that our friends soon had that part of the outpost clear. They were thus obliged to come again within range of our muskets.

While my friend Mr. Hardingham, another of the volunteers, was actively engaged in firing, a bullet from behind whistled so close to his ear, that he turned round and saw the terror-struck countenance of one of our own sepoys. Hardingham made an advance towards him, and was about to bayonet the fellow, when his officer's command arrested him. "Never mind, Hardingham," said he, "don't bayonet him yet, there's lots of time afterwards." The look of sorrow and deprecation the sepoy cast on him proved sufficiently that it was not by treachery, but by accident, that the piece had so nearly killed my friend.

While this was going on in one part of the compound of Innes's house, another portion of it, called the cock-loft, was in the most imminent danger of being taken. Mr. Erith, the Corporal of the Volunteers, saw the peril, and intending to reinforce our party there, advanced amidst a volley of musketry that opened upon that part from the elevation opposite, known as the "Mound." But a bullet struck him in the neck, and he fell like a log of wood. His friends were obliged to leave him there, nor could they remove him till some hours after, when the fire slackened a little.

Meanwhile another part of the outpost was stoutly held by a little fellow of the name of Bailey, a volunteer, the son of a native Christian captain formerly of the king's service, and a couple of sepoys. The young man spoke Hindostanee so well, that the mutineers, whom he, native like, abused from behind the palisade that sheltered him, fancied him a Mohammedan or Hindoo sepoy, and offered to spare his life, if he would throw down his arms and assist them. A very interesting and animated conversation took place. "Come," cried one of the rebels, who had found shelter in one of a large number of huts, not five yards away from the palisade which Bailey defended, "come over to us, and leave those cursed Feringhees, whose mothers and sisters we have defiled, and whom we shall kill this day. Come over to us; what have you to do with them? Will you be made a Christian too? (pop, pop) or have you already lost your caste?" "Take that," firing his piece, cried Bailey; "do you think that I have eaten pig's flesh like yourselves. Do you think that I too shall disgrace myself, by proving unfaithful to my salt? Take that, thou son of a dog! (pop.) Thou whose grandfather's grave I have dishonoured!" (pop) "Wait, you offspring of a dishonoured mother," cried another, "we are coming. I shall just be with you, and jump over your wall. My sword is sharp." "Is it," cried Bailey, "but thy heart is craven. Come along then, boaster. My bayonet is ready, scale the wall. We are all prepared, and as for you, I shall catch you on the point of my bayonet. But first, here's for you."

Off went a dozen of our muskets that had meanwhile been loaded by our two sepoys, who now also joined in abusing the enemy. Showers of abuse, which it is impossible to render as forcible in English as it is in Hindostanee, and an unceasing fire of musketry, were interchanged between the two parties for some time longer, Bailey firing off his spare muskets with great rapidity, when at last his ammunition failed him. He could not venture to leave his post, for to do so would have been to make our own sepoys desert it also; and he dared not send one of them, lest he might not return, nor did he even venture to call out too loudly, lest the enemy, aware of his deficiency, should leave their shelter and carry this point by storm.

Fortunately the guns from the Redan commanded this position, and the shells thrown by Lieutenant Macfarlane, of the artillery, and Lieut. Bonham, did no little mischief among them. This prevented their advance, and Bailey at last succeeded in making his wants known. Accordingly, one of the volunteers, Hardingham, amidst a heavy fire, brought him the required ammunition, and the combat continued till Bailey's party was reinforced, but not before one of the sepoys was knocked over. He himself was very dangerously wounded. A musket ball had smashed his chin, and effected an exit through his neck, — a most singular wound; the more so as, contrary to expectation, he recovered from it.

The fire still continued all round the outposts; two other soldiers and two more sepoys were severely wounded, and all the remainder had the most narrow escapes. Gately, a corporal of the 32nd, had his stripes torn off by a musket-ball. At last the enemy, beaten at all points, slowly retreated, our muskets and the tremendous fire from the Redan having killed a very large number. Not less than a hundred were borne off the ground by their comrades from this outpost alone.

At the Financial and Sago's garrisons the enemy made a scarcely less fierce assault. One of their fanatical preachers, bearing the green standard of Islamism in his hands, and shouting, " Deen deen " (for our religion, our religion), " maro faringeeun ko " (kill the Europeans), led a very numerous party of sepoys and matchlockmen through a gateway which they burst open, while a ceaseless fire was kept up by a regiment of insurgents outside. Both garrisons were almost entirely defended by non-military men; and Mr. Bryson of Sago's, and Mr. Kight of the Financial, the serjeants of their respective garrisons, kept the enemy in check for some time, till Lieutenant M'Cabe, with a small detachment of the 32nd, reinforced Captain Saunders, commanding Sago's, and were covered by a well kept up fire from the Judicial and Anderson's garrisons.

The officers commanding there, Post-Captain Germon and Captain Anderson of the 25th, and the garrisons under them, behaved with great spirit, and contributed to the dispersion of the rebels, not only from their own, but also from the two most exposed outposts of Sago's and the Financial. All behaved well and gallantly; but among those who most distinguished themselves were Messrs. Bryson, Lawrence, Sequera, Kight, Anthony, Wharton, Chick, Capper, Barsotelli, and Jeoffroy.

After some hours' hard fighting, the enemy retreated with their commanders all dead, and perhaps fifty or sixty of their comrades slain. Several of their bodies they were obliged to leave behind them, and about three or four corpses were lying for several days unburied in the compound; but they succeeded in carrying off the holy standard of the Mohammedan faith, and the remainder of their dead.

At the Brigade Mess and Gubbins's garrison, the enemy made equally unsuccessful attempts to storm, and at the Cawnpore battery they succeeded in coming under our very guns, but hand grenades thrown among them caused great slaughter, and made them retreat, after about half an hour's opposition. It would be taxing my readers' patience too far were I to enter into minute details of every separate assault. I shall, therefore, merely mention that during the whole of this furious fusilade and cannonade, we lost only from fifteen to seventeen Europeans in killed and wounded, and about ten natives. Among the wounded were Lieut. M'Farlane, a portion of whose skull was torn away by a musket ball, but who eventually recovered from this very dangerous wound. He had during the whole of that day done excellent service by his artillery practice. Of the 32nd, Lieut. J. Edmonstone was slightly, and Captain E. W. D. Lowe, severely wounded. Of the 48th N. I., Adjutant O. L. Smith, and Captain Forbes, of the Oude Irregular Force, received each slight wounds. Of the civilians, besides those already named, Mr. Blaney, at Sago's outpost, was wounded in the back, and Mr. Morgan, attached to the artillery, in the hand.

The enemy on the other hand had lost not fewer than 1000 men, perhaps even more. The fight had commenced at 9 o'clock in the morning, and the fire did not cease before 4 o'clock in the evening. After it had quite terminated, the rebels sent a flag of truce, and begged permission to remove the slain and wounded whom they had not been able to carry away. This permission was readily granted, for their stench might have created a pestilence. We afterwards saw whole cart-loads carried away. They are a cruel set, and threw their wounded promiscuously among their dead, so that many must have died of suffocation.

I had not eaten anything the whole day, and when the combat was over and I found myself alive and with a whole skin, I mentally thanked Heaven, and then enjoyed my chupattees and a glass of brandy and water, which Deprat gave me, with a relish which is inexpressible in words. I was filthy and black with dust and gunpowder; and a wash, a little repose, my poor dinner, and a cigar after it, put me into the most enviable frame of mind. I had not been so happy for a long time; — not even before I had been imprisoned by these cursed insurgents.

CHAP. IX.

OUR TROUBLES INCREASE.

Constant cannonading. — Death of Major Banks. — Brigadier Inglis and Mr. Gubbins. — Mr. Polehampton, the Chaplain, dies. — Hospital Scenes. — Death and Disease. — Erith's Death. — Pigeon killed. — Friends in Hospital. — Mr. Thompson's Kindness to the Sick. — Dr. Scott. — Hospital Surgeons. — The Plague of "Flies." — The Martinière Pupils. — Rain. — News of coming Reinforcements. — The Enemy's Interruption to our Songs. — A sham Attack. — " Hope deferred maketh the heart sick."—The Enemy's Mines. — Captain Fulton's Master-mind. — Our Casualties. — Dr. Brydon of Jellalabad and Lucknow.

THOUGH beaten at all points, the enemy, every day after the memorable 20th of July, unceasingly annoyed us, keeping up a furious cannonade from not only their old positions, but from new batteries which they had erected. Their artillerists also seemed to have improved, and their shots were excellent. For some days after their grand attack, our casualties were very heavy. On the very next day we lost no fewer than twelve Europeans, among whom were our chief commissioner, Major Banks, our chaplain, Mr. Polehampton, and a civilian, Mr. Pigeon.

Major Banks was at Gubbins's battery, examining one of the houses occupied by the enemy. A round shot took off a portion of his brain and skull, and killed him instantaneously: he never uttered a groan. Major Banks was a leader in whom we had every confidence, farseeing, careful, and brave. His loss was deemed a great misfortune. Brigadier Inglis now assumed the supreme command of our little garrison, but not without some opposition made by Mr. Gubbins, the financial commissioner.

This disagreement between the two personages was, at a time when all our lives were in jeopardy, to say the least of it, very unseemly. Mr. Gubbins, I have heard, had been in the habit of writing to our Government, and sending away spies with his letters, who never returned, and who most probably were seized with their despatches by the enemy, thus revealing to them our positions and difficulties. To this the Brigadier very justly objected, and he even menaced Mr. Gubbins with arrest, if he should ever attempt to despatch another letter without his consent; alleging, that in time of war, civil authority was at an end; and that the only service he could recognise in him was his shouldering a musket and fighting in the ranks like other civilians and officers. Both maintained they were in the right, but Mr. Gubbins struggled for precedence, and was in the minority. That this dispute existed and was carried on for some length of time I am convinced; but as to the details, I write under correction, and merely state the rumours then current in the Residency. Both individually and collectively, most of us deplored this sad disagreement at so critical a period.

The death of Mr. Polehampton was also a serious loss: for that reverend gentleman had been unremitting in his kindness to the sick and wounded in hospital. From morning to night Mr. Polehampton was constantly by the bedside of some poor sufferer, inspiring him with confidence in Providence, and hope in his recovery, or, if hope was at an end, with the prospects of salvation in a better world. He never swerved from this self-imposed duty, and only left the hospital to go to his meals.

His wife even more generously devoted herself to the task of relieving the temporal wants of the sick. Mrs. Polehampton was ever to be found where she was most wanted. No Sister of Charity could have acted more kindly. It was not long, however, before the chief object of her attention was her own husband. He had been wounded in the shoulder by a bullet while in the act of shaving. From the effects of this wound he slowly recovered; but his system had received a shock which it could not get over. He died some weeks after of cholera.

The hospital at this time was always full; and the spectacle which it presented was heart-rending. Everywhere wounded officers and men were lying on couches, covered with blood, and often with vermin. The apothecaries, hospital attendants, and servants, were too few in number, and with all their activity could not attend to everybody; and as for a change of linen, where was that to come from? We had one or two dhobbies, it is true, who at most exorbitant prices now and then washed, —badly, insufficiently, and without soap, of which there was a great dearth in the garrison; but they were overwhelmed with labour, and would do little; and besides, there was very little linen. This was, indeed, a luxury which few were permitted to enjoy. There were not even bedsteads enough for all.

Many of the wounded were lying groaning upon mattresses and cloaks only. Everywhere cries of agony were heard, piteous exclamations for water or assistance. The fumigations to which recourse was had were not sufficient to remove the disagreeable, fetid smell which pervaded the long hall of the sick, and the air in it was pestilential and oppressive. Owing to the unceasing fire of the enemy, the windows had to be barricaded, and it was therefore only by the doors facing the Residency, and those fronting the Bailey-guard wall at the back, that light and air could penetrate the building. The upper story was quite untenable; and, indeed, the lower was far from safe.

One poor fellow, in a fair way of recovery, while smoking his pipe, was shot in his bed, and several of our sick had most narrow escapes from the bursting of shells. At a subsequent period, too, a carcase fell into the midst of one of our barricades, and set not only the whole of it on fire, but consumed also a great number of hospital appurtenances. It was with difficulty extinguished. Dysentery and diarrhœa swelled the numbers in hospital almost as much as the balls of the enemy. The exposure we all had to bear at last affected the majority of us. Though all did not go into the hospital, many were ailing at their posts, or in their apartments, and the bad food we had to swallow did little towards invigorating us. The children, however, mostly felt the privations. More than a score had already died.

About this time I often wandered about in the hospital to see my wounded friends. Poor Erith was lying still sensible, but unable to move, on a bed clotted with his blood. His wife was bending over him, weeping bitterly. She had been told that no hope remained. As I approached the poor fellow's bedside he opened his eyes, looked at me, and calling me by name, asked if all was right at his garrison (Innes's outpost). Poor Mrs. Erith, who was so soon to be a widow, had only been married three months, and seemed devoted to her husband. Though I had become accustomed enough to these sights, I could not help being moved by the image of despair which she presented. Poor Erith! he died tranquilly during the night, and without pain.

Next to his bed lay Mr. Pigeon, a civilian attached to the Judicial garrison. He was mortally hit, and was likewise attended by his afflicted wife. I had helped to carry him to the hospital, but we had been obliged to put him down at the post-office to rest ourselves for a moment. "Let me lie here," cried he; "I know I shall die, so let me die in peace. Moving me hurts me." But we took him on. We thought his wound dangerous but not fatal; but on reaching the hospital we soon learnt that the ball had entered the spine and that he could not live, nor did he survive above three hours.

I also went to see little Bailey, whom I found sitting up, his chin bleeding profusely, but as soon as he saw me he would talk, though with his teeth set. He chiefly expatiated on his valiant deeds of the day before, and seemed to feel no little pride in not having left his firelock at his post. Sinclair, too, I found stretched on his bed, with the bullet still in his thigh.

But wherever I went, and whomsoever I went to see, whether officer, soldier, or civilian, Mr. Apothecary Thompson, who had been in medical charge of one of the Oude Irregular Infantry regiments, and who now acted as the medical officer in charge, was everywhere to be seen. Not a patient that recovered but could testify often to his professional skill, but always to his unremitting kindness. Many a recovered friend afterwards assured him that, next to God, Dr. Thompson had been the means of saving his life. Mr. Thompson lived in a room in the hospital, and was therefore constantly in attendance when required. As a surgeon, Mr. Thompson undoubtedly was most skilful, and there was no patient, who had not, at some time or other, an encouraging word or some little personal comfort from this gentleman.

But before speaking of Mr. Thompson, I should first have mentioned the superintending surgeon, Dr. Scott. Though apparently rough, his arrival was always hailed with pleasure by every one in hospital. For some poor soldier, he usually had a trifling present, and though he bestowed his favours with a degree of roughness bordering on rudeness sometimes, he did so in order not to have the thanks of the recipient. The 32nd always speak of him with gratitude, and say, with pride, that their surgeon had never been absent from his regiment since he joined it. They all looked to him as to a father.

Dr. Darby, Dr. Boyd, Dr. Bird, Dr. Partridge, and the other gentlemen who were attached to the hospital, were also always busy, cutting and slashing, as well as doing their best to alleviate the sufferings of the sick. And last, though not least, Mr. Higgins, the head apothecary, often acted the good Samaritan to the poorer class of sufferers. This good and humble-minded man, never let an opportunity pass by to do a charitable action, not the less acceptable because it was done in silence and unostentatiously. The lower the rank of the patient, the more did Mr. Higgins consider him entitled to his good offices.

And yet, with all this numerous and well-intentioned medical staff, the hospital was always so crowded, that it was impossible to attend to all.

To one nuisance, the "flies," I have already alluded; but they daily increased to such an extent that we at last began to feel life to be irksome, more on their account than from any other of our numerous troubles. In the day flies, at night musquitoes. But the latter were bearable, the former intolerable. Lucknow had always been noted for its flies, but at no time had they been known to be so troublesome. The mass of putrid matter that was allowed to accumulate, the rains, the commissariat stores, the hospital, had attracted these insects in incredible numbers. The Egyptians could not possibly have been more molested than we were by this pest. They swarmed in millions, and though we blew daily some hundreds of thousands into the air, this seemed to make no diminution in their numbers. The ground was still black with them, and the tables were literally covered with these cursed flies.

We could not sleep in the day on account of them. We could scarcely eat. Our beef, of which we get a tolerably small quantity every other day, is usually studded with them; and while I eat my miserable dall and roti (boiled lentil soup and unleavened bread), a number of scamps fly into my mouth, or tumble into the plate, and float about in it, *impromptu* peppercorns and — I was about to say something wicked — but really even the reminiscence of this annoyance is enough to make a saint swear.

The poor Martinière pupils, who go about the garrison more filthy than others, and apparently more neglected and hungry even than we are, are made use of to drive away these insects from the sick in hospital, and others. That they, too, should contribute their share of usefulness is but just and fair; but that they should be placed in menial attendance upon the healthy great in the garrison is, in my opinion, far from right. But I shall say nothing more on this subject, lest I assume a tone of censure.

Rain, rain, rain, almost constantly. This is unpleasant, for though one shower cools the air after a hot day, when it lasts too long the heat, instead of being dry, is moist, like a vapour bath, and suffocating to a degree. And to stand sentinel at night when it is as cold as the day is hot, and to shiver in the wet, is also far from agreeable.

On the 25th (July) we were first delighted with authentic news from the outer world, in the shape of a letter from the Quarter-Master-General of General Havelock's force, telling us to be of good cheer, for forces were coming in overwhelming numbers, and that we should be relieved in two or three days. With what joy we received this communication my readers can perhaps imagine. We had been much depressed of late, notwithstanding the elation which succeeded our victory of the 20th, but this joyful intelligence reanimated us, and we were full of hope. Though Angud, the spy who had brought us this good news, spoke only of 700 Europeans and a regiment of natives, we believed this to be merely the advance guard, especially as he assured us that our force had retaken Cawnpore, had fought and gained a battle at Futtypore, and that we had Benares, Allahabad, and Agra in our possession.

We were all very happy, and the night of the 26th found me talking in high glee and singing with Captain Boileau, my new commanding officer, who, while second in command in the Volunteer Cavalry, had so much distinguished himself at Chinhutt, and with a number of other officers and gentlemen. We had just encored " Cheer, boys, cheer," and were chorusing it with stentorian lungs, when our sentinel sent one of our men from the terrace of the Bhoosa-guard outpost, where we were, to report to us his having seen forms in the dark; and immediately after it was "rattle, rattle," and a heavy fire of musketry and great guns. We never stopped to finish our song, accoutred ourselves without an instant's delay, and were ready to meet the enemy with joy and hope in our hearts, for now we were certain of success and sure of a speedy deliverance. The rebels, however, never put us to the proof. Their attack was only a sham one, and they only marched from one house to another, and kept up a furious fusilade in order to harass and annoy us. This trick they afterwards played us often enough.

But the 27th passed, and no troops came; the 28th, and still no aid; the 29th, the 30th, the 31st; yet no sign of reinforcements coming to our assistance. It was sad, indeed! We had so trustfully buoyed ourselves up with hope, we were so sanguine in our expectations, so confident that our friends outside must soon arrive and beat the rebels, that our depression, on not seeing our hopes realised, was proportionately great. Our hearts began to sink, and many (of whom I, however, was not one) gave up even the last glimmering of hope, and delivered themselves up to a sullen, obstinate, silent despair. Thus, hopeless of life, and hoping only to kill before being killed, their existence became almost a burden to them, and many a one cast envious glances at the poor fellows carried to their grave every evening.

Rumours of mining began now to be circulated. One was said to have been under the Cawnpore battery, another under the Brigade Mess, and a third under Sago's garrison. My friend Lawrence never saw me but he reported to me the progress that the enemy was making in their subterraneous galleries there. He seemed certain of one day being blown up; "So, hurrah, my friend," cried he, "for a celestial trip up in the air."

But we had in the garrison a master mind, a great man, who foresaw all, who opposed science to force and superior numbers, who was indefatigable in taking precautions against all contingencies, who directed everything; for the Brigadier was too sensible a man not to listen to his advice, and Major Anderson, the chief engineer, was too ill, not to devolve his duties upon his active subordinate. All acknowledged his genius. This was Captain Fulton of the Engineers, the man to whom, next to Sir Henry Lawrence, we, under Providence, owe our lives. And by dint of his prompt and scientific measures we beat off a danger which, from the vast labour the insurgents had at their command, we had most to dread. Captain Fulton, by countermining the enemy's subterraneous galleries, either stopped their works, or, by blowing them up, made them innocuous.

I shall now again continue my story in the shape of a journal; but before I conclude my narrative of the month of July, I have to record several casualties. Lieutenant A. S. Arthur was shot through the eye at the Cawnpore battery while aiming at one of the enemy. He had belonged to the 7th Light Cavalry. He expired nearly at the same time as he was hit, the 19th July. Lewin, of the Artillery, was shot through the head, and died almost instantaneously. Indeed this branch of the service suffered immensely.

Our gunners are constantly knocked over, and though the artillery has been reinforced by volunteers from the civilians and the 32nd Regiment, we cannot man the guns sufficiently. Captain Sheppard, of the 7th Light Cavalry, was hit on the night of the same day, 26th July, during the sham attack of the enemy. My officer, Captain Graydon, had occasion to go to the terrace of the Brigade Mess, to report to the Brigadier a move of the enemy towards the Bhoosa-guard, and I accompanied him. On passing through the first square we saw the body of this unfortunate officer wrapped up in a sheet, red with blood. We heard then that, while at the Cawnpore battery, the 32nd soldiers, stationed on the top of the Brigadier Mess, believing the enemy to be approaching, — for it was a dark rainy night, — and thinking they saw a form passing, fired in that direction. It was, unfortunately, Captain Sheppard, who had left the battery itself, and moved to the wall to make a reconnaissance. He was shot dead. When we arrived we found Brigadier Inglis anxiously investigating the affair.

A young man, the son of an old uncovenanted servant, Mr. Wittenbaker, the head of the Financial Commissioners' Office, was killed about the same day at the Financial Office. He was a very promising young lad.

Lieut.-Colonel Halford, who had been long ailing, died on the 29th of July of a carbuncle in his back. He had commanded the 71st Native Infantry.

Dashwood of the 48th, was slightly wounded. He had been playing with his revolver, which went off, and lodged one of the balls in his leg. He was rapidly getting better, and during the attack of the 20th slept so very soundly that, wonderful to relate, the tremendous thunder of the enemy's and our guns never woke him. He recovered, but only to die of cholera afterwards.

Mrs. Dorin, who had effected her escape, was killed by a musket ball at Mr. Gubbins' house.

Surgeon Brydon, of the 71st Native Infantry, who had been very useful in attending to his patients in hospital, became (29th) an inmate of it himself. He was shot while performing an operation, I believe, in the back. His wound was considered dangerous, but he recovered eventually. This gentleman had been at the siege of Jellahabad, and was now destined to go through the dangers and sufferings of a second siege.

CHAP. X.

AUGUST. — THE MONTH OF MINES.

Our daily Food. — Captain Fulton's mining Operations. — Hely's Death. — Cholera. — Hope. — Disappointment. — Revelry of the Insurgents. — Their Taunts. — The Enemy's Mines discovered and blown up. — Attack of August 10th. — Explosion of their Mine at Sago's, and miraculous Escape of two Soldiers. — Explosion and Attack on the Brigade Mess. — "Turk" as "Luchminia." — Blenman wounded. — Brice's Death. — Death of Major Anderson. — Anecdote. — Refractory Conduct of a Civilian. — Retribution.

August 1st.— THE siege continues as usual; but the coarse insufficient food is playing the mischief with us. Many of the officers know, however, nothing of this, and one civilian, if report says true, enjoys even luxuries. As for myself, my good things have long been expended. The authorities, before the siege commenced, purchased for Government all the stores of the different merchants, but we never see anything of them. Our grand diet consists of coarse, exceedingly coarse, "attah" (ground corn with all the husks unsifted), "mash dall" (a nasty black slippery kind of lentils), and bitter salt, with, every other day, a small piece of coarse beef, half of it bones. The whole of this, when passed under the hands of my *chef-de-cuisine*, a filthy black fellow, who cooks for three or four others, and whom I am obliged to pay twenty rupees a month, results in an abomination which a Spartan dog would turn up his nose at. I have been robbed of nearly half my cigars, too; and a smoke is now a luxury which I must only occasionally indulge in. Eight poor fellows killed to-day.

August 2nd.—As usual, "rattle rattle,"—musket, rifle, jingal (a sort of huge blunderbuss, moved on pivots fastened to walls), matchlock, cannon from a 2- to a 36-pounder, swell the diapason of uproar. And besides, we hear of mines everywhere. Captain Fulton, however, organises a body of miners, partly European, partly native, and begins a series of defensive mines. We are, when doing sentinel's duty, particularly warned to be careful, and listen to the sounds of excavation.

Hely, veterinary surgeon, 7th Light Cavalry, had been shot in the arm some days ago. I found the poor gentleman lying in the Thuggee jail, and fainting from loss of blood. Apothecary Hyde was soon at his side, and by his directions I got a glass of brandy from one of the masters of the Martinière.

This revived him. He was carried to hospital, had his arm amputated, and died to-day.

August 3rd.— Heavy rain. The enemy's fire slackens. Nine Europeans buried to-day, among them, Oswin Brown, who died of cholera,—the gentleman who, on my last trip to Lucknow, had treated me so hospitably at Bunnee, where he was toll-collector. He was the son of Colonel Brown. Cholera, indeed, is making many awful ravages, but particularly among the children.

August 5th.— We hear firing of cannon in the city. Can it be our long expected friends? Is it possible that our reinforcements have at length arrived, and have actually penetrated into the city? God grant it be so. We all think so, and are frantic with joy; we shake hands with each other as if our deliverance were already at hand, and congratulate each other, and run to the tops of houses, regardless of danger, to see them coming. But we perceive nought but smoke; and now it ceases, and we hear the sound of cannon in cantonments. Have they veered round, and will they come across the iron bridge, after fording the river at Constantia? This must be so! How otherwise can we account for their guns being heard in two different quarters? This night we sleep little, for we are full of suspense and anxiety, and yet fearful, lest our hope be turned into disappointment. They will come to-night or early to-morrow morning without fail.

August 6th.— What bitter, bitter disappointment! We have a solution of yesterday's fire in the city, but it is one which makes our hearts sink with despair. The enemy are the first to give it us. At some parts of our entrenchments the insurgents are so near that we can hear them talking distinctly. At the school-houses and the brigade mess, almost every night might be heard the sounds of revelry, music and dancing, in Johannes' house, not twelve yards away from us, and separating us only by a street from the insurgents. At one of these places or at the Bailey-guard, I do not know which, some of the rebellious sepoys, having no doubt witnessed our delight, and guessed the cause of our shout and "hurrahs," were not slow in undeceiving us, by taunting us with "So you think your reinforcements have come, do you? reinforcements forsooth! why we have beaten them long ago" (this we knew to be a lie), " and we have crowned our king. The rule of the Feringhees is over, and we'll soon be in your Bailey-guard."

As we afterwards heard, the insurgents — it being full moon — fired a grand salute at various points, in honour of their new king; for they have a king; nothing short of royalty suits them.

Rain again; a dreary day, quite in keeping with our melancholy mood.

August 7th.—A spy comes in from the city, and brings us authentic news,—at least, so it is said,—that an action has taken place at Futtypore, between the Cawnpore insurgents and our fellows, the result of which was a good beating to the Babalogue, and the loss of all their guns. Can it be believed? is the next question. We have been so often disappointed that we fear to believe in good news. At no time did I feel so strongly as this the truth of the proverb, "Hope deferred maketh the heart sick." Aye, indeed it does! We were so sanguine before, that the natural result of our disappointments is that we believe in evil tidings, and doubt all good news.

August 10th.—The last two days had been of the same stereotyped character as the preceding; but on this day the insurgents made another attack, but not of the same determined character as that of the 20th of July. Since then they had become more wary; and Captain Fulton, aided by Lieutenants J. Anderson, M'Leod, Innes, and Hutchinson, had discovered and obtained possession of two of the enemy's galleries,—one under the Brigade Mess, and another under the Cawnpore battery,—which they blew up.

This also had annoyed and disgusted the enemy; and they attacked to-day in great force. They fired off an unusual amount of ammunition, sounded the bugle, shouted, advanced, and retreated, but without giving us many opportunities of knocking them over. We were, of course, all under arms, and at various places, where they attempted to storm, drove them back with the loss of some of their men. But their attack was so short-lived and comparatively so feeble, as far as actual storming was concerned, that we soon had nothing more to do than keeping well under cover. Our victory was cheaply purchased with the loss of only two or three men; but we were not the less on that account cheered by it. We began now fairly to despise our enemy.

Two of the enemy's points of attack on this day had been Sago's garrison and Innes' outpost. My friend Lawrence's predictions had at last proved true; the enemy had really begun a mine, but it was not in a direction to injure our friends there. It exploded, but hurt no one, and only brought down some outhouses; so that the garrison had to strengthen their defences within. Two European soldiers, who had stood sentinel at one of these out-house piquets, were also blown into the air, but both escaped with their lives. One fell within our compound, slightly bruised, but in no way seriously injured, and the other was thrown into the middle of the road which separated us from the enemy. He no sooner found himself unhurt, than he got upon his legs again, jumped over our wall, and made his escape to us in perfect safety, notwithstanding the shower of bullets that whistled past his ears.

Another mine of the enemy's had been sprung between the brigade mess and the Cawnpore battery, and blew down the stockade traversing the lane leading from Johannes' house to the post office. A few, more bold than the rest, attempted to enter, but they were received by a well-kept-up fire from the brigade mess and the earthen-work parapet crossing the road near the post office, and this made them quickly retreat.

Another attempt to assault on the part of the insurgents had been made at Innes' outpost. The fire there had been incessant, particularly from the large gun taken at Chinhutt, the 8-inch howitzer which our men had christened "Turk," and which the enemy, as one of our spies reported, had dignified with the name of one of their favourite divinities, "*Luchminia*." It played on the devoted outpost with fatal effect, bringing down beam after beam of the roof, and making a great number of breaches in the walls. Unfortunately, a friend of mine, Mr. D. Blenman, a volunteer of that garrison, was standing firing in the bath-room, when one of Luchminia's round-shot displaced the bricks of the wall he was near, and, covering him with the debris, almost buried him beneath the ruins. He was extricated by a brother volunteer some time after; but his injuries had been very severe. His eyes were both inflamed, and one of them is supposed to be for ever useless. Next day, when I visited him in hospital, he was so disfigured, that I did not know him again. He could not see with either eye for very many weeks after.

Poor Bryce, of the Artillery, died yesterday or the day before. He had saved one of our guns at Chinhutt, had succeeded in reaching the Residency safe, though wounded, had recovered, and, as had been the case with many convalescents, had become predisposed to cholera, and fallen a victim to it. I saw him in hospital, looking frightfully emaciated, a short time before his death. Ensign Studdy, of the 32nd, also expired about the same time. Wounded in the arm, by a gun-shot which broke the bone, he had to suffer amputation, which, as usual, proved fatal.

August 11*th*.—We are destined, it appears, to lose almost all our chief men; first Sir H. Lawrence, then Mr. Ommaney, then Major Banks, and now Major Anderson, the chief engineer. This gentleman had long been ailing, but notwithstanding his ill health he had worked unremittingly. When, during the first days of the siege, I had occasion to deliver reports at night, I found him almost always awake, either writing or looking over the plan of our garrison, or consulting with the other engineer officers. He had seldom left the post office, his headquarters, whence he directed all engineering operations, till he could no longer attend to any, and his duties were performed by Captain Fulton instead. Major Anderson died of a dysentery contracted in the hills, at first slight, but which became fatal by over exertion, anxiety of mind, and want of repose.

Connected with Major Anderson's death I must relate an anecdote. In our garrison there was a person of the name of Schmidt, whose grandfather had been a German, but who was himself born in India, and who was well known as a man of dissipated habits, and as having an utter disregard of truth. He had no situation, having been dismissed from some appointment under Government, but he pleaded in the Deputy Commissioner's Court at Mullapore in Oude, in favour of native clients. He was, however, a hard-working man in the garrison, being always ready to lend a hand at anything, as fearless as any other European, and constantly visiting one battery after another. One day he was one of a fatigue party in the post office, when Major Anderson saw him, and asked him what business he had there, and why he did not join his garrison, as an attack was expected? The reply was uncourteous enough. "Who the d— are you, to put me such a question?" "I am an officer," was the Major's reply. "D— officers," retorted Schmidt; "we have too many of them here that are not worth their salt, and who are fonder of bullying civilians, now that they can do so with impunity, than fighting the insurgents. Who *are* you?" "I am Major Anderson, and will soon show you who I am." Whereupon he called two Europeans, and had him conveyed to the quarter-guard, ordering him to be detained for forty-eight hours. As soon as Schmidt found himself in trouble, he did his best to get out of it; sent for his friends and begged them to endeavour to get him off. They succeeded, and Major Anderson ordered his release next day.

Instead of being grateful for having his punishment thus remitted, Schmidt was no sooner set free than he cursed Major Anderson and every officer in the garrison, swore he would return his firelock to Captain Boileau, his commanding officer, and vowed he would no longer lift a musket in defence of " such bullies." He would also try to revolutionise the other garrisons where the uncovenanted were ill-treated, and if possible cause a mutiny in the entrenchments. It was in vain that he was told that neither he nor any other civilian in Lucknow fought out of love to the officers in the garrison, but for his own life, for his friends, for the women and children under their common charge, and for the honour of the European name. None of the arguments had any effect. He was furious with rage at the indignity that had been offered to him, and attempted to incense the civilians in other garrisons against their superiors, assuring them that if they were all of one mind they would soon bring down the pride of these detested officers.

Of course no one would listen to his nonsense, and on his return he called the civilians a parcel of cowards, and then, taking his musket, went up to Captain Boileau. He there threw the firelock at his officer's feet, swore he would not take it up again, and continuing his insolence, begged the Brigadier to let him have a horse, and have the gate opened for him, and he would risk being cut up by the insurgents, but whom, if they allowed him, he would join. He then broke his sword in two, and was walking away, when he was ordered back; and, as such insolence could not be allowed, he was sentenced to be put into irons, and to receive twenty-five lashes. Before he was stripped to receive the cane, he said to the provost, "Remember, sir, I am a British subject, and a European." "Are you, indeed?" said that gentleman, affecting surprise; "well, judging from your face, I did not think so, but now that I see your body, I am of opinion you are;" adding, just as the culprit entertained some hope of being let off, "However, lay on, my lads."

He received his punishment stoically enough, went to hospital for treatment, recovered as soon as the period of his arrest had expired, and then returned to his duty as if nothing had happened. This flogging had not been very public, and he invariably denied that the sentence had ever been executed.

This happened in July. To-day, while we were all assembled on the terrace at the Boosha-guard, Schmidt suddenly called out, "Boys, I have some capital news to give you. Will you cheer if I tell you?" "Yes, yes, of course," was the reply. "Well, then (with an oath), Major Anderson is dead this afternoon." Every one cried out "Shame! shame!"

I felt the greatest inclination in the world to knock the fellow down for his brutality, but I restrained myself, and merely said, " How easy it is to forgive, when one's enemy is dead; even supposing Major Anderson was your enemy, it is horrible and unmanly to speak thus of the dead." " Forgive him!" cried he, with a sneer and an oath; " no, never would I forgive him;" and he uttered a curse, with which I shall not disgust my readers.

I shall finish this episode, though I might be thought guilty of an anachronism. Schmidt from that day began to ail, and at last became so ill that he could no longer rise from his bed. He lingered on for weeks, but just as our troops had at last gladdened us with the hope of relief, *he* expired. He had been in the thickest shower of musket balls, and even often exposed himself uselessly, without ever being touched; but to die of disease, and to die at such a moment, when all other hearts were full of joy, to die neglected and unnoticed in the midst of rejoicing, made many think, and think justly, that his death was a direct punishment from Heaven, and that the curses he uttered over the corpse of poor Major Anderson had met with their deserts by a higher power than even martial law.

CHAP. XI.

AUGUST CONTINUED.—SORTIES.

Despair.—Captain Fulton's Successes.—War with Brickbats.—Our Artillery Officers. — Deaths. — An Episode of War. — Bitter Thoughts. — Hairbreadth Escapes. — Successful Explosion of the Enemy's Mine.—Orr's Miraculous Escape.—The Enemy repulsed. — Sortie.—" Bob the Nailer."—Sally out. — Other Sorties.—The Mohurrum. — Desertion of Sergeant Jones and others. — Our Natives disheartened.—News from the outer world.— Character brought out by the Siege.—Our Casualties in August.

August 14*th.* — The last few days had been of the same character as before, with this addition merely, that our hope of relief had become daily more feeble. Still I doubt if even my friend Barsotelli, than whom I never knew a man less hopeful, had not also a glimmering of hope. But it was distant, so very distant indeed, that the inkling of its light could scarcely be perceived, — however, yet existing, yet present in the midst of the surrounding darkness. Our loss of European lives had of late been very heavy also, and we had reason to look at everything as *couleur de deuil.*

But Captain Fulton at least never despaired. He had now become our chief engineer, and was ever on the watch for the enemy's mines. He soon discovered them at work near Sago's garrison, and our sentries there were enabled to learn the very spot where they had sunk a shaft. A sortie had therefore been resolved upon, in the view of taking possession of it and destroying it. They had sallied out towards noon, expecting to be able to surprise the guard they believed they would find there. But instead of only a small number of men, they found an overwhelming force prepared to meet them. They accordingly retreated and miraculously succeeded in reaching our entrenchments without the loss of a man.

Captain Fulton, therefore, ordered a countermine to be made, and so expeditious was he that in the space of three days it was completed. Its gallery led right under one of the houses they occupied in great force, with riflemen particularly; for we could see their dark-green uniform often enough, and still more frequently hear the sharp whiz of the rifle ball. Lieutenant Birch, in order to see if it was full, this morning threw a few brickbats into its courtyard. Immediately fifty other similar missiles were shied at the place where he had been. We were satisfied, and shortly after the mine was fired. It exploded, and the house was instantly one mass of ruins, burying under them from forty to sixty of the enemy. Many were not killed, and endeavoured to escape from their tomb, but only to fall by our rifles. Seeing our success, we set up a shout of joy, and our foes out of spite immediately began a furious fusilade all round, which, however, did no harm.

August 16*th.*—Two of our artillery officers were wounded yesterday, Lieutenant J. Alexander and Lieutenant Bonham. The latter had recovered from his first wound at Chinhutt, and now received a contusion at his side. Of our artillery officers we have now none but Lieutenant Thomas (Madras) and Lieutenant Cunliffe who remain untouched. Bryce and Lewin are dead, and Captain Simons is dangerously wounded, and M'Farlane, Clare Alexander, and J. Alexander, and Bonham are in hospital. Of our gunners, out of ninety, half are already laid low, and among them a civilian named Wells, a first-rate fellow, who never failed to go where danger was to be faced. He was shot through the head while serving his gun.

I had been going about the whole of the last few days, and among other places to Sago's garrison. Poor Lawrence, whom I visited there, is a living proof of the miseries which war entails. He has the misfortune to be a family man; for to have a wife and children to think of and to work for, in his circumstances, must indeed be terrible. He had at first told me of his wife being feverish and quite overcome with the abominable life she had to lead, herding together with a number of other women, and the stuff she had to swallow. And then he talked to me of his boy Herbert; how he was attacked with cholera, and feared he was very ill; and how, instead of being able to watch by his bedside, he had been all night digging at Captain Fulton's mine; and then how his child next night was convulsed, and what little hope he had of his darling being spared to them — how heart-rending his sufferings were to his parent's feelings — how even his iron constitution was at last giving way — how he had neither medicine nor attendance nor proper food for the child, and how the blowing up of the mine so close to his sick couch had frightened him. And then to-day he told me with tears in his eyes, that yesterday — the anniversary of his birthday, when he was exactly twenty-nine years of age, his poor child was called away. "God's will be done," said he, "but it is terrible to think of. At night we dug a hole in the garden, and there, wrapped in a blanket, we laid him. Oh, my God!" Lawrence's case is not singular. Many another poor parent's heart is thus torn. These episodes, alas! occur daily. May Heaven's curses fall on these miscreants!

August 17*th.* — Much as usual. The heart aches while watching for relief, but none comes. Will Cawnpore be repeated in Lucknow? Alas! it seems so. Our number is visibly decreasing. Besides, how do I know whether I shall escape even before the final catastrophe, which, unless our forces come to our aid, must take place sooner or later? How do I know whether I shall not be knocked over before? That is soon done. A covering to wrap my corpse up in, a dooly borne by sweepers to serve me as a hearse, a shallow hole, a short prayer over it, and half-a-dozen other dead bodies, and the thing is done, and no one can afterwards tell where my bones are laid. These reflections come frequently enough, but I banish them as quickly as they come. What is the use of thinking?

As for death it stares one constantly in the face. Not daily, not hourly, but minute after minute, second after second, my life, and every other's, is in jeopardy. Balls fall at our feet, and we continue the conversation without a remark; bullets graze our very hair, and we never speak of them. Narrow escapes are so very common that even women and children cease to notice them. They are the rule, not the exception. At one time a bullet passed through my hat; at another I escaped being shot dead by one of the enemy's best riflemen, by an unfortunate soldier passing unexpectedly before me, and receiving the wound through the temples instead; at another I moved off from a place where in less than the twinkling of an eye afterwards a musket-ball stuck in the wall. At another, again, I was covered with dust and pieces of brick by a round-shot that struck the wall not two inches away from me; at another, again, a shell burst a couple of yards away from me, killing an old woman, and wounding a native boy and a native cook, one dangerously, the other slightly; at another, again—but, no; I must stop, for I could never exhaust the catalogue of hairbreadth escapes which every man in the garrison can speak of as well as myself. The wonder is not that we lose so many men, but that so few of us are hit amidst the constant dangers we are exposed to.

August 18*th*.— Captain Adolphe Orr, who commanded the Sikh Square, had already reported two of the enemy's mines there, and Captain Fulton accordingly began a countermine, which the insurgents no sooner discovered than they at once stopped their operations. But a few days after they began a third mine, directed also to the Sikh Square, which Captain Orr also reported, but the engineers and other officers, who listened to the suspicious sounds, pronounced them to be caused not by the excavations of the hostile miners, but by the tramping of the horses, tied up close to the Sikh Square. This was indeed the most probable solution of the question, and no further notice was taken.

Early this morning, however, we discovered our mistake. The 2nd Sikh Square was garrisoned by about fifteen Christian drummers and musicians of the regiments that had mutinied in cantonments, and about as many Sikhs. One of the sentries on the look-out, suddenly called out, "Mine, sir." The words were scarcely out of his mouth, when a loud explosion shook the earth, buried seven Christians and two Sikhs under the ruins it made, hurled Captain Orr, Lieutenant Mecham, and three drummers into the air, and slightly bruised Lieutenant Soppitt and a few men. Captain Orr fell back into the square, receiving merely a slight contusion in the hand and back, and Lieutenant Mecham escaped likewise with a few bruises. Of the three drummers, one fell on the enemy's side, and two came down unhurt to us. The former was either killed by the fall or murdered by the mutineers, for the next day we saw his headless trunk lying on the road side. Of the other two drummers, one was killed, and the other, owing to the darkness caused by the smoke and dust, mistook his way, and was just about to run over to the enemy's side, when he was called back by his commanding officer, and thus saved.

A large breach had been effected, and the enemy made a feeble attempt to enter by it, but a bullet from the Brigade Mess killed the leader, and the rest retreated. But still we could not approach the breach. No sooner did any one of our men show himself, for the ruins of the building were now taken possession of by the foe, than he was fired at. Indeed, we lost several wounded in making the attempt. Nine of our fellow-creatures were buried there, some alive, and making piteous exclamations for assistance, but we could not help them. Brigadier Inglis then ordered a 9-pounder gun into the 1st Sikh Square, and Lieutenant Hutchinson made a temporary embrasure. But it was not before twelve o'clock that we could complete all these arrangements, and begin to drive out the enemy. Some of our gallant 32nd were then made to advance, protected, as they did so, by bullet-proof doors, which they held before them. Having once reoccupied the corner of the 2nd Sikh Square which we had temporarily lost, we tried to assist the victims of the explosion; but they had expired of suffocation and thirst by two o'clock, so that our aid came too late.

We did not, however, content ourselves with merely recapturing a point we had lost, but, headed by Captain Fulton, a party of volunteers, consisting of 84ths, 32nds, and a few civilians, sallied out, killed a number of insurgent matchlockmen in a house known as "Young Johannes," put the rest to flight, and then attacked a bazaar of Golahgunge, known as the Goenda Barracks. Captain Fulton's party not only destroyed a number of small houses in the neighbourhood, but also blew up the shaft of another mine they had begun. Before the enemy could recover from their surprise, and attack us, our party was already safe again in our entrenchments. My friend Deprat was severely wounded in the face to-day.

August 20th. — One of the houses from which we suffered most was that opposite the Cawnpore battery. We had already, in July last, made a sortie upon this house, known as "Johannes," which I omitted to notice It was the private property of a merchant of that name; and had been stored with goods of all sorts. One of the late king's African eunuchs, a first-rate rifleman, had picked off dozens of our men during the first days of the siege. Our men had christened him "Bob the Nailer," because he nailed every man he fired at with his double-barrelled rifle. The sortie, headed by Lieutenant M'Cabe, of the 32nd regiment, had been perfectly successful. An entry had been effected by blasting open a little doorway. A number of the enemy had been found asleep, and were bayoneted in grand style. Bob himself — found seated at his elevated post, where he was engaged in returning the fire kept up by the officers on the terrace of the Brigade Mess to divert his attention, perfectly unconscious of the entrance of our men — then paid for the death of so many brave Europeans, with his own life. Several others had been found hiding, with a view to plunder, in chests, which our men were searching in a godown or magazine, attached to the building, and had been killed after a hand-to-hand struggle.

However, it was soon after re-occupied by the enemy, and filled with other capital sharpshooters. We had tried shells and cannon-balls to dislodge the enemy, but without effect; and Captain Fulton, therefore, began a mine right under it, beginning from the cellar in Deprat's house, near the Cawnpore battery. The mine was fired to-day, and perfectly succeeded, killing from sixty to eighty of the rebels, as we afterwards heard. Immediately after the explosion, our men made two sallies. One was under Captain Fulton himself, who attacked some of the adjacent buildings, drove out the insurgents that occupied them, and blew them up. The other party, under the gallant Lieutenant M'Cabe, who had won his commission at Mooltan, where he was the first man that placed the British standard there, was not less successful. He spiked two of the enemy's guns, and returned without losing a man; only one of the 32nd being slightly wounded.

The enemy, as usual, showed their disgust at these manœuvres immediately after recovering from their surprise, by invading the Residency with shell and shot from all sides.

August 25th.—During the last few days nothing of consequence occurred. The siege went on as usual, with this difference only, that the enemy seem to have become reinforced again, and to fire with greater effect and more judiciously. We undergo the same privations, the same sufferings, the same annoyances, the same hopelessness of relief, the same or even greater loss of men daily, the same dangers. In the language of the Psalmist, " One day certifieth another."

The Mohurrum has now come on, so that the stimulus of fanaticism will probably add to the courage of our despicable foe. We hear the "tom tom" of their processions, and the shrill tones of their buffalo-horn bugles more frequently. This Mohammedan festival is held in commemoration of the deaths of Hossein and Hussen, who are regarded by the Shiahs as martyrs to their faith, and are reckoned in the number of their twelve imaums or saints. Nine days after the first of the forty days of the Mohurrum, is the "*Kutl ka rath*," or Night of Butchery, when the Shiah Mussulmans are wont to kill goats as a sacrifice to heaven. This time, however, we expect they will endeavour to kill us, who are in their eyes, infidel Feringhees; for to die in such an attempt is a certain way of going straight into the sixth heaven of Paradise.

Among those who were particularly alarmed about the result of another attack, was a man named Jones, who had been made sergeant of the Bhoosa-guard. He was a fair, European-looking man, though he had Asiatic blood in his veins, very stout, very phlegmatic, and very fond of brandy, but more so of opium. Indeed, he was a confirmed opium eater; and having been all his life in Lucknow among Mohammedans, he had imbibed their prejudices, habits, and ways of thinking. Some said he had even been circumcised; but whether or no, he was an excellent Christian during the siege, for he never went to sleep without praying in company with four or five hangers on, men of his set and stamp. Fear, I believe, made them pious for the nonce.

The battle of Chinhutt had overtaken us so suddenly, that he and his companions had been obliged to leave their wives and children in the city. Anxiety to learn their fate, his terror of a general massacre on the Night of Butchery, the want of opium, and a sort of reliance upon his native friends, made Mr. Jones think seriously of deserting. I fear he had even carried on treasonable correspondence with the enemy. At all events, he succeeded in persuading ten others, mostly native Christians, to follow him, and to endeavour to leave the Residency. Accordingly, in the dead of night, while one of their set was doing sentinel's duty, they undid a barricade before a door in the bullock sheds, and, leaving it wide open, effected their escape without being discovered.*

We had got rid of rubbish, that was true; but the moral effect of their desertion was highly injurious. Our natives argued that our position must be

* We afterwards learnt that Jones and his companions had been seized by the insurgents and killed, and their blood sprinkled on the "tazeas," or images of Hussen's tomb, as a sacrifice.

very bad indeed; for if Feringhees themselves considered our cause hopeless, why should they risk certain death with us? Many of our servants, who had remained with us, now deserted, and the rumour became current, and was generally believed, that the sepoys who were with us would leave by the 1st of September, if no reinforcements should come to our aid, or if we had not certain tidings of their coming.

August 29*th.* — We were gladdened to day with news from Cawnpore. The same spy who had already succeeded in smuggling in a letter, returned to-day. After having been confined by the insurgents under suspicion, on going out of our entrenchments, he effected his escape to Cawnpore one dark night, and came back to us with a letter. It stated in a few words that we were not forgotten, but that this time we were certain of being relieved, but not before three weeks. This damped our ardour a little, but still it encouraged all to persevere, and we looked upon the future now with renewed hopes. It is a long period to look forward to, but still it serves as a bright beacon of light to lessen the darkness of despair. Even our sepoys are more cheerful, though they do grumble a little, and in grumbling they are not singular.

Through Ungud (this was the name of the messenger), we for the first time learned how our troops had re-crossed the river, after beating the enemy everywhere; but that their victories had cost them so dearly, that they were obliged to fall back upon Cawnpore for other reinforcements, and that a large force was assembled there. Is this true? *Nous verrons!*

August 31.—A siege is certainly the best school to learn character. People show themselves in their true light, and throw off the mask they wear in society. One's good or bad character becomes apparent at once. Many a kind action here I have seen performed by people whom I had considered harsh and proud; and men with smiling faces, polite, and noted for their obliging disposition, proved themselves selfish in the extreme. They might enjoy delicacies before your face, and though they knew you to be hungry, would never ask you to partake of them, even if they had more than enough for themselves. People to whom, during the first month of the siege, I had given all sorts of little luxuries, afterwards refused me a handful of flour, a teaspoonful of sugar, or a few leaves of tea, and yet they had stores of all. It was infamous! Self, self, self,—how general that feeling was, especially among the rich. And a poor sergeant's wife, or a common soldier, would occasionally give me a something that, though in the every-day course of life one would scarcely say a "thank you" for, is now prized above gold, pearls, diamonds, and rubies, of which, *à-propos*, one may have as many as one pleases for a few rupees, for a cigar, a glass of brandy, or a little tobacco.

Selfishness, which proceeds from a disinclination to deprive oneself of some benefit, I can understand; but the dog-in-the-manger style of selfishness is what I really cannot comprehend. Yet even this existed, and I knew people to hoard up luxuries, neither enjoying them themselves nor allowing others to enjoy them, and being in a perfect agony of mind at seeing others use their kettle, or avail themselves of the services of a domestic. And pride too still existed, though I must say most men put it into their pockets. Cowardice was, however, a failing which I saw very conspicuous in only one man, and that man, I am ashamed to confess, was a European. Surliness too was not quite uncommon. A siege sours one's temper considerably. One or two officers whom I shall not name were like rabid dogs, snapping at whoever addressed them. But the generality could bear scrutiny well enough, and yet not suffer in estimation. There are many good men with us still.

An old acquaintance of mine, known as Captain W. W. Need, formerly of the King of Oude's service, and of gold-seeking celebrity, was shot this month. He had been very careful to keep under cover, and he was besides old and ailing. But his children wanted food, and he had to get firewood. No sooner had he however made his bundle, than he was shot through the breast. This happened near Innes's outpost.

Two men who had done excellent service in the magazines here, superintending the manufacture of fusees, shells, &c., and had been indefatigable throughout, were also killed. Conductor Woods received a bullet through his breast at the hospital, and Sergeant White was shot dead through the head, near the Bailey-guard.

Captain G. P. Barlow, of the 50th Native Infantry, who had commanded the church garrison, died this month (21st August). His complaint was slight at first, but by his fretting it had become fatal.

A gallant young fellow, Mr. Edwin Sequera, who had distinguished himself at Chinhutt, as well as throughout the siege, for his coolness under fire, died of a wound received in his breast. He was more fortunate than others, for he expired in the bosom of his family, was carried to the grave by his friends, and buried alone, for on that day (29th August) his was the only death that took place.

Two officers were wounded this month, besides those I already named. Lieutenant H. Inglis was wounded by a piece of shell in the leg at Anderson's garrison, and Lieutenant and Adjutant Graves slightly wounded. Mr. M'Rae, a civil engineer, had his shoulder-bone injured by a bullet at the post office; and a hospital attendant, Brown, was shot through the shoulder in the hospital.

Captain Kemble, an officer, who, while in command of the Cawnpore battery, had been conspicuous for his coolness and gallantry, had a most narrow escape at his exposed post. A shell, which severely wounded one of our men, burst close to him without hurting him.

Mr. Bickers, an uncovenanted member of Innes's outpost, was very severely wounded. Though his jaw-bone was smashed, he yet lives, and is doing well.

CHAP. XII.

THE SEPTEMBER MONTH.

Famine Prices. —Valuable Cigars. —Commotion among the Rebels. — On the Alert. — Mines and Countermines. — Attack of the 5th September. — Quiet Days. — Sudden Death. — Death of Captain Fulton. — His Eulogy. — Fatal Error. — Deprat's Death. — The Protestant and Roman Catholic Clergymen. — Deprat's Military Experiences in Africa. —Offer of Service from the Nana. — Conversation with the Insurgents.— Characteristic Anecdote.— — The only Effective Artillery Officer. — Casualties. —Suicide. — Continuation of my Journal. —Signs of Coming Reinforcements.

September. — HERE we are, in the grouse-shooting season of merry England; but here in India, we shoot black men instead. Articles of consumption are sometimes obtainable, how and where from we do not ask. "Attah" (coarse flour), one rupee per seer; "ghee" (melted butter), very rancid, 10 rupees per seer; sugar, 16 rupees a seer; country leaf-tobacco, 2 rupees a leaf; a dozen of brandy, 150 rupees to 180; a dozen of beer, 70 rupees; a ham, 90 rupees; a bottle of pickles, 20 rupees; and all other things in proportion.

I have given up smoking tobacco, and have taken

to tea-leaves and neem-leaves, and guava fruit leaves instead, which the poor soldiers are also constantly using. I had sold my gold chain and watch for 250 rupees to one of the men who had more money than he could keep, and I was, therefore, enabled to enjoy the luxury of a cigar as long as I could get it for a rupee, but the price has come up to three rupees each now, and I cannot afford that. Provisions are not always to be had even at the abovementioned fearfully high prices, and money is of no use to me now, except for the immediate requirements which I can occasionally have for it. Indeed, I never thought I could ever come to care so little for rupees as I do now, and my only wonder is, how any of us can at such a time at all attach importance to such dross.

On the 3rd of September we observed some movement among the "Babalogue," and distinctly saw their regiments marching off towards Cawnpore. Ungud had assured us that Nana Sahib and his troops had been beaten and driven out of Cawnpore and Bithoor, and that the massacre of our women and children there had been fearfully avenged. But he also affirmed that the Nana had escaped, he believed, to Lucknow, and that, at all events, a great number of the troops and guns of the beaten army of that ruffian had joined the forces of the insurgents here. We might, therefore, expect an attack; as the insurgents said, the Bailey-guard once in their possession, they could easily withstand the forces that were coming to our relief.

We were, therefore, constantly under arms, day and night, and slept with our accoutrements on and our muskets by our sides. We were often, during the night, called out; for the enemy, in order to harass us, several times began a tremendous fire, and shouting and screaming, as if about to attack us. These were, however, only false alarms; except once, when they actually made an assault, but a very feeble one, on the Bailey-guard, easily repulsed by our sepoys, under command of a gallant officer, Lieutenant Aitkin.

On the 4th, we observed a stir and unusual bustle in the city. A thousand conjectures were accordingly afloat about it. Whether they were preparing for another assault, or making ready to oppose our coming troops, or plundering the town over again, we, at the time, could not tell.

Captain Fulton and the engineer officers under him meanwhile had discovered other mining operations of the enemy. One mine was found to be directed at the Financial garrison; and a counter-mine was at once commenced, under the superintendence of Lieutenant M'Leod Innes, who succeeded in not only blowing it up, but also the miners who were in it at the time. Lieutenant Hutchinson also countermined against another gallery of theirs, intended to destroy the Brigade Mess. The enemy perceiving this, however, stopped in their work, and left it unfinished. A third mine, which they then constructed against the Financial garrison, was taken by Lieutenant Innes, who entered it by a subterranean passage he had excavated, and blew the whole of it up.

We had, also, under Captain Fulton's directions, strengthened our defences near the Cawnpore battery, which had become now a very strong place, and fortified the Bailey-guard and Dr. Fayrer's garrison with newly constructed batteries.

On the 5th, the insurgents made another attack upon us. They began, as usual, with the explosion of mines. One they sprung near the Brigade Mess, the uncompleted one; it was innocuous. Another they blew up near Sago's garrison; the house rocked and shook as if it were about to fall down, but the mine proved short of its aim. A third they fired near Gubbins's battery; but it, too, did no harm. They advanced to the Brigade Mess boldly enough;

but more than a hundred bodies were soon strewn on the ground, and they retreated. The officers who garrisoned the Brigade Mess had not missed a single shot. They then attempted to assault the Bailey-guard, against which point they opened a terrific fire of great guns; but ours soon silenced them, and a few withering rounds of grape made lanes of death in their ranks, and scattered the assailants like chaff before the wind. At Innes's outpost, also, where they approached close enough, we drove them back, and the Bhoosa-guard, Gubbins's, Sago's, and the Financial garrisons, were equally successful. The attack lasted scarcely an hour. We had again vanquished the foe.

The next two days were unusually quiet. We were so accustomed to the constant unceasing crack of the enemy's musketry, that we felt uncomfortable if we did not hear it. And, besides, we always suspected the "Babalogue" to be up to mischief on those quiet days, which, indeed, were generally the precursors of explosions of mines or of assaults. And at such times, too, we usually lost more men than on fighting days. During the latter, we were careful to keep under cover, and to kill, without, if possible, exposing ourselves to being killed. But during the former a few well-aimed shots from the rifles of the late king's African eunuchs and other first-rate sharpshooters, often deprived us of three, four, and even more stout English hearts. We were then more careless of walking about the premises, and were picked off in the midst of the most peaceful occupations. One poor soldier, I remember, who was standing talking with me, every now and then giving a few puffs of guava-leaf smoke from his self-manufactured wooden pipe, suddenly fell dead at my feet. A rifle bullet had pierced his temples.

Things, however, began to take their usual course,—fusilade and cannonade all round, the latter particularly from sunrise to nine o'clock A.M., and from four o'clock P.M. to sunset. Their shots are usually well directed, and their shells are principally aimed at the centre of the Begum Kothy, where the officers of the commissariat and staff, and of the brigade mess, usually discussed their dinner. From the manner in which they aim their shots and shells, I suspect they are acquainted with the nature of all the different localities within our entrenchments. They no doubt obtain more correct information of what we are doing, than we do of them. For aught we know of what is going on in the city of Lucknow twenty yards away from us, we might as well be in Kamtschatka as here. I fear also we shot several of our own spies attempting to come to us with letters. Indeed, Ungud says it is less dangerous to pass through the enemy's ranks, than to come under the vigilance of our own sentries.

I had from the beginning of this month joined Innes's outpost. There was greater honour in being attached to this place,—more fighting to be seen; and having, besides, no longer a room to myself, I was desirous of some tolerable shelter. It was martyrdom to attempt to sleep at the Bhoosa-guard; the musquitoes, the fleas, the pestilential atmosphere from the slaughter-house close by, were all far worse than the balls, carcases, and shells which were constantly discharged at our outpost, with a view no doubt to set fire to so combustible a material as the Bhoosa.

On the 14th of September we had to deplore an irreparable calamity, the death of the gallant Captain Fulton. He had been visiting Gubbins's battery to examine the enemy's movements, when a 9-pounder, entering by an embrasure, took his head clean off. The universal grief with which this news was received by all classes of the community in the garrison was second only to that of Sir Henry Lawrence's death. Captain Fulton, like that much-lamented chief, was kind to all who acted under him.

He was one for whose genius all had the highest respect, and who commanded the gratitude of us all. As I said before, during a siege, a man's value easily becomes known, particularly when his office is one of importance.

Brigadier Inglis, who lost in him one of his ablest counsellors and most active subordinates, thus speaks of him in his report on the siege: "Captain Fulton, who was also struck by a round shot, had up to the time of his early and lamented death, afforded me the most invaluable aid; he was indeed indefatigable."

Captain J. C. Anderson (Madras Engineers), who succeeded Captain Fulton as garrison engineer, and who in his report to the Brigadier of the Residency defences, with a noble self-denial (rarely to be met with in a man) depreciating his own important services in order that those of others, high and lowly, might appear more prominent, thus mentions Captain Fulton and the officers working under him:—

"Captain Fulton became the senior engineer officer on the demise of Major Anderson, on the 11th of August. He had constructed the greater portion of the defences, powder magazines, &c., and up to the day of his death displayed the most unremitting energy, in spite of bad health, in advancing our work. In particular, he took a most active part in foiling the enemy's attempts to destroy our advanced posts by mines, and the manner in which he conducted the blasting operations during our sorties invariably excited the admiration of all who were present, officers and men.

"In the performance of the above-mentioned and engineering operations generally, he received the most able and untiring assistance from Lieutenants Hutchinson, Innes, and Tulloch, and the late Lieutenant Birch; and latterly, since Captain Fulton's death, I have received much assistance from Lieutenant Hay. The active part I myself have taken in the superintendence of works has been small, owing to my having suffered from continued ill health.

"Finally, I beg to bring to the notice of the Brigadier the excellent services performed by the late Mr. Carey, head accountant to the chief engineer, who had been sergeant-major of Sappers, and who was recommended by Major Anderson for the rank of assistant field engineer; of the late Mr. Supervisor Barrett; Mr. Beale, overseer, and Sergeant Ryder, assistant overseer,—all of whom have left families behind them."

The mention of the other names in Captain Anderson's report reminds me of several other losses we sustained. Lieutenant Birch, the son of the late Colonel Birch, of the 41st Native Infantry, who was shot at Seetapore by his own men, met with his death by a European hand. He was attached to the engineering department, and, with Lieutenant Huxham, of the 48th, Captain Boileau, and Lieutenant Keir, proceeded, towards eight o'clock in the evening, out of our entrenchments, at the Bhoosa-guard, to examine a suspected mine. Captain Boileau and Lieutenant Keir were returning, when Lieutenant Birch again went to the place he had started from. He had a cigar in his mouth, and the light of it was very plain in the dark. A soldier of the 32nd, at Gubbins's garrison, next to the Bhoosa-guard, seeing this, and believing the object to be an enemy with mischievous intent, to blow up a mine for aught he knew, fired.

The ball struck Birch in the abdomen. He fell. Huxham left him for an instant, and came hurriedly in to ask for assistance to carry him inside. I went out along with him and Mr. Keir. The unfortunate gentleman was perfectly conscious, and on our attempting to reassure him, smiled sadly, and said, "I know it's all over with me." He expired the same night.

A message had been sent to Major Apthorp, commanding Gubbins's garrison, apprising him of

Lieutenant Birch's intention of proceeding out, and requesting him to order the sentinels not to fire. The order had accordingly been given; but unfortunately it just then happened that the sentries were relieved, and the relieving sentinel was not made aware of the fact. The man who had fired was, therefore, held blameless; but the soldier who had failed to convey the order to his comrade was placed under arrest. It was sad, very sad, to meet death at the hand of a countryman!

The death of my poor friend Deprat affected me considerably. Generous in the extreme, hospitable, warm-hearted, kind,—one could forgive his faults, though they were many. With a head to conceive, he lacked perseverance to continue. Trusting implicitly in his honour, I discovered, when too late, that his habitual idleness and culpable negligence rendered nugatory all his principles of honesty. He died above 4000 rupees in my debt, and his books scarcely showed half that amount. His testament was informal, and his papers in the greatest confusion. He had documents proving a very large claim against Government, in the hands of Mr. Martin, the deputy-commissioner; but as he leaves no relatives who would prosecute these claims, it is not likely that his creditors will ever benefit by them. But I little thought of this at the time. We,—that is, three of his friends and myself,—carried him to his grave.

The corpse of Captain Cunliffe, who died the same day, was thrown into the same hole, and a short prayer finished the ceremony.

On this occasion, I observed the striking difference of conduct between our Protestant chaplain and the Catholic clergyman. During the lifetime of Mr. Deprat none received greater favour at the deceased's hands than Father Bernard; yet because it poured bullets and rain, forsooth! the Padre objected to accompany the body to the churchyard, alleging that Mr. Deprat's religious views were of a very loose kind, and that he did not deserve Christian burial. Mr. Harris, however, the Protestant clergyman, prepared to go, and thus at last shamed the Father into compliance. He reluctantly went, and mumbled a few unintelligible words, meant to be Latin, and hurriedly took himself off, leaving the poor French gentleman's body to be buried like a dog, for there were not even gravediggers ready; and we were obliged, therefore, to lower it ourselves, as best we could, into a hole almost filled with water. Mr. Harris, however, read the beautiful burial service over poor Captain Cunliffe's body, and we took it as intended for Deprat as well. I have known many very excellent Roman

Catholic clergymen, men who deserved honour and esteem; but Father Bernard was certainly none of these.

Deprat, a man of a good family in France, formerly a soldier and afterwards an officer of the Chasseurs d'Afrique, had gone through all the campaigns in Algiers under Lamoricière, Cavaignac, Changarnier, Pelissier, and Canrobert. The Nana of Cawnpore, who visited him when last at Lucknow, long before the mutinies broke out, knew this; and, instigated by Azimoollah, his chief adviser, a man who had travelled in Europe and had a perfect acquaintance with the English, and a tolerable one with the French language, sent a letter and messenger to Deprat, offering him the command of his troops and a fortune, if he would join him. Deprat's imperfect knowledge of Hindostanee made me become the repository of this secret, and to convey the reply. "No!" said he; "I cannot do so. It is too late now; for I have already sought the protection of the British, and shall not desert them at such a time as this. Besides, what can there be in common between myself and assassins of women and children? Tell this to the Nana and Azimoollah, and be off; for if you are here half an hour hence I'll have you hanged. Here are twenty rupees. Go quickly!" I urged Deprat strongly to report the matter to the chief, and to have the messenger hanged,—who, by the bye, was also the first to communicate to us the Nana's success, as he called it; but Deprat would not hear of it; and having taken the precaution to enjoin me to secrecy before, I could not then speak of it. Besides, it would have done no good; for the messenger had lost no time in returning into the city, and probably to Cawnpore.

Throughout the siege Deprat behaved splendidly. At Gubbins's battery he acted as an artillery officer as well as a rifleman, and he performed some deeds of bootless boldness which none but a Frenchman or a madman would think of. "Come on!" would he often shout in his broken Hindostanee; "come on, ye cowardly sons of defiled mothers! are you afraid to advance? Are you men or women?" And then the reply. "Cursed dog of an infidel! I know thee! Thou art Deprat the Frenchman, living near the iron bridge. We'll yet kill you. Be sure of this. Here goes!" and a rifle-ball would whistle past his ears.

Deprat died in the greatest agony. His facial bone was shattered to pieces; but he was actually recovering, when his own imprudence aggravated the wound, and he expired above a month after he had received it. Some time previously we had a theological discussion together. "I deny," said he, "that there is a Providence. Just see the justice of your Providence. Here is a good man like Polehampton dead, and a rascal like myself still living, and likely to get out of it too. I am sure I shall not be killed." He was mistaken. He must know by this time whether there is a Providence or not.

There were several other casualties of officers and civilians besides those I have named. Captain Cunliffe, who died of typhus fever, was a sad loss to us. We could little spare artillery officers. Captain Thomas is now the only one not wounded. Let us hope no misfortune may befall him. Several sergeants, who acted as artillery officers, were also killed. Unfortunately I do not remember their names. Carey and Barrett, whom I have already noticed, were most invaluable men; indefatigable and active. Both died from over-fatigue. A civilian named Clausey, was shot dead at the Judicial garrison; and another, named C. Brown, had a bullet through his stomach near a passage where fifteen others had been wounded before him. This poor fellow, while actually dying, no sooner recognised me than he whispered, while I bent over him, " How is poor Deprat?" To forget his own sufferings and to be able to think over those of another fellow creature, was indeed sublime. Here, at least, was no selfishness.

The death of Lieutenant Graham, of the Oude Irregular Cavalry, was more than ordinarily frightful, even in times like those of the siege. He died by his own hand. A pistol ball through the head ended his life. Poor Graham! we had become great friends. He was so kind, so amiable, so good, so brave! But his privations and sufferings, and fretting, and a slight fever he had had in consequence deranged his intellect, and he was half crazy when he committed suicide.

Of wounded there were fewer than killed. The enemy's rifles are usually fatal. At our garrison (Innes's outpost) young Mr. Alone was shot through the right hand; his bone was fractured, but he eventually recovered.

I shall not weary my readers now with a detailed narrative of the events which succeeded the attack of the 5th of September. The fire of the enemy, our annoyances and troubles, the deaths of our unfortunate European comrades, the feeble attacks the insurgents afterwards made, are of a sameness that will not interest the reader. I shall, therefore, hurriedly pass over this period of the siege, and merely copy a few brief notes from my diary.

September 21*st.* — Much the same as usual. The weather is now getting pleasant; the mornings and evenings are quite cool. Yesterday, however, we had heavy rain, and to-day the same pelting rain continues quite steadily all night. This I know to my cost, as I am nearly blown off my legs in the hurricane of wind and rain while on night sentry.

September 22*nd.* — Raining still. Spies came in last night. Generals Outram and Havelock are actually coming to our relief. This is true! How can I describe my joy at even the bare thought of our being relieved!

September 23*rd.* — From ten A.M. to four P.M. a furious cannonade is raging outside the city, at a considerable distance from it. Our fellows must be hammering the very souls out of the insurgents' carcases. The commotion in the city seems tremendous. The fire keeps approaching. Hurrah!

September 24*th.* — We hear a distant cannonade, but our troops are evidently quieter. The city, however, seems awfully disquieted. Noises of all sorts are heard day and night. The bridge of boats can be seen with a telescope from the terrace of the post office covered with flying " Babalogue."

CHAP. XIII.

HAVELOCK'S REINFORCEMENTS ARRIVE. — THE TWENTY-FIFTH OF SEPTEMBER.

Our Reinforcements arrive. — Street Fighting. — Providence. — Our Friends enthusiastically received. — The Cawnpore Massacre. — My Agent's Death. — News of the Indian Stations. — A Feast. — The Hornpipe. — Havelock's Victories. — The Nana. — A fit Retribution. — The Cawnpore Slaughter-house. — Havelock defeats the Enemy in every Engagement. — His Return to Cawnpore. — General Outram's characteristic Generosity. — Advance upon Lucknow. — The Volunteer Cavalry. — The Storming of the Alumbagh. — Reception of the Enemy's Cavalry. — The Battle of the Charbagh. — A wily Foe. — Fire from the Kaiserbagh. — The Bagpipe a rare Instrument of Salvation. — Every House a Fort. — The "Forlorn Hope." — General Neill's Death.

We were now pretty certain that a severe conflict was raging outside. Though strict orders had been given not to leave our respective garrisons, I felt too excited to obey the command, and quietly stole off to the Residency terrace. I could see nothing but smoke, and hear the crack of the musketry. Street-fighting was evidently going on. The fire advanced gradually and steadily towards our entrenchments, and at last a loud shout proclaimed the arrival of the long expected reinforcements.

The immense enthusiasm with which they were greeted, defies description. As their hurrah and ours rang in my ears, I was nigh bursting with joy. The tears started involuntarily into my eyes, and I felt, — no! it is impossible to describe in words that sudden sentiment of relief, that mingled feeling of hope and pleasure, that came over me. The criminal condemned to death, and, just when he is about to be launched into eternity, is reprieved and pardoned, or the shipwrecked sailor, whose hold on the wreck is relaxing, and is suddenly rescued, can alone form an adequate idea of our feelings. We felt not only happy, happy beyond imagination, and grateful to that God of Mercy who, by our noble deliverers, Generals Havelock and Outram, and their gallant troops, had thus snatched us from imminent death; but we also felt proud of the defence we had made, and the success with which, with such fearful odds to contend against, we had preserved, not only our own lives, but the honour and lives of the women and children entrusted to our keeping.

As our deliverers poured in, they continued to greet us with loud hurrahs; and, as each garrison heard it, we sent up one fearful shout to heaven, "Hurrah;" it was not, "God help us,"—it was the first rallying cry of a despairing host. Thank God, we then gazed upon new faces of our countrymen. We ran up to them, officers and men without distinction, and shook them by the hands, how cordially who can describe? The shrill tones of the Highlanders' bagpipes now pierced our ears. Not the most beautiful music ever was more welcome, more joy-bringing. And these brave men themselves, many of them bloody and exhausted, forgot the loss of their comrades, the pain of their wounds, the fatigue of overcoming the fearful obstacles they had combated for our sakes, in the pleasure of having accomplished our relief.

How eagerly we listened to their stories! With what sentiments of gratitude, and pride, and pleasure, we heard what sympathy our isolated position had excited, not only throughout India, but in all classes of people in England! With what anxiety we, who had been shut out of all communication with the rest of the world, listened to the news they brought us of the other stations of India! We now heard the true particulars of the Cawnpore massacre for the first time. But we also heard how fearfully that gallant officer, Brigadier

Neill, had exacted vengeance for the dishonour and murder of our countrywomen, the relatives and friends of many in the garrison. It was with grief and sorrow, mingled with a savage delight at the vengeance inflicted upon at least some of the murderers, that we received this news.

My poor agent and friend, S. Greenway and his whole family, I now heard, had fallen victims to the brutality and treachery of the mutineers, and my agent, Mr. Archer, had shared the same fate at Allahabad. The particulars of the mutinies at Benares, and Dinapore, and Allahabad, and the defence of Arrah, Futtygurh, and the fighting before Agra and Delhi, and the account of the state of the Punjab, all interested us intensely. We put question after question, faster than they could answer; and now our gallant deliverers went over their victories and triumphs again, and we listened with breathless attention. It was now their turn to question us; and as they expressed their admiration and surprise at the struggle we had maintained, we felt, if possible, still greater pride and pleasure.

But our new friends were hungry and thirsty, and in our selfish joy we had forgotten this. They at last sat down to the repast that was spread out for them unsparingly, for who could think of economy amid such general rejoicing. It was not sumptuous, but it was good, and was seasoned by that best of all sauces, hunger. But one grief, one great sorrow damped the universal joy, — the death of one of their bravest and most beloved leaders, General Neill. Yet even this loss was momentarily forgotten, and the evening found some of us dancing the hornpipe to the sounds of the Highlanders' pibroch. The remembrance of that happy evening will never be effaced from my memory. Of course we could not sleep that night. It was three o'clock when I retired to bed.

The next morning we learnt how dearly the accomplishment of the noble enterprise they had undertaken had been paid for. The first force destined to relieve us had been very small. Still, with scarce more than fifteen hundred men, General Havelock succeeded in beating the enemy wherever he met them. The first engagement had been at Futtypore. Nana Sahib's army consisted then of about 7000 men; the manœuvres of their General were excellent, but the hostile cavalry, as usual, had not much pluck. Our troops beat them with the loss of some 2000 killed, and took almost all their guns. Two more actions were fought before they arrived before Cawnpore. In both Havelock was successful.

The Nana, furious at the defeat of his armies, like the coward and ruffian he is, ordered the murder of all the women and children who had been saved from the first Cawnpore massacre. But Neill now approached with his 1st Madras Fusiliers, 78th Highlanders, Sikhs, and Coopers' Artillery, and Volunteer Cavalry, and, notwithstanding the inferiority of his numbers, defeated the enemy's forces in a pitched battle, not far from the town of Cawnpore itself.

At last the Nana's craven heart gave way. He fled, and his army of boasting sepoys with him. They set fire to the magazine, and deserted the station: a fortunate circumstance, since, had any resistance been made from the houses, it is more than probable that our troops would have been so fearfully cut up, that they, with their reduced numbers, would scarcely have kept possession of Cawnpore, even if successful. Neill's men had fought for some hours, and were too exhausted to follow up their victory. They encamped before Cawnpore, 15th July, and entered it next day.

Some prisoners were made, Mohammedans and high-caste Brahmins, to whom the mere touch of a dead man's bone is pollution. They were taken to the house where our unfortunate ladies and children had met death at the hands of ruffians whom no entreaties or tears had moved, and who in the execution of their horrible office had felt no remorse and no pity; who had torn infants from their mothers' breasts, and bayoneted the babes before their very eyes, in order to make the few minutes before the murder of the parents themselves even more agonising.

The floor was still black with congealed blood; and large bunches of long hair, probably torn out by the cowardly executioners of the Nana's will, were scattered about; the walls were covered with the bloody finger-marks of little babes and children and the delicate hands of wounded females; and bibles, ladies' apparel, and even a complete diary, strewed about, showed that the ladies had occupied the room. General Neill took fearful vengeance.

The prisoners — some of whom, if not all, were no doubt actors in that wholesale slaughter of defenceless women and helpless children — were made not only to clean the whole house, but forced to lick up the blood, which, by throwing water on it had been made liquid again: and after they had thus completely lost their caste, and were, in their own opinions, no longer fit to approach their gods after death, they were hanged, or blown from the cannon's mouth. The well into which the victims to sepoy cruelty had been thrown, was blocked up, and a prayer read and a hymn sung over this their common grave.*

Neill had now joined Havelock with a small reinforcement, and after having fortified Cawnpore, or rather erected a strong entrenchment opposite the bridge of boats at that station, he crossed the river to effect our relief. At Magarwar, at Unnao, at Busheergunge, the insurgents were everywhere defeated. Havelock's victories had, however, cost dear, and another foe still more terrible — the cholera — had swept away many of the brave men, who had advanced to our relief. He was, therefore, compelled to recross the river. Again, however, they advanced; again they beat the foe in every engagement, and battled successfully with unheard of hardships, — the most inclement weather, cold, heat, rain, sleepless nights, fatigue, hunger, thirst. Another engagement at Unnao, and one at Busheergunge, ended in the dispersion of the rebels, the loss of several of their guns, and the death of many hundreds of their men.

But the Nana had reassembled a considerable force, and threatened not only to harass his rear, but to at-

* It has been proposed to erect a church over this monument of barbarian cruelty. May this intention be carried out!

tack Cawnpore itself, now denuded of all but a few hundreds of our troops. Havelock accordingly again fell back, made the Nana fly before him a second time at Magarwar, and, returning to Bithoor, took that place by storm, killed more than a thousand sepoys, and again dispersed the rebels. It was useless to endeavour to fight his way into Lucknow with the handful of men that remained. The loss they subsequently experienced goes far to prove that the course General Havelock had pursued was a wise one. His apparent vacillation was condemned at the time; but he could not have done otherwise than return. Had he pursued the enemy into their strongholds at Lucknow, the likelihood is, that scarcely one of his 800 men would have come out of the fight alive. Lucknow would have been another Thermopylæ, and our own position within the entrenchment would have been endangered, perhaps hopelessly.

Havelock remained at Cawnpore as short a time as possible, but did not again leave before he had obtained ample reinforcements. General Sir James Outram had joined him with a considerable number of detachments from various regiments, and might, had he felt so disposed, have assumed the command to which his superior rank entitled him: but with rare generosity he placed himself under Havelock's orders, saying, "It would be unfair, after all the efforts he had made to secure Lucknow, that Havelock should be debarred from the honour of having succeeded in relieving the beleaguered garrison."

Again Havelock re-crossed the Ganges about the 19th of September, in a little steamer which had been brought up to Cawnpore, as well as over the bridge of boats. The enemy attempted to prevent the crossing, but one of our shells, thrown right among their horse batteries, killed eleven or twelve of their gunners, and the rest decamped after we had once crossed.

Havelock's little army, composed of about 2500 men of all arms, was formed into two brigades. The first consisted of H. M. 5th Fusiliers, detachments of H. M. 64th and 84th regiments, and the invincible 1st Madras Fusiliers, who had been present at all the previous engagements, fighting by the side of those well-known gallant fellows the 78th Highlanders. The second brigade consisted of H. M. 78th Highlanders and H. M. 90th Light Infantry, and was commanded by Brigadier Cameron. To the latter were also attached a body of Irregular Cavalry (natives) and Captain Olphert's horse battery, while to the former were added Captain Maude's bullock battery and the Volunteer Cavalry, who were about 150 strong. The left wing of the Volunteers was composed of men drafted from various infantry regiments and the right was composed of officers, private gentlemen, and civilians, who had volunteered to assist in aiding us, more for the sake of seeing some service, than for the handsome salaries they got. These were constantly exposed to the enemy's fire, not only in action, but during the numerous reconnoitring parties they had to undertake.

Havelock's army had not advanced very far when they were attacked about five miles away from their first encamping ground. The enemy had planted several batteries of light field-pieces behind some broken ground, and began firing as soon as they came within reach. The first shots were aimed with great precision and did our men some injury; but as they advanced, and our heavy guns began to play on them, their artillerymen lost heart, fired less carefully, and at last fled, leaving in our hands four 12-pounders and a considerable amount of ammunition. Our cavalry was soon after them, and cut up about sixty or seventy of their infantry.

On the next day, the 23rd, our men came to within a short distance of the Alumbagh ("the garden of the Lady *Alum*," or beauty of the world). This consists of a very fine pukka (brick-built) house, a mosque close by, an emumbarah, or place of worship, several smaller outhouses, and a very fine building, containing a magnificent well. A splendid garden is attached to it, and the whole is surrounded, as far as the main road, by a splendid and extensive park.

They found the enemy drawn up before the buildings in excellent position; their left resting on the Alumbagh itself, and their centre and right protected by some rising ground. As soon as our forces appeared, the enemy's guns opened upon them, killing several of our officers and men; but as regiment after regiment deployed into line, and our guns, which were brought up with some difficulty, owing to the heavy rain which had fallen, and had made the fields one extensive morass, at last played upon the insurgent columns, the enemy gradually retreated, and fell back upon Alumbagh. A large gun, placed between Havelock's position and the building, was captured with a shout, and maintained, notwithstanding an infernal fire kept up by the cannons in the Alumbagh. Our men then stormed and took the garden itself, after an obstinate resistance; for the sepoys, though cowards in the field, fight well behind walls. Four more guns were also captured, — one by Capt. Holmes's Irregulars, another by the Volunteers, and two by our gallant infantry. Sir James Outram himself, heading Captain Burrows's cavalry, pursued them towards Lucknow, a portion of our infantry also following. The enemy's guns, however, continued now to vomit forth grape and round shot, and our men were compelled to halt. This encouraged the mutineers, who continued to fire the whole of that and the next day.

It was raining as it only rains in India. Torrents poured down from the heavens, and our men, drenched to the skin, were too exhausted to follow up the enemy into the city on that day, the 23rd. Their baggage had by this time arrived; and, though wet and uncomfortable, they halted on the 24th at the camp formed at Alumbagh. Our men had lost, on the 23rd alone, above sixty officers and men, killed and wounded.

A regiment of the enemy's cavalry meanwhile, stealing round by the canal, came on us to cut off our baggage; and the soldiers of H.M. 90th, in charge of it, believing them to be our own Irregulars, allowed them to approach quite close; nor did they perceive their mistake till some brave officers and men had been cut down by them. Then, however, they turned upon them, and charging them with the bayonet, after firing their Enfields, killed and unhorsed about thirty or thirty-five, and, aided by Captain Olphert's battery, that had come opportunely to the rescue, put them to flight.

On the 25th, early in the morning, the assault of the city was determined on by General Havelock. Lucknow is encircled by a deep canal, dry in the hot season, but at that time—during the rains—swollen considerably. Its banks are precipitous and steep. Had the enemy broken up the bridges leading over it, the difficulties to be overcome would have increased a hundred-fold. But they probably trusted in the resistance they had determined to make. At the bridge of the *Charbagh* ("four gardens"), at the outskirts of the town, they found the enemy's guns planted in great number behind a strong palisade, ready to receive them. They did dreadful execution; but, nothing daunted at the lanes of death constantly opened in their ranks, Sir James Outram himself, with Brigadier Neill and his gallant Madras Regiment, and the men of the 5th, 64th, and 84th regiments, advanced and, surmounting every obstacle, took the guns at the point of the bayonet, cutting down the gunners or putting them to flight.

General Havelock, with the brave 78th and 90th, following up the advantage gained, dashed in after them. They had to fight for each inch of ground; but they successfully drove the enemy from one enclosure into another, and from garden to garden. The captured guns they threw into the canal, after spiking them.

Natives expect defeat; and, foreseeing the event of our men being successful in taking their first battery, they had studded the road leading direct to the Residency with all manner of obstacles,—palisades, guns, stockades, barricades. One of their apparently strongest batteries, too, had (as we afterwards learnt) a deep ditch in front of it, covered over with thin bamboos and earth; so that, on our men making a rush upon it, they might all be precipitated within. Havelock, however, avoided all these obstacles, and making a detour to the right, skirting the canal, the whole force debouched at a street called Huzrutgunge, and proceeded on their way to the palaces on the riverside.

At the Kaiserbagh, or "King's Palace," the enemy's fire was tremendous. Musketry, grape, and round-shot poured in upon them with tremendous effect. Hundreds fell, and, what was still worse, a portion of our force lost their way. Unfortunately, some officer had called out "Cavalry to the front," and the Cavalry accordingly galloped up, but so crowded were the narrow streets, that they could not return to protect the baggage from falling into the hands of the enemy. Among it were two cartloads of shot, eight of provisions, and several camels.

On this occasion the Highlanders' piper, who had lost his way, suddenly found one of the enemy's cavalry, sabre in hand, about to cut him down. His rifle had been fired off, and he had no time to use his bayonet. "A bright idea"—said he afterwards, when relating the story—"struck me. All at once I seized my pipe, put it to my mouth, and gave forth a shrill tone, which so startled the fellow, that he bolted like a shot, evidently imagining it was some infernal machine. My pipe saved my life."

Meanwhile the enemy still kept up an incessant fire from the houses, which were all loopholed. Each house was a fortress, each fortress well garrisoned. Desperate at their immense losses, without being able to touch the rebels themselves, our men pushed forward, and many rushed to the loopholes, and fired into them. A party of ours had, however, stormed the palaces of the Feradbuksh and Lehree Kothee, and kept possession of them. Darkness was fast coming on, and still the fight continued, still our men dropped off one by one.

Generals Havelock, Outram, and Neill, taking a

detour, rushed forward at the head of the brave Madras Regiment and 78th Highlanders, captured another battery that opposed them, and, in spite of every obstacle, carried all before them, and reached the Residency. Lieutenants Hargood, Hudson, and Havelock, Captain Alexander Orr, and Mr. W. Money, General Outram's private secretary, had accompanied this party, which might almost be styled the " Forlorn Hope." They well deserved the praise for their gallantry which was afterwards, in the despatches, bestowed on them.

General Neill, that gallant soldier, here lost his life. He had accomplished his object, having actually arrived within our entrenchments, when he heard that some of our heavy guns were in jeopardy. He galloped out again; but scarcely had he done so, when a bullet struck him in the head, and he fell. Our guns were, however, saved by the intrepidity of our Madras Regiment and Highlanders, who captured two standards of the enemy's 5th Oude Irregulars.

CHAP. XIV.

THE TWENTY-SIXTH OF SEPTEMBER.

Horrible Fate of some of our Wounded. — Captain Arnold's frightful Situation. — Colonel Campbell's Position. — Colonel Napier and "Hellfire-Jack." — Attack of Colonel Purcell and the 32nd. — Noble devotion of our Sepoys. — Honour to whom Honour is due. — Heroic Deaths. — Sir James Outram. — Wounded Officers. — Losses of the Volunteer Cavalry. — The 1st Madras Fusiliers and 78th Highlanders. — Sorrowful End of Lieutenant Jolie. — The 84th and 90th Regiments. — Havelock's heavy Sacrifice. — Our true Saviours. — Ruined Condition of our Entrenchments.

The next day only, the 26th, when the remainder of our troops, a portion of our baggage, almost all our camels, and a number of our wounded came in, we learnt what sacrifices our noble deliverers had had to make in order to reach our position. Horrible to relate, a considerable number of our wounded had fallen into the enemy's hands, and were partly burnt alive in their hospital litters (doolies), and partly cut up. Many had died in the greatest agony, on the plain before the Motymahal. Some of our dooly-bearers having left the doolies on the roadside, a few were next day brought in.

I was present when an unfortunate gentleman of the name of Arnold, of the Madras Fusiliers, was carried in. He was in perfect possession of his senses, the loss of blood from two wounds having no doubt prevented a fever at the time. The agony of mind on being left alone during the whole night, far more than the pain of his wounds, one in the arm the other in the leg, was, according to his own description, frightful. Often, he said, during that horrible night, did he take his revolver to blow his brains out, that he might not fall alive into the hands of the enemy; but he was allowed to remain unmolested, and the next day had, as he said, the unspeakable happiness of again seeing his brethren in arms. He lingered some days and then expired.

The whole of the heavy guns, both our own and those captured from the enemy, had been in an enclosure near the Motymahal, together with a number of our wounded, guarded by a party of about a hundred men under Colonel Campbell. These were hard pressed, and it was in fact there that we had lost so many of our wounded. They were reinforced, by order of Colonel Napier on Sir J. Outram's staff, by a party of about 250 men, guided by Captain Moorsome, consisting of the 5th Fusiliers under Major Simmons, and the Sikhs under Captain

Brasyer. They were themselves however surrounded in a gateway which they occupied, and only relieved on obtaining a further reinforcement of a company of the 78th Highlanders under Colonel Stisted.

Mr. Kavanagh, a civilian, the head-assistant of the Chief Commissioner's office, directed Colonel Napier on this expedition through some intricate passages, by a short cut, to the party they came to reinforce.

During the night, Colonel Napier managed to convey all the remaining sick and wounded into the Residency. Captain Hardinge of the old garrison also aided the Colonel in every way with his sowars, and brought in some camels loaded with Enfield rifles also. One of our 24-pounders, which we had been obliged to leave in a very dangerous position, was saved in a daring manner by Captain Olpherts (Bengal Artillery). This officer, who had always been in the very thickest of the fight, and whom no bullet seemed to injure, was the pride not only of his own men, but of all the Europeans of the force. They had given him the *sobriquet* of "Hell-fire Jack," for wherever the fire was hottest, and the greatest danger was to be faced, Captain Olpherts was sure to be there. Aided by Captain Crump (Madras Artillery), and private Duffy, who has since been mentioned in the despatches and recommended for the Victoria Cross, he succeeded not only in extricating the gun from amidst the greatest difficulties, but also in getting it safe into our entrenchments. Captain Crump (Artillery), a most brave officer, was killed during this operation.

Our wounded had scarcely reached the palace gate, meanwhile, when the enemy attempted too late to prevent it, and attacked the rear guard. They were driven back, however, with great slaughter.

Another party at the same time, under Colonel Purcell, and reinforced by one of our most gallant soldiers, Captain M'Cabe, of the 32nd, came upon a party of sepoys, and drove them, after a fierce resistance, from one of the gardens. Lieutenant Aitkins, and Captain Loire of the 32nd, each commanding detachments, had also an opportunity of distinguishing themselves, which they were not slow in seizing. The former was accompanied by the gallant Lieutenant Cubitt, who was wounded, and the latter by Captain Bassano and Lieutenant Cooke.

But to detail all the various operations performed on those days, the 25th and 26th of September,—to enter into all particulars, and to note down the distinguished gallantry of our officers and men,—would weary the reader. Suffice it to say, that we (the old garrison) not only were relieved, but the palaces of the Furrad

Buksh and Tehree Kothee were taken possession of, and formed into new entrenchments, which were afterwards of the greatest service to us. I must not omit relating an incident which revealed great nobleness of character in one of our native soldiers. The 78th Highlanders coming upon the Bailey Guard Battery, guarded by our sepoys, and not knowing it to be within the Residency, stormed it, and bayoneted three of our men, whom they mistook for insurgents. They never resisted, and one of them waved his hand, and crying "*Kootch purwanni* (never mind); it is all for the good cause; welcome, friends!" fell and expired.

Havelock had done that with 2500 men which could scarcely have been hoped for from twice that number. I have since heard the successful defence that we had made lauded; and, indeed, when Generals Outram and Havelock visited the various outposts, and witnessed our roofless houses and battered walls, they expressed the greatest admiration at what they were pleased to call our "unparalleled gallantry;" but our defence of the entrenchments is obscured by the immense obstacles which Havelock's own army had to overcome. To them, far more than to us, is praise due.

What we did was, after all, only what every European in similar circumstances would have done. We fought for ourselves, Havelock for us. Our defence was prompted by the love of life and the honour of preserving our women; but the gallant troops of General Havelock relieved us, out of a chivalrous feeling of honour and compassion for our distresses. And I may safely aver that the commonest soldier of that brave army was actuated by the same sentiments as the general. In other wars soldiers fight because they are ordered to do so. But Havelock's efforts were responded to by every private in his force. Each man burned to avenge the massacre at Cawnpore, each man strained every nerve to save us from a similar fate.

Alas! many, too many, brave men had fallen, to accomplish that object. Brigadier-general Neill was killed; Major Cooper, of the Artillery, had fallen, Major Eyre, who had already gained laurels at Arrah and Jugdispore, succeeding to the command of the Artillery. The gallant Lieutenant Colonel Bazeley, Lieutenant Cramp, and Dr. Bartrum, of the same corps, were all shot at the guns they had made so terrible to the enemy. Of the 12th Irregular Cavalry, Lieutenant Warren was killed, and of H. M.'s 64th, Lieutenant Bateman. The brave 78th Highlanders lost Lieutenant Webster and Lieutenant Kirby; the 84th, Captain Pakenham and Lieutenant

Poole; and the 90th, Lieutenant Moultrie, over whose grave, and that of Captain Denison, of the same corps, their men erected a marble monument.

Sir James Outram, who, throughout the 25th, showed the greatest coolness under fire, and was ever at the head of the troops, received a wound, fortunately only a slight one, in the right arm. Captain Becher, his assistant adjutant-general, was also wounded, and Captain Alexander Orr, who had escaped from Fyzabad, where he had been a deputy commissioner, and who was invaluable as a guide to the relieving army, had his horse shot under him, and was himself slightly wounded in the leg.

Captain Crommelin, of the Engineers, whose engineering operations at Cawnpore and Bunnee, and subsequently at Lucknow, earned for him the well-deserved praise of Government, received also a slight wound. Captain Dodgson, the assistant adjutant-general, and Colonel Tytler, the deputy assistant quarter-master-general, Lieutenant Havelock, deputy assistant adjutant-general, the general's son, and Lieutenant Sitwell, aide-de-camp, on the 25th, and Captain Olpherts, the bravest of the brave, on the 26th, were also wounded; the latter only slightly, however.

Of the Volunteer Cavalry, who had covered themselves with glory, not only at Lucknow, but wherever they had met the enemy, Lieutenant Lynch, Her Majesty's 70th, was wounded in the arm; Lieutenant Palliser, 63rd Bengal Native Infantry, in the head slightly; Lieutenant Birch, 1st Bengal Light Cavalry, severely; and Lieutenant Swanston, 7th Madras Native Infantry, the quarter-master, slightly. Of the gentlemen serving in the ranks four were also wounded; Mr. Erskine, dangerously, Mr. R. Goldsworthy, slightly in the hand, and Mr. Green, their corporal, severely in the head. Their body had lost, besides, in killed, three rank and file, and in wounded, eleven. Captain Burrows himself, their commander, had had two horses shot under him, but escaped untouched.

Of the 1st Madras Fusiliers, Lieutenants Arnold and Bailey were both severely wounded. They died afterwards in our entrenchments. Captains L'Estrange and Johnston, of the 5th, and Captains Lockhart and Hastings, Lieutenants Grant and Swanston, were severely, and Lieutenants Crowe and M'Pherson, all of the gallant Highlanders, slightly wounded.

Lieutenant Jolie, who had been doing duty with this corps, was also most dangerously wounded. This gentleman, belonging to our 32nd, had been absent on leave from his regiment, and had therefore not assisted in the defence of the Residency. He had joined Havelock's force, delighted at the prospect of again seeing his brother officers and his old regiment, and in having shared in the honour of their relief. But he was destined to enjoy the looked for pleasure for a few hours only. Dangerously wounded at the storming of Alumbagh, he expired in sight of his old friends, a short time after his arrival in the Residency, more deeply regretted, than if his death had occurred under ordinary circumstances.

Of Her Majesty's 84th regiment, Lieutenants Woolhouse and Oakley were severely, and Captain Willis and Lieutenant Barry, slightly wounded; and of the 90th, the gallant Colonel Campbell and Lieutenant Knight were severely, and Dr. Bradshaw and Lieutenant Preston, slightly wounded.

Altogether we had lost, as far as could then be ascertained, about 550 officers and men, killed, wounded, and missing, a heavy, heavy sacrifice for our relief, but which made us the more grateful to our gallant deliverers. Our own number of fighting men was scarcely more, but our women and children were at least treble that number.

That the honour of having, under Providence, saved our lives is really due to Generals Havelock and Outram is unquestionable. But for their timely arrival, our native troops, who had up to that time behaved nobly and adhered to us with exemplary fidelity, would certainly have abandoned us. Nor could we have reasonably found fault with them had they done so, for life is sweet, and hope had almost entirely left us. Their desertion would have caused the most fatal depression in our own breasts, and with our diminished numbers and our continual losses we should soon have been obliged to give up our outposts.

Reduced within the narrow compass of the Residency itself, and exposed to the enemy's harassing fire from what would lately have been our outposts, it would have been utterly impossible to have held out. Nothing short of a miracle could have saved us then. Cawnpore would have been re-enacted in Lucknow, or we would, as we once talked of doing, have been compelled to blow up our women, children, and wounded, to prevent their falling into the hands of the insurgents, and to have died fighting on the ruins ourselves.

Our houses had been already perforated with cannon balls. The Cawnpore battery was one mass of ruins, our outpost at Innes's house was partly roofless, and the other garrisons were as badly off. From one alone, the brigade mess, 435 cannon balls that had fallen within it were actually counted. It would be, therefore, by no means an exaggerated statement to affirm, that not less than 10,000 cannon balls had struck our various buildings. As for musket bullets, they are only to be counted by myriads.

More than 400 of the defenders of the garrison lie buried in our churchyard.

CHAP. XV.

LUCKNOW AFTER HAVELOCK'S ARRIVAL.

Our extended Positions. — African Rifleman's Contempt of our Shells. — The Tehree Kothee. — The Order of the Day. — Embarras de Richesses. — Luxuries. — The Second Chapter of the Siege. — Sir Henry Lawrence's Foresight. — Purchase of Food. — Hunger imperative. — Kossids. — Position of our Men at the Alumbagh. — Our Colours and Band. — Indomitable Perseverance of our Foe. — Effect of our Shot and Shell upon the Enemy's Positions. — Picturesque Aspect of the City of Lucknow. — Meeting with old Friends. — Captain Alexander Orr. — Goldsworthy. — Berrill. — The Intelligence Department. — The rebel King. — His Minister and Council. — The Commander-in-Chief of the Insurgents. — Danger of high Offices with the Mutineers — The People of Lucknow. — Punishment for Adhesion to our Cause. — European Prisoners in the hands of the Enemy. — Rajah Man Sing of Sultanpore. — A Friend turned Foe. — The Rebels offer to treat with Sir James Outram. — An insolent Proposal. — Mutual Threats. — Fate of the Native Prisoners with the Insurgents. — Native Gratitude.

THE Residency now again wore an animated aspect. Every now and then troops were coming in, new faces might be seen, and horses and camels were lying about our enclosure in plenty. Though we could not go into the city, yet our position was far more extended. We had possession of the Tehree Kothee, the Furrad Buksh, and the Chutter Munzil, palaces situated on the river side and facing our north. This was an immense advantage to us. The enemy's fire had been particularly fatal from that point, and their strongest batteries had been placed near a gateway called the "clock tower," from there being a clock dial painted on it.

The late Sir H. Lawrence had ordered a number of the adjacent houses to be blown up, but our engineers had not quite succeeded in converting the gateway and other buildings into ruins; the siege had come on so suddenly that they had had no time to repeat the blasting operations. One of the late king's sharpshooters, an African eunuch, had made this clock tower his favourite haunt. Like his friend, "Bob the Nailer," his shots were almost always fatal. So troublesome had this man become to us, and we had lost so many good soldiers by his rifle, that Captain Thomas (Madras Artillery) had been directed to shell the fellow's place of refuge, merely to enable us to get rid of this one man. The shells had been thrown with beautiful precision, and we had seen them bursting just where they should burst; but immediately after a rifle bullet whistling through the air as if in defiance of our efforts, proved that we had not succeeded in killing the marksman. Nor could we solve the riddle till after the capture of that gateway: then we learnt how it was that he had escaped so often.

The Residency was perfectly commanded by the clock tower, and the eunuch, as soon as he had observed through his telescope that we were about to shell, retired by a ladder into a sort of cavern he had caused to be scooped out for his safety, and, returning at once to the scene of action, recommenced his firing as soon as the shell had burst. He was killed by our men at last, and the telescope and rifle were found by his side.

The Tehree Kothee, the late residence of the General Sahib, the ex-king's brother, adjoined the Feradbuksh, which had formerly been the throne and levee room of the kings of Oude. They consisted of a perfect labyrinth of courtyards, inner gardens, balconies, gateways, passages, verandahs, rotundas, outhouses, and pavilions. Though I had afterwards often been loitering there, I invariably had lost my way in some of the numerous intricate places of those buildings.

Plunder was the order of the day. Everywhere might be seen people helping themselves to whatever they pleased. Jewels, shawls, dresses, pieces of satin, silk, broadcloths, coverings, rich embroidered velvet saddles for horses and elephants, the most magnificent divan carpets studded with pearls, dresses of cloth of gold, turbans of the most costly brocade, the finest muslins, the most valuable swords and poniards, thousands of flint guns, caps, muskets, ammunition, cash, books, pictures, European clocks, English clothes, full-dress officers' uniforms, epaulettes, aiguillettes, manuscripts, charms; vehicles of the most grotesque forms, shaped like fish, dragons, and sea-horses; imaunns or representations of the prophet's hands, cups, saucers, cooking utensils, chinaware enough to set up fifty merchants in Lombard Street, scientific instruments, ivory telescopes, pistols, and, what was better than all, tobacco, tea, rice, grain, spices, and vegetables, — the provisions, however, unfortunately, in very small quantities.

I had gone to bring something home. I generally returned from my expeditions empty-handed. I now knew what an *embarras de richesses* was. Where I could take everything, I usually took nothing but a few eatables. The things which I had sometimes actually carried away, I not unfrequently would leave on the road-side. I afterwards often regretted not having taken what I was subsequently obliged to pay very dear for; but at the time I became utterly indifferent about property, which I might have had only for the taking. Several men, more prudent than myself, however, made fortunes. One of them, an overseer, named B——, succeeded in obtaining several boxes of tea, tobacco, soap, candles, and other useful articles of household furniture, which a few days afterwards fetched very high prices; so that, when we finally evacuated the place, he must have had above a thousand pounds in cash alone; and, with singular good fortune, he not only managed to convey all his valuables away, but was enabled to travel in a magnificent phaeton, which had been abandoned by the owner, and to which he had succeeded in yoking bullocks, that he had obtained equally cheap. There are some men on whom Fortune smiles even in the worst of times. This was one of them, and there were several others similarly favoured by the blind goddess.

We had, for some days after Havelock's arrival, luxuriated in a number of good things. The spices I had found served to make capital stews and curry, and, as we hoped to be soon released from our imprisonment, we were rather profuse with our few vegetables, which tasted deliciously after that unvaried round of plain coarse beef and dall. Those eternal chupatties were, however, still our staple food.

Though we had extended our positions, yet we were far from being free. Contrary to expectations, the enemy, so far from abandoning the city, or suing for terms after the arrival of Outram and Havelock, continued to blockade us, and our gallant deliverers were now besieged along with us. They had brought in no provisions or stores of any kind, and in point of food we were worse off than even before. The number of additional mouths, owing to the very great multitude of camp followers, made considerable diminutions in our commissariat stores; but by dint of the very strictest economy, we managed to make them last longer than was expected,— down to the end of November.

Again had we reason to bless the memory of the late Sir Henry Lawrence, whose foresight had thus enabled us to drag on our lives with comparative safety. Our rations, which had previously been reduced to one quarter, were now brought down to just half of what we originally got. Instead of attah or flour, we obtained wheat, which we had to grind ourselves or get ground as best we could; dall was stopped entirely, and our modicum of salt reduced. Of beef we now got only six ounces a day, bones included. Many grumbled and growled at these reductions, but they were absolutely necessary.

Yet food was still now and then obtainable. Several persons had hidden stores of something or other, of which for money, — exorbitant sums, however,—I succeeded in getting part now and then. And wheat, too, plundered from the palaces, or stolen from our own commissariat, I fear, was also sometimes to be had. One enterprising man actually set up a sort of bakery, and sold biscuits at six rupees per seer, but this did not last long. The stock of corn was soon exhausted, and then I too had often to go to sleep with an empty stomach. On one occasion I went to see a friend, whom I did not find at home. He had just finished his breakfast, of which a solitary bone remained as evidence on a plate. Hunger was imperative, and I actually took the well-gnawed bone up and picked it clean afterwards.

But I saw others far more in want than myself. I could at least *sometimes* procure an extra chupatty: but most of the new force were less fortunate; so that I was therefore often able to give a picking to some of my new friends, particularly of the Volunteer Cavalry, who were principally stationed at my garrison (Innes' outpost).

Soon after the arrival of General Havelock, we had

been cut off from all communications with Alumbagh, except by means of the Kossids, who occasionally brought in letters in quills, or inserted into the soles of their shoes, at considerable risk to themselves. Owing to our now having the river one of the boundaries of our position, the chance of eluding the vigilance of the enemy's sentries was, however, far less than before we had possession of the Tehree Kothee, Chutter Munzil, and Feradbuksh palaces.

The baggage and ammunition of the relieving force had been deposited in the Alumbagh: four guns had been left with them to defend themselves with, should they be attacked by a party of the enemy; but that the 300 men left as an escort to protect the immense number of elephants, camels, horses, and camp followers, with hundreds of laden carts, should afterwards themselves be besieged without our being able to assist them, was never contemplated by any individual of the force. Indeed from the confident manner in which our new friends spoke, we could easily see that, even after those dearly-paid-for victories of the 25th and 26th of September, they expected the city to be cleared in a few days.

Before the storming of Lucknow they had even expected to come into the city, after one defeat of the enemy, with bands playing and colours flying;

but their colours had to be brought with difficulty, the bandsmen had to be converted into soldiers, and their instruments had to be left behind at Alumbagh.

We who had had experience enough of the indomitable perseverance of our foes, whatever their courage might be, knew well that they would never think of leaving the city unless driven out of it at the point of the bayonet; that unless each fortified house and each battery had been stormed, we could hold no portion of Lucknow; that they would fight, return, be beaten, and fight again; and, knowing themselves to be rebels and murderers and worthy of death, that we would spare none of them, and therefore it was better to die by the bullet while fighting, than to be sent out of the world in so ignominious a manner as being hanged at the hands of a despised member of the sweeper caste.

This we knew, and we, the old garrison, looked upon being besieged anew as a natural event. The houses to the south and east had never been deserted by the insurgents, and we still lost a number of good and brave soldiers from the houses commanding Innes's outpost, Gubbins's battery, the slaughter house, and Bhoosa-guard, as well as the brigade mess. In our new entrenchments our men were daily fired upon; and Captain Crommelin, the superintendent engineer, lost no time in pushing on our fortifications towards the Kaiserbagh and the positions commanding the Feradbuksh.

We had now opportunities of seeing more of the injury our shot and shell had done the enemy. The Captanka Bazaar and the enclosure before the Residency were now open to us without any great danger to ourselves. The ruins of these buildings, and the deserted air that hung over all those large structures before us, gave one almost as much an idea of desolation as a city of ruins. All within was still, scarcely a movable object was seen, and the sharp crack of a rifle or the flight of an occasional round shot alone showed life.

Yet even these did not always disturb the ear. At noon particularly, when our enemies, as is customary with natives, ate their food and took their siesta after dinner, perfect silence would reign. There was something really grand and majestic in the now sombre and, as it were, defiant aspect of this really magnificent and picturesque city. Seen from the terrace of the Residency, the *tout ensemble* of the view presented to us was perfect. The gilded minarets, the rich domes, the splendid mosques and palaces, the regular and thickly crowded houses were charmingly relieved by gardens, and parks, and trees, along and opposite the banks of the river, and interspersed in the middle of the city. And those green fields! that luxuriant vegetation! how often we longed to be there! I never could look on them without a sigh, without panting for them, without feeling almost an ungovernable longing for freedom. Only those can know the sweets of liberty who have gone through the pain of captivity.

General Outram had organised an Intelligence Department, at the head of which he placed Captain Carnegie and Captain Alexander Orr, an old friend of mine, whom I was delighted to see again after three years' absence. I had also the pleasure of meeting several other friends and acquaintances in the field force that had come to relieve us. One of them, Mr. Roger Goldsworthy, had joined Captain Burrows's cavalry as a volunteer, and was present at all the engagements which that gallant body had fought. As a reward for their distinguished gallantry, he, Lieutenant Chalmers, Price, and several other officers and civilians, received the temporary appointments of assistant field engineers, in which they had still further opportunities of doing good service to the state. Goldsworthy afterwards, several times, in his capacity as engineer, accompanied Captain Crommelin in sorties, and to places where the greatest danger was to be faced. He was so fortunate as afterwards to obtain a commission in the cavalry of Her Majesty's army, and none more deserved that advancement.

Another young friend of mine, Berrill of Allahabad, had similarly distinguished himself. He was a very little fellow, and scarce nineteen, but plucky like a veteran soldier. Every one of his comrades bore witness to the gallant manner in which he would rush on and attack the rebels; he had been in all the fifteen battles which Neill and Havelock had fought. They had massacred two of his brothers at Cawnpore, and he had resolved to kill their murderers in revenge.

The intelligence supplied by Captain Orr to General Outram was secret, and for many days we knew nothing of what was going on in the city. We heard, however, that the insurgents had crowned a ruler, called Burges Kadr, a natural son of the ex-king, who we learnt had been made a state prisoner at Calcutta. He was to be called "Badshah," King, but was to hold his crown under the Emperor of Delhi, as a sort of tributary prince. He is but a child of eight or ten years of age, and all the real power was vested in a minister and a council of state.

The former was one Shirf-ood-Dowlah (Ibrahim Khan), who had, under the ex-king's father, held the reins of office with considerable credit to himself, and was always considered by the then Resident, General Sir H. Sleeman, as a friend to the British. The council of state consisted of the king's principal servants, of the rajahs and great landed proprietors of the country, and of the self-created high dignitaries of the army. These also deliberated upon the mode of conducting operations against us.

They had a commander-in-chief, Hissamut-ood-Dowlah, a brother-in-law of the ex-king (but he was merely a name, and nothing more). They had their generals, and generals of division, their brigadiers and colonels, their majors, captains, and subaltern officers, and in fact an apparently well constituted and well regulated army.

But these great dignitaries were never treated with that respect and obedience we ourselves had commanded. Their offices, too, except the very highest, were replete with danger. The sepoys themselves elected their officers, and the officers their commanders, though in the name of the king. But if, as was not unfrequently the case, they happened to displease the gallant "Jacks," a debating assembly would immediately be held by the privates, at the conclusion of which, they would usually signify to their officers, either that they were degraded, or, what suited their cowardly and sanguinary minds better, they attacked and fired on their victim.

The least suspicion of a hankering after the British, of being a spy, or of attempting to escape or to treat with us, was instantly punished with death. Nor were they able to refuse these dangerous nominations to army rank. Refusal was death. As for the citizens, they had no voice in the matter. In oriental phraseology, "they lived but to obey." Many were no doubt well affected towards us, but they dared not show it; and the majority, though they hated us as Feringhees, could not but long for our rule, plundered, and in continual dread of their lives, as they were. The king's adherents however, were also very numerous, and the ambitious of all classes, the bravoes and the vagabonds of the city, and the old servants of the former government, were all of that class.

We heard also that the enemy had some European, and many native prisoners. The former consisted of officers and their families, who had been saved from the first fury of the mutineers, and had been protected by rajahs and landholders from the military rebels, either from a desire to propitiate Government in the event of our being successful, or in order to sell them to the insurgent leaders should they continue to be in power. The rajahs of Mithowly and Bulrampore, who had concealed and entertained them for some time, probably were sincere in the beginning, but had been afterwards led away to join the majority either from fear of their revenge, or from treachery, or from ambition.

Whatever the motive, they were then prisoners in the insurgents' hands, and actually within the precincts of the Kaiserbagh. They were Sir Mountstuart Jackson and Miss Jackson; a very valued and dear friend of mine, Captain Patrick Orr, late a deputy commissioner in the Mallaon district, his wife, and his child, three or four years old; Lieutenant Burns, Serjeant-Major Norton, and little Miss Christian, whose parents had both been murdered at Seetapore,—altogether eight souls.

Their fate is indeed horrible to contemplate.* Constantly in dread of their lives, in the hands of savage and remorseless barbarians, in the hearing of our guns, knowing assistance was near, and yet unable to obtain it, they must indeed have been leading a miserable existence. They had been very cruelly,

---

* Before I left Calcutta for England, I called on the sister-in-law of Captain Patrick Orr, who told me, she had received news from Captain Alexander Orr that these prisoners were yet alive. This was in the beginning of January.

even brutally, treated by a party of sowars who had charge of them, being all placed in irons, even the delicate ladies and the late Commissioner Christian's orphan. Only on their arrival in Lucknow, where they were placed in safe custody at the Kaiserbagh, was their treatment more humane. The rebel government were, no doubt, not insensible of the political use to which these prisoners might be turned; and afterwards, indeed, made them instrumental in treating with Sir James.

Among the most distinguished of the insurgent rajahs, and the most powerful landed barons of the province, Man Sing holds one of the first places. He had at first sided with us, and during the whole of the siege, I believe, his troops never aided the other insurgents in their operations against us. He had saved twenty-nine European lives, gentlemen, ladies, and children, refugees from Fyzabad and Sultanpore, and had them safely escorted to Allahabad. But Man Sing knew his power, and, being an ambitious man, intended to make use of all his influence to aggrandise himself. He could raise 10,000 armed men from among his retainers and tenants, and these were mostly rajpoots, high caste Hindoos of the warrior class; and he had guns and ammunition, and money besides. Having also, by saving European lives, established a claim of gratitude upon Government, he wanted to derive all possible advantage from it, and, accordingly, sent proposals to our local Government at Allahabad, so it was stated, to put the district of Sultanpore in order, if he were nominated its governor, and if his estates should be increased by neighbouring ones to which he laid claim; but the Commissioner of the Peace would listen to no terms. "Do so unconditionally," was the reply. Man Sing was enraged; yet he never took active measures against us even then, but preserved a sort of armed neutrality. On the failure of Havelock's relieving army to clear the city, an impossible task, Man Sing at last definitively sided with the rebel government; but he must still be looked upon as one of the most powerful, though best intentioned, of our enemies.

Not long after Sir James Outram's assumption of the command of the Oude Field Force, Man Sing sent a messenger to him, offering to mediate with the rebel government, and stipulating as the price of his doing so, and fighting for our cause, the guarantee of his own life being spared, and the restitution of all his estates. He was told that, if he wished to prove his fidelity to Government, he must leave with all his troops, and return to his estate; Government was generous, and would, no doubt, act well towards him; but he must trust to that generosity alone. A few days after, another messenger, a person of rank, came in with a letter from Captain Orr to his brother in the garrison, evidently meant for the eyes of the Chief Commissioner, and written under compulsion. The letter was signed by all the prisoners in the enemy's hands, and mentioned the facts I have already noticed respecting themselves. The writers offered to be of assistance to our authorities, should they feel inclined to treat with the "*Oude Government;*" but there were no particulars. Several more visits were made by the same messenger; but the treaties were at last quite broken off.

The demands of the rebel leaders were extravagant; not only their lives were to be spared, but their newly elected king and all the insurgent chiefs were to be pensioned according to the rank they had given themselves. Of course, such proposals were at once rejected. To have accepted the submission of a foe we had everywhere vanquished, would be to give a premium to rebellion, and to legalise the usurpation of their rulers.

After this, Man Sing had the insolence to offer to escort our women, children, and wounded to Cawnpore, with his 10,000 men. This would have been like entrusting the safety of a flock to a wolf. We had learnt to distrust natives now.

They threatened to murder their prisoners if we refused to listen to terms. Sir James replied, that if they did so, he would hang the state prisoners in our hands. They said, we might do so, for they cared nothing about them. General Outram then hinted, that they should remember we had the Ex-King Wajid Ally Shah in custody at Calcutta, and our executing him would by no means be something improbable. This frightened them, and I believe they are still alive. We were even furnished with the names of the individuals in whose charge they were, and who will, no doubt, be held to be responsible. Sir James did all he could to obtain the release of these unfortunates, and would probably gladly have given 10,000*l*. for each of their lives; but the insurgents wanted terms, not money. They were evidently very suspicious of the future, and no doubt believed that they would succumb in the end; as they of course really must, sooner or later.

I had said the enemy had a number of native prisoners. These were the servants and others who had deserted, and who were seized as spies. Every one of them was hanged or shot. They well merited their fate. The Kotwal of the city, of whom I spoke in the beginning of the book, was seated on a donkey, carried through the streets with his face blackened and head and beard shaved, and then beheaded. All the native Christians, and even the servants of Christians, were murdered. One old man, a domestic of Mr. Johannes, who had been fifty years in his employ, and was treated more like a friend than a servant, plundered his master's own property, and cursed the Feringhees and fathers of Feringhees, as a true-hearted Mussulman should; but, notwithstanding his apostacy, he was at last also killed. He had been a living example how little our servants are attached to to us by our kindness. There is no such word as gratitude in the Hindostanee language. "Nimakhalaly" only means "fidelity to one's salt." Natives, in future, must be ruled with a rod of iron.

CHAP. XVI.

OUR SORTIES AND DEFENSIVE OPERATIONS.

Lieutenant Lowe's Sally. — Lieutenant Hughes and Mr. Sinclair wounded. — Major Stephenson's Sortie unsuccessful. — Lieutenant Hardinge's Gallantry and Success. — Sorties of the 29th September. — Major Apthorp. — Death of Mr. Lucas. — Captain M'Cabe falls while leading his fourth Sortie. — Captain Shute's Attack on Hill's House. — Anecdotes. — Colonel Napier's Attack on Phillips' Battery. — Repairs of our Entrenchments. — Our Engineering Operations. — Easy Capture of "the Mound." — Strengthening our Position. — Sergeant Purdell shot at my side. — Death of my Captain. — Our Losses. — Affecting Death-bed Scene. — Sorrow and Joy. — Scientific Construction of the Enemy's Batteries. — Captain Crommelin's Engineering Works. — The Enemy's Mines. — Successful Repulse of the Enemy's Attack. — Our Mining Operations.

I HAVE somewhat anticipated events in the previous chapter, and must now return to the occurrences which followed the capture of the palaces opposite our entrenchments. On the 26th of September, Lieutenant Lowe, of the 32nd, sortied with a party of about 150 men of this regiment, with a view to clear the Captanka Bazaar, in front of the Residency kitchen garden, and the adjacent houses. Two of his detachments, one under Captain Bassano, and another under Captain Hughes, 57th Native Infantry, issued under cover of the long grass and shrubs near the Redan. A third party, under Captain Lawrence, left from Innes's outpost, took three guns, and drove the enemy, completely taken by surprise, into the river, killing almost all of them.

Captain Hughes also took the direction of the iron bridge, spiked two mortars, and before retiring blew up a powder magazine of the enemy. Captain Lowe, who commanded the three detachments, was thus everywhere successful, and himself as well as all the officers and men behaved with that gallantry and bravery so conspicuous in Englishmen. Lieutenant M'Leod Innes, of the Engineers, was also present at this affair as guiding officer.

My friend Sinclair, of our garrison, had also accompanied this sortie, though scarcely recovered from his former wound. He was here again wounded in the arm, and severely too. Unfortunately, two men were killed, Lieutenant Lawrence and Captain Hughes wounded, the latter mortally, and eight soldiers wounded, some fatally. As trophies of his success, Captain Lowe brought in an 18-pounder, a 9-pounder, a 6-pounder, and four smaller guns, two without carriages.

On the 27th, Major Stephenson, with the whole of his 1st Madras Fusiliers, made another sortie. They were divided into three divisions, Captain Galway had one, Captain Raikes another, and Captain Fraser the third. Another party of 32nd men were conducted by Lieutenant Warner, 7th Light Cavalry. Lieutenant Huxham, 48th Native Infantry, Lieutenant Mecham (Madras), and Captain Kemble. These were under the orders of Lieutenant J. C. Anderson, Engineers, and Lieutenant Innes. The sortie was designed to attack the Garden battery. The enemy on their approach, after a short time abandoned their guns, but fired on the assailants from all points. The insurgents were, however, in such force that our men could not maintain the position they had taken, and were obliged to return eventually after spiking three guns and burning the battery. The delay in bringing up the blasting party prevented their bursting the guns as they intended to have done. Had the advice of Lieutenants Anderson and Innes, however, been attended to, the result would have been far more satisfactory. The men had drunk most of the water intended for bursting the guns, and the party had to return sooner than they had expected. Four of the Madras Fusiliers were killed, and seven wounded, two mortally; and of the 32nd three men were killed; one of them, Cooney, and another, Smith, two soldiers of the most lion-hearted intrepidity, who had throughout the siege always been where danger was most to be faced. One of the sergeants and four others also, were wounded, belonging to the 32nd regiment. Lieutenant Huxham was also severely wounded on this occasion, and a young man, a civilian, named Crabbe, a volunteer, was killed.

Lieutenant Hardinge, commanding Irregular Cavalry, led the first sortie. His party was composed of 90 Madras Fusiliers, under Captain Galway; 140 Highlanders (78th), under Captain Lockhart; and 20 of the 32nd, under Lieutenant Cooke. The first gun, a 12-pounder, was taken by the 32nd; Lieutenant Cooke and Sergeant Keily being the first at the gun. Of the Highlanders, Sergeant Young bayoneted a man at another gun in the act of reloading, and was severely wounded. The batteries and barricades were completely destroyed, one heavy gun burst, and three smaller ones brought in. Our loss was three killed and ten wounded, among them Captain Lockhart himself. Lieutenant Hardinge had throughout these difficult operations acted with that cool judgment and bravery which had ever distinguished him.

On the 29th there were three sorties. The reserve was commanded by Major Apthorp, a gallant officer who had done excellent service while commanding Gubbins's battery. He took several guns, spiked others, and discovering two mines, had them blown up by Lieutenant Innes and Lieutenant Ouseley, 48th Native Infantry, who, aided by Sergeant Higgins, Madras Fusiliers, captured a large gun. The Honourable Lieutenant Fraser, Captain Galway, Lieutenant Aitkin, 13th Native Infantry, and Lieutenant Cleveland particularly distinguished themselves. Major Apthorp had been perfectly successful in clearing and examining all the enemy's guns in front of Gubbins's garrison. The detachment under his command, consisting of six officers and 100 men of the Madras Fusiliers, had lost four killed and four wounded. Among the latter I regret to name Mr. Lucas, a traveller and speculator, who had come to India more for pleasure than business. He had safely come within our entrenchments, but in returning to aid in bringing in the captured guns he was shot. He expired an hour after his return.

The second sortie was commanded by Captain M'Cabe of the 32nd Regiment, and directed by

Lieutenant J. C. Anderson. Major Simmons also led a party of the 5th Fusiliers (H.M.'s). A great number of the enemy were killed, and the objects of the sortie fully attained. Unfortunately, Captain M'Cabe was mortally wounded. This was indeed a severe loss. Next to Captain Fulton, this officer was one to whom we had most reason to be grateful during the siege for the zeal, gallantry, and devotion with which he aided in the defence? Brigadier Inglis in him lost one of his most able advisers and most trusted friends. Captain M'Cabe fell while leading his fourth sortie. A braver soldier never stepped. Poor gallant Major Simmons was also killed, and nine others killed and wounded besides. Lieutenant Anderson, aided by Captain Evans (attached to artillery), here again did good service. He blew up three large houses, whence we had most suffered, destroyed the principal musketry cover of the enemy between the Cawnpore battery and Brigade Mess, and demolished the guns in front of the former.

The third sortie was under the direction, as guiding officer, of my commanding officer, Lieutenant Graydon, 41st Native Infantry, and was composed of 150 officers and men of H.M.'s 84th, 64th, and 5th Regiments, under the command of Captain Shute.

A party under Lieutenant Edmonstone of the 32nd also accompanied this column. They issued from our outpost at early dawn, and proceeded towards the iron bridge, stormed the house known as Mr. Hill's shop, close to our garrison, where Lieutenant Tulloch, who accompanied them, after our men had succeeded in driving the enemy out and killing a great number, blew up their favourite gun called Luchminya, which had been captured by the insurgents at Chinhutt, and which had played with such fatal effect upon our garrison and the Residency.

Lieutenant Graydon's order to occupy the houses near the iron bridge, and near the lane commanded by our outpost, was unfortunately not executed. The consequence was, that the insurgent guards there, who in their first surprise had fled across the river, on recovering from their panic, reoccupied them, and fired at our men murderous volleys. We lost no fewer than *thirty-five* men, killed and wounded, exactly the third part of the strength of the detachment which had gone out, and our men were obliged to retreat without being able to maintain the positions they had taken temporary possession of.

A large part of the enemy attacking our party from the lane opposite our garrison, were fired on by us, and I had the good fortune to shoot two more natives on that day. Lieutenant Graydon was slightly wounded in the ear, and Lieutenant Edmonstone received his third wound in the arm.

On this occasion a party of our soldiers on entering a house found among its defenders a man paralysed with age. On seeing the hostile faces enter, far from begging for mercy, which, owing to his extreme age would have been granted perhaps, he took up a horse-pistol and aimed at one of the men. The pistol missed fire, and the soldier, enraged at the opposition made, fired, but before he had time to pull the trigger, a woman interposed her body between the old man's, and received the bullet in her breast. The man was bayoneted afterwards.

On this day one of the Madras Fusiliers was saved from the most dangerous position imaginable, and the most horrible of all deaths. On the afternoon of the 26th he had been suddenly cut off from the sortie party which he had accompanied. To return to the Residency was impossible — a considerable force of the enemy having taken up a position between him and his comrades, and he therefore thought the best plan was to escape into a house and endeavour to return at night. But the house, too, was occupied, and unwilling to fall alive into the hands of the insurgents, he threw himself into a well. Fortunately it was a dry one. Near him lay the dead body of a native that had been thrown into it. For nearly three days and two nights the poor fellow remained concealed there. The pestilential atmosphere of the cistern was horrible to bear, and he could only at night venture out to breathe a little fresh air. He had nothing to eat or to drink, and hope almost began to desert him, when the shouts of our men gave him notice of their approach. He emerged from his hiding place to the great astonishment of our men, who were about to shoot him for an insurgent, so filthy and black had he become, when he was recognised and saved.

On the 1st October, under the personal superintendence of Coloniel Napier, an experienced and very able officer, whose cool judgment and courage elicited the praise of all the officers and men who acted under him, the position to the left of the Cawnpore battery was attacked by us. They were of all the corps, and were commanded by Major Haliburton, Her Majesty's 78th; Captain Shute, Her Majesty's 64th; and Captain Raikes, Madras Fusiliers; and consisted of about 570 men. They occupied on that day the houses to the left and front of Phillips's battery, the point they designed to storm, and one of the enemy's strongest positions. Lieutenant Groom, with his Madras Fusiliers, had, in a most gallant manner, led the advance. Colonel Napier, then restraining the ardour of his men, remained in the same position all night, and attacked the battery next day.

The assault had been so carefully and scientifically planned by Colonel Napier, that we lost only two killed and eleven wounded. It was stormed by our men with their usual gallantry, three guns were taken and burst by Lieutenants Limend, Innes, and Tulloch, Engineers, and the house in the garden was destroyed. Major Haliburton here particularly distinguished himself, as did also all the officers with him. Mr. Kavanagh and Mr. Phillips had also accompanied the party as guides.

In order, if possible, to make the Cawnpore road our line of communication with Alumbagh, Sir James Outram directed openings to be made from one house to another. But we were obliged afterwards to relinquish this idea, for a mosque which intervened was filled with riflemen, and so strongly fortified, that we could not have taken it without very great loss. We were therefore compelled to abandon the houses we had occupied on the Cawnpore road, for we had not men enough to hold them, and the musketry of the enemy upon them was incessant. During these operations, that very gallant officer, Major Haliburton, was mortally wounded. His successor, Major Stephenson, fell next day.

Brigadier Inglis, who still continued to command our garrison, and General Havelock, who had the command of the palaces occupied by his force, were ably carrying out Sir James's instructions to repair the defences of the old position, and make batteries and entrenchments for the new.

The engineering operations of the old garrison were superintended by Lieutenant J. C. Anderson, garrison engineer, actively seconded by Lieutenant M'Leod Innes, by Lieutenant G. Hutchinson, who was attached to the Engineers, by Lieutenant Hay and Lieutenant Tulloch, assistant field engineers. The buildings which had given us shelter were many of them in a very precarious state, and there were several breaches in the walls.

Owing to the great number of camp-followers, such as dooly-bearers, camel-drivers, bullock-drivers, syces, and grass-cutters, which had come in with the Oude Field Force, and were placed at the disposal of Brigadier Inglis, our labour went on far more rapidly than before. Our sepoys, too, though in time of peace they would have urged their caste as a reason for not putting their hands to the spade, worked now right willingly.

Two large gaps on either side of the Brigade Mess,

which had been during the siege so gallantly defended by Colonel Masters and his garrison of officers, were now repaired. Earth-works and barricades were also thrown up at our outpost, and the Sikh Square, and the Cawnpore battery. The latter was greatly improved; the platform being made low. The left side was formed into a gun-battery, armed with two 18-pounders and a 9-pounder, and the left into a strong musketry battery.

Towards our outpost (Innes's) our position had also been extended. The mound commanding it, where we had suffered so much in the early part of the siege, had been now taken possession of. The enemy had seriously molested us during a feeble attack they made on us in the middle of October; and we were warned to prepare for its capture. It was easily effected. We left at five in the evening, and silently stole up, with bayonets fixed, and our muskets loaded. On we went, made a sudden dash, and found — nobody. We set up a loud laugh, and congratulated ourselves on the ease with which the conquest was effected. The enemy had apparently only occupied the mound temporarily, on extraordinary occasions.

In our hands the mound soon became one of our strongest positions. Lieutenant Hutchinson, who conducted the operations, was indefatigable, and by his personal exertions, pushed on the works during the night as well as the day. The tombstones on it, for it had been a Mohammedan cemetery, were made use of to serve as bastions; and deep trenches were dug to ensure the safety of our going to it from Innes's. The position had been recommended by Lieutenant Graydon, who commanded our outpost. This officer was ever going about remedying defects; and suggesting and superintending any possible improvements in our defences.

The mound commanded the iron bridge, Hill's shop, and the houses adjacent to it. Towards the enemy's side it was naturally steep, and difficult of access. An attack upon it by the insurgents would have been repulsed with the greatest ease by its garrison. A mosque to the right of it, and likewise commanding our outpost, had also been taken up as one of our positions. It had sheltered the enemy's riflemen in great numbers, and we had been particularly exposed to their musketry from that direction.

A sergeant of the 32nd, named Purdell (a man who had always been foremost, not only in fighting, but also in the peaceable occupations of carrying out sanitary improvements in our garrison), a volunteer, Mr. Alone, and myself, had been ordered to put up a barricade in an exposed place, during a hot fire of the enemy. The sergeant fell dead at our feet, struck by a rifle ball in the forehead. This event stimulated our captain in his endeavours to obtain possession of the mosque. A gun was brought to bear on it, and we occupied it the next day. It was well barricaded, and earth was thrown on the dead bodies of the insurgents who had there fallen by our hands.

Our captain, Graydon, was soon afterwards shot, while superintending some works on the mound. He received a rifle bullet in his breast, and expired next day. Brave, active, and kind to all those he had commanded, his was, indeed, a serious loss. In him, we in the garrison had all lost a friend, and the news of his death cast a gloom over it for many days. Lieutenant Thaine, his second in command, succeeded to the command of these important garrisons of Innes's outpost, the mound, and the mosque.

The enemy, meanwhile, continued to molest us: and we had almost daily to deplore the loss, by wounds or death, of one or two men. Of the Volunteer Cavalry several were wounded. I remember only the names of young Ensign J. Hearsey and Mr. Volkers, a civilian. Poor Mr. Erskine, too, who had been wounded at the storming of Alumbagh, died about the end of October. He had dwindled down to a skeleton, and was so changed that he could no longer be recognised by his friends. To one of them who had visited him in hospital, he whispered "It is hard to die so young, but the grief of my poor mother, when she hears of my death, is what afflicts me most."

Alas! how many many tears will be shed for those fallen at Lucknow; how many parents will be childless, — how many widows have been made so by this cruel war,— how many sisters have to mourn the loss of their brave brothers! On the other hand, how they who will hear of the safety of their sons, husbands, and brothers, will have reason to rejoice! They may indeed be grateful to Providence; for their dear ones have been given to them a second time. How we ever escaped is something I cannot comprehend even now.

In my numerous walks round our old intrenchments and into our new positions, I could never withhold my admiration at the enormous labour the insurgents had undergone, not only in their offensive but in defensive operations. Before their batteries, deep trenches, some twenty feet deep and three feet wide, were excavated. Ladders were placed at intervals for sentries to go down and see that our mines did not go under their batteries. Deep trenches intersected one another all round us, along which the rebels could crawl unperceived to the very edge of our entrenchment. Some of the batteries were within forty yards of us, and all were well and stoutly made. How we resisted all these is truly a wonder. The right hand of the Lord is manifest in all this plainly enough, for in spite of all our courage, we could never have kept them out.

The chief engineer, Captain Crommelin, meanwhile superintended the defensive works of the new palaces. With the miners placed at his disposal he soon foiled most of the enemy's mining operations, and sunk shafts and began galleries in every direction. In carrying out these labours he owed much to the energy and courage of Lieutenant Russell, his Major of Brigade; Lieutenant Limond, the only engineer officer under his command; Lieutenant Hutchinson, directing engineer; Captain Oakes, 8th Native Infantry; Lieutenant Hall, 1st battalion Fusiliers; Lieutenant Tulloch, Mr. Goldsworthy, Lieutenant A. Chalmers, and Mr. Kavanagh, assistant field engineers; and among the non-commissioned officers and men, who acted as overseers, Sergeants Duffy and M'Hale, Corporal Horey, of the Madras Fusiliers; Baylon of Her Majesty's 8th Fusiliers; and of the 32nd, Sergeants Farrer, Banetta, and Callimore, and Corporal Dowling, who, during the first siege, had several times distinguished himself. He also connected the Tehree Kothee, Chutter Munzil, and Feradbuksh together, forming a labyrinth of gardens and courtyards, without flanking defences, and put them in position to resist the enemy up to Sir Colin Campbell's arrival. In a military point of view they were not necessary, but they afforded our troops and camp-followers the best shelter they could have had. The Residency was already far too crowded to receive into it many more inmates.

On several occasions, notwithstanding the vigilance of Captain Crommelin and his subordinates, the enemy succeeded in blowing up portions of our walls, and we lost several good and valiant men by these explosions. Generally, however, their mines were innocuous, and were countermined and blown up by our engineering department, not unfrequently the miners with them. Rencontres between our miners and the enemy's occasionally took place. Ours generally surprised them, and were of course always successful in these contests under ground. The Sikhs of Captain Brasyer, separated though they were by only a very narrow passage from the enemy, worked their own mines and defended their position in spite of the heavy fire of musketry directed against them.

The enemy had once even penetrated into their enclosure. I was at the time not far from the point of attack, and being unarmed, most narrowly risked being shot or made prisoner; but our men drove them back with immense slaughter. No less than a hundred dead bodies were afterwards dragged away by our sweepers and thrown into the river, but more than three times that number must have been carried off by their comrades. The 5th Fusiliers, the 78th Highlanders, and the Sikhs rushed on them, intercepted them in some of our passages, and finally cleared the palaces of them.

Captain Crommelin also erected several strong and scientifically built batteries; one, the Cavalier battery, directed against the more eastern buildings of the enemy, was a perfect *chef-d'œuvre* of engineering operations under difficulties. Trenches cut here and there protected the soldiers going from one place to another. During all these works, Colonel Napier, the chief of the staff, was invaluable. I cannot express greater admiration of his services than by comparing him to the late excellent Captain Fulton. Like that gallant officer, he was ever present at all the points of operations, advising, directing, and encouraging all.

According to General Outram's report to General Mansfield, chief of Sir Colin Campbell's staff, twenty-one shafts, aggregating 209 feet in depth, and 5291 feet of gallery, had been executed. The enemy advanced twenty mines against the palaces and outposts. Of these they exploded three, which caused no loss of life, and two which did no injury; seven had been blown in, and out of seven others the enemy had been driven, and their galleries taken possession of by our miners, results of which the engineer's department may well be proud.

CHAP. XVII.

CONTINUATION OF THE SIEGE.

Notes from my Journal. — News of the Fall of Delhi. — Position of Alumbagh. — Death of Mr. Thornhill. — Reward to the Uncovenanted. — Injustice to non-Government Volunteers. — Prize Jewels. — General Outram's Division Order. — Reward of our Sepoys. — Auctions in our Garrison. — Brigadier Inglis's Improvements within the old Entrenchments. — Dr. Scott's Hospital Arrangements. — Commissariat Reductions. — Our Treasure Exhumed. — Sanitary Measures. — Fortifying of our New Positions. — Successful Explosion of our Mines. — Loss of the Enemy. — Captain Brasyer's Sikhs and our other Troops. — News of Sir Colin Campbell's Approach. — Our Intelligence Department. — Telegraph Signals.

I BEGIN this chapter with a few notes from my diary.

October 8th. — Still hazy, close, and warm. Firing as usual. A shell burst in the midst of Sago's garrison, and nearly blew off the head of Mrs. Lawrence, smashing her almirah to pieces. Ensign G. W. Greene, a most pleasant companion and brave officer, died of dysentery to-day.

October 10th. — News came in to-day that Delhi has at last been taken, with the loss of 1300 killed on our side, of the enemy 7000! This is glorious news! Troops are also said to be coming to our aid from three or four quarters.

October 12*th.*—Three regiments are said to be at Alumbagh, which was besieged. Sir James had attempted to send out the Volunteer Cavalry some time ago, but they found the enemy in such overwhelming numbers, and so heavy a fire was opened on them, that they were at last obliged to return to us. With us things are much the same; firing as usual. It is truly annoying to have these faithless mercenaries of ours still firing at us from behind loopholes, and working guns within fifty yards of us.

Mr. Thornhill, of the civil service, died to-day. He had been wounded a second time in his arm, which, necessitating amputation, as usual, proved fatal. He had long ago recovered from his bayonet wounds, received on the 18th June in his encounter with the rebels of the military police.

October 15*th.*—Sir James Outram had called at the various garrisons a few days ago. The volunteers of the uncovenanted service were called together, and were told that, owing to the vigilance, gallantry, zeal, and valour they had displayed in the defence of the siege, they were to receive three months' gratuity.

No general reward is without injustice. Men like

Hill, who had made himself particularly useful in carrying out conservancy duties, Sinclair, Parry, and myself, being in no Government employ, of course get nothing. I tried my best to obtain a few rupees, for, owing to Deprat's death, and the absence of all communications with Calcutta, I had no means of replenishing my purse. Yet with all my endeavours I succeeded in getting only seventy-five rupees. It is really unjust. Why I should have nothing, while others, who did as much or as little as myself, should receive from 150 to 1500 rupees, I really do not see. Money is again valuable, for one can occasionally make purchases, particularly of clothes, of which we are much in need.

October 16th. — A sham attack to-day. A great search of prize property is making, but most things will end in nothing. People who have the great hauls of jewellery take care of such things. Apropos of valuables: it is stated the Government possess no less than 800,000*l.* worth of jewellery, lately belonging to the ex-King of Oude, a prisoner of ours, in Calcutta. I myself saw cartloads of the most costly diamonds, stones, pearls, gold and silver, in the Residency. Is the army to have no share of this spoil?

The General has issued the following division order, which I copy entire:—

"DIVISION ORDER BY MAJOR-GENERAL SIR JAMES OUTRAM, G. C. B.

"*Head Quarters, Lucknow, October 5th,* 1857.

" The incessant and arduous duties which have devolved on Brigadier Inglis and his Staff since the arrival of the Relieving Force had hitherto prevented him from furnishing to the Major-General Commanding the usual Official documents relative to the siege of the garrison.

" In the absence of these, the Major-General could not with propriety have indulged in any public declaration of the admiration with which he regards the heroism displayed by Brigadier Inglis and the glorious garrison he has so ably commanded during the last three months, and he has been reluctantly obliged to defer therefore so long the expression of the sentiments he was desirous to offer.

" But the Major-General having at length received Brigadier Inglis' Reports, is relieved from the necessity of further silence, and he hastens to tender to the Brigadier and to every individual member of the garrison, the assurance of his confidence that their services will be regarded by the Government under which they are immediately serving, by the British nation, and by Her Gracious Majesty, with equal admiration to that with which he is himself impressed.

" The Major-General believes that the annals of warfare contain no brighter page than that which will record the bravery, fortitude, vigilance, and patient endurance of hardships, privation, and fatigue, displayed by the garrison of Lucknow, and he is very conscious that his unskilled pen must needs fail adequately to convey to the Right Honourable the Governor-General of India, and His Excellency the Commander-in-Chief, the profound sense of the merits of that garrison which has been forced on his mind by a careful consideration of the almost incredible difficulties with which they have had to contend.

"The term 'illustrious' was well and happily applied, by a former Governor-General of India, to the garrison of Jellalabad, but some far more laudatory epithet, if such the English language contains, is due, the Major-General considers, to the brave men whom Brigadier Inglis has commanded, with undeviating success and untarnished honour, through the late memorable siege; for while the devoted band of heroes who so nobly maintained the honour of their country's arms under Sir R. Sale were seldom exposed to actual attack, the Lucknow garrison of inferior strength, have in addition to a series of fierce assaults, gallantly and successfully repulsed, been for three months exposed to a nearly incessant fire from strong and commanding positions, held by an enemy of overwhelming force, possessing powerful artillery, having at their command the whole resources of what was but recently a kingdom, and animated by an insane and blood-thirsty fanaticism.

"It is a source of heartfelt satisfaction to the Major-General to be able, to a certain extent, to confer on the native portion of the garrison an instalment of those rewards which their gallant and grateful Commander has sought for them, and which he is very certain the Governor-General will bestow in full; and though the Major-General, as regards the European portion of the garrison, cannot do more than give his most earnest and hearty support to the recommendations of the Brigadier, he feels assured that the Governor-General of India will fully and publicly manifest his appreciation of their distinguished services, and that our beloved Sovereign will herself deign to convey to them some gracious expression of royal approbation of their conduct.

"Brigadier Inglis has borne generous testimony to the bravery, vigilance, devotedness, and good conduct of all ranks; and to all ranks, as the local representative of the British Indian Government, the Major-General tenders his warmest acknowledgments. He would fain offer his special congratulations and thanks to the European and Eurasian portion of the garrison whom Brigadier Inglis has particularly noticed; but by doing so he would forestall the Governor-General in the exercise of what the Major-General is assured will be one of the most pleasing acts of his official life."

The native soldiers who had, through so many dangers, adhered to us, were well rewarded. All were promoted one or two steps, and we have no private native soldiers now any longer in the garrison.

Oct. 17th. — I attended an auction of deceased officers' property; the prices which prevailed were as high as ever. For an old flannel coat, 51 rupees; 15 cheroots for 51 rupees; 25 rupees for three old cooking utensils; and other things equally exorbitant.

No more news of troops, so the three regiments at Alumbagh are myths.

Oct. 20th. — The cold weather is setting in fast. The "Babalogue" were very quiet yesterday, but last night they made a determined rush at the Cawnpore battery, under some idea that our guns had been removed, but a smart dose of grape, promptly administered, had the effect of soon dispersing them.

Oct. 21st. — Siege progressing much as usual. Heavy firing is heard in the Alumbagh direction, so that it is evident our men there are attacked.

An apothecary apprentice, named Dallicott, was killed to-day in his bed in the Convalescent Hospital. Both his legs and a portion of his stomach were carried off by a round shot.

Oct. 23rd. — We have spies in. The firing on the 21st was an attack on Alumbagh. We lost some elephants while out foraging, some say two, others eleven.

Oct. 26*th.* — An auction of prize property to-day. Old shawls sold at very high prices.

Oct. 28*th.* — News brought in that the Delhi brigade has arrived at Cawnpore after fighting two battles, in which the insurgents were well beaten.

Oct. 30*th.* — Attended an auction to-day. Brandy sold at 54 rupees the bottle; some hermetically sealed provisions at equally ridiculously high prices. People gladly pay any sum for provisions. After our meals are over we feel a deplorable emptiness; over eating is no complaint with us. We live in a perfect Great Sahara of wants. However, the Commander-in-Chief is coming to relieve us. Let us see if this proves true, or if it is only to be added to the great mass of unredeemed expectancies.

In the interior economy of the old entrenchments many improvements had been effected by Brigadier Inglis and his staff. The magazine was remodelled, and the laboratories removed to the post office and the Bailey-guard treasury, where cartridges for the musket and Enfield rifle, fusees for shells, quick and slow matches, wads, sacks for sandbags, &c. were prepared. The shots and shells were piled up, and the spare wood, lead, and iron collected from the palaces. Captain Thomas, commissary of ordnance, had the superintendence of this labour.

DR. SCOTT'S HOSPITAL ARRANGEMENTS.

Dr. Scott, the superintending surgeon, busied himself in making arrangements for the comfort of the sick and wounded. A room in the emambarah of the Begum Kothee had been made over by the Brigadier for the reception of wounded officers, and the jail had been converted into a convalescent hospital. Two large tents were pitched before the general hospital, to give shelter to the very large number of wounded who had hitherto been crowded into one room. Beds and beddings were also made from the plunder in the palaces.

I have already alluded to the commissariat reductions, and their absolute necessity. I should, however, mention that praise is due to the economy enforced by Captain James, the assistant-commissary-general, and Captains Boileau, 7th Light Cavalry, and Vanrenen, commissariat officers, as well as to Mr. Yerbury, the head assistant in the department. For the Oude field force, Captain M'Bean efficiently carried out the commissariat arrangements.

We had about 23 lakhs of rupees buried under ground, near the Residency; this was exhumed, and made over to the officers of the treasury.

In the palaces similar improvements were carried out, and Dr. Ogilvie, the Sanitary Commissioner, now again became active enough. In every corner of the gardens and outhouses were dead bodies at one time to be seen, in the most horrible and disgusting positions, and with the most frightful wounds about them. Several of them were Africans. These were dragged by ropes to the river side and thrown into the Goomtee; horses were buried, and cleanliness again enforced as much as possible.

The palaces, as I have already observed, were continuing to be fortified as much as lay in the power of our officers. The enemy's fire and attacks seemed now more directed at these new entrenchments than at the old ones. Captain Lockhart and his gallant 78th Highlanders had to defend a very dangerous and exposed post, and so had Captains Rattray, Wade, and Moorsome. The latter officer had placed a piquet at a building commanding the Khas bazaar, whose long colonnades formed a complete street. Our piquet house was blown up by the enemy; and during the attack of the 6th, to which I have already alluded, in which the insurgents were so completely defeated, Lieutenant-Colonel Purnell and Captain Moorsome particularly distinguished themselves.

The enemy, however, could not then be driven out of a portion of the palaces, which they had maintained possession of after having exploded a mine. Colonel Napier, accompanied by Colonels Purnell and

Moorsome, however, reconnoitred the enemy's position one dark night with perfect success, and Lieutenant Russell, of the Engineers, was then directed to attempt to blow up the mosque which the enemy maintained. He was perfectly successful; a great number of insurgents were blown into the air, and we obtained a capital point to command the Khas bazaar from. This was maintained by the daring Colonel Purnell (H.M. 90th), in spite of every attempt of the enemy to drive him out.

Captain Brasyer with his Sikhs, Captain Galway with his Madras Fusiliers, Lieutenant Meara with his 5th Fusiliers, and Captain Shute with his 64th, and Captain Willis and his 84th men, maintained also very difficult positions in the new entrenchments.

We now heard that Sir Colin Campbell, urged by Sir James Outram, was approaching Lucknow. The joy which this news diffused is more easily imagined than described. We thus looked forward to certain relief, and already anticipated the pleasure we should have in again seeing our friends in other stations in India; for we doubted not that we should be permitted to leave with the ladies and the wounded, for none of us either desired or contemplated the entire evacuation of Oude.

Owing to the excellent arrangements carried out by Captains Alexander, Orr, and Carnegie, at the head of the Intelligence Department, many messengers could be despatched, who were able not only to reach their destination but also to bring in replies to the letters of our generals. We thus learnt that Sir Colin Campbell had arrived at Alumbagh on the 10th of November, and had relieved the gallant little garrison that had been besieged there, but who had many more luxuries than we had. The natives, servants, and camp followers, however, most of them, had deserted on account of there not being sufficient wheat in the store-room. They all had to work at the fortifications, which they carried on with great vigour, nor did they receive any rations until they had performed a certain amount of labour.

Our authorities had invented a capital way of communicating with the Alumbagh by means of different coloured flags, the key having been transmitted by a spy. This superseded the necessity of sending messengers through a hostile country, and we could converse from the terrace of the Residency somewhat in the same way as ships signal to each other, but far less perfectly. And here I would take this opportunity of recommending the advisability of our commanders being furnished with signal books, like those published by Lloyd's. Had we had these means of communication during the first siege, what anxiety would have been spared to us!

CHAP. XVIII.

KAVANAGH'S EXPLOIT. — OUR OFFENSIVE OPERATIONS.

Mr. Kavanagh volunteers to carry Despatches. — His interesting Narrative. — Mrs. Kavanagh. — Lieutenant Hutchinson's Mines. — Havelock's offensive Operations. — Explosion of our Mines. — Our Attacks upon the Hirukhana, Engine House, King's Stables, Captain Lockhart's Post. — Ardour of our Troops. — Havelock's Success. — Our Casualties.

PLANS were to be forwarded to Sir Colin Campbell; but as it was necessary that he should have them explained by some intelligent person, who could give him every information respecting the different localities, and who could act as a guide in whom every confidence could be reposed, Mr. Kavanagh, a civilian, who had already distinguished himself in several sorties, which he accompanied in his capacity as assistant-field engineer, volunteered to go himself into the Commander-in-Chief's camp: and, notwithstanding the very great dangers he would have to face, trusting in his own courage and his good fortune, he set out, and succeeded in reaching Sir Colin Campbell in safety. Had he fallen into the enemy's hands he would undoubtedly have suffered a death of the most refined cruelty which these barbarian insurgents could invent. But I will let Mr. Kavanagh tell his own story.

"*Narrative of my escape from the British Entrenchment at Lucknow to the Camp of Sir Colin Campbell near Bunnee, for the purpose of acting as his Guide in his advance for the relief of the besieged Garrison.*

"While passing through the entrenchment of Lucknow about ten o'clock A.M. on the 9th instant, I learnt that a spy had come in from Cawnpore, and that he was going back in the night as far as Alumbagh with despatches to His Excellency Sir Colin Campbell, the Commander-in-Chief, who, it was said, was approaching Lucknow with five or six thousand men.

"I sought out the spy, whose name is * * * * and who was in the Court of the Deputy-Commissioner of Duriabad before the outbreak in Oude. He had taken letters from the entrenchment before, but I had never seen him till now. I found him intelligent, and imparted to him my desire to venture in disguise to Alumbagh in his company. He hesitated a great deal at acting as my guide, but made no attempt to exaggerate the dangers of the road. He merely urged that there was more chance of detection by our going together, and proposed that we should take different roads and meet outside of the city, to which I objected. I left him to transact some business, my mind dwelling all the time on the means of accomplishing my object.

"I had some days previously witnessed the preparation of plans which were being made by direction of Sir James Outram to assist the Commander-in-Chief in his march into Lucknow for the relief of the besieged, and it then occurred to me that some one with the requisite local knowledge ought to attempt to reach His Excellency's camp beyond or at Alumbagh. The news of Sir Colin Campbell's advance revived the ideas, and I made up my mind to go myself, at two o'clock, after finishing the business I was engaged upon. I mentioned to Colonel R. Napier, chief of Sir James Outram's staff, that I was willing to proceed through the enemy to Alumbagh, if the General thought my doing so would be of service to the Commander-in-Chief. He was surprised at the offer, and seemed to regard the enterprise as fraught with too much danger to be assented to, but he did me the favour of communicating the offer to Sir James Outram, because he considered that my zeal deserved to be brought to his notice.

"Sir James did not encourage me to undertake the journey, declaring that he thought it so dangerous that he would not himself have asked any officer to attempt it. I, however, spoke so confidently of success, and treated the dangers so lightly, that he at last yielded, and did me the honour of adding that if I succeeded in reaching the Commander-in-Chief, my knowledge would be a great help to him.

"I secretly arranged for a disguise, so that my departure might not be known to my wife, as she was not well enough to bear the prospect of an eternal separation. When I left home about seven o'clock in the evening, she thought I was going on duty for the night to the mines, for I was working as an assistant-field engineer by order of Sir James Outram.

"By half-past seven o'clock my disguise was completed, and when I entered the room of Colonel Napier no one in it recognised me. I was dressed as a Budmash, or as an irregular soldier of the city, with sword and shield, native-made shoes, tight trowsers, a yellow silk koortah over a tight-fitting white muslin shirt, a yellow-coloured chintz sheet thrown round my shoulders, a cream-coloured turban, and a white waistband or kumurbund. My face down to the shoulders, and my hands to the wrists, were coloured with lamp black, the cork used being dipped in oil to cause the colour to adhere a little. I could get nothing better. I had little confidence in the disguise of my features, and I trusted more to the darkness of the night: but Sir James Outram and his staff seemed satisfied, and, after being provided with a small double-barrelled pistol, and a pair of broad pyjamahs over the tight drawers, I proceeded with Kunoujee Lal to the right bank of the river Goomtee, running north of our entrenchment, accompanied by Captain Hardinge of the Irregular Cavalry.

"Here we undressed and quietly forded the river, which was only about four feet and a half deep and about a hundred yards wide at this point. My courage failed me while in the water, and if my guide had been within reach, I should perhaps have pulled him back and abandoned the enterprise. But he waded quickly through the stream, and, reaching the opposite bank, went crouching up a ditch for three hundred yards to a grove of low trees on the edge of a pond, where we stopped to dress. While we were here a man came down to the pond to wash, and went away again without observing us.

"My confidence now returned to me, and with my tulwar resting on my shoulder, we advanced into the huts in front, where I accosted a matchlockman, who answered to my remark, that the night was cold, 'It is very cold; in fact, it *is* a cold night.' I passed him, adding that it would be colder by and bye.

"After going six or seven hundred yards further, we reached the iron bridge over the Goomtee, where we were stopped and called over by a native officer, who was seated in an upper-storied house and seemed to be in command of a cavalry piquet, whose horses were near the place saddled. My guide advanced to the light, and I stayed a little back in the shade. After being told that we had come from Mundeon (our old cantonment, and then in the possession of the enemy), and that we were going into the city to our homes, he let us proceed. We continued on along the left bank of the river to the stone bridge, which is about eight or nine hundred yards from the iron bridge, passing unnoticed through a number of sepoys and matchlockmen, some of whom were escorting persons of rank in palanquins preceded by torches.

"Recrossing the Goomtee by the stone bridge, we went by a sentry unobserved, who was closely questioning a dirtily-dressed native, and into the chouk, or principal street of the city of Lucknow, which was not illuminated as much as it used to be previous to the siege, nor was it so crowded. I jostled against several armed men in the street without being spoken to, and only met one guard of seven sepoys, who were amusing themselves with some women of pleasure.

"When issuing from the city into the country we were challenged by a chowkeedar or watchman, who, without stopping us, merely asked us who we were. The part of the city traversed that night by me seemed to have been deserted by at least a third of its inhabitants.

"I was in great spirits when we reached the green fields, into which I had not been for five months. Everything around us smelt sweet, and a carrot I took from the road side was the most delicious I had ever tasted. I gave vent to my feelings in a conversation with Kunoujee Lal, who joined in my admiration of the province of Oude, and lamentation that it was now in the hands of wretches whose misgovernment and rapacity were ruining it.

"A further walk of a few miles was accomplished in high spirits. But there was trouble before us. We had taken the wrong road, and were now quite out of our way in the Dilkooshah Park, which was occupied by the enemy. I went within twenty yards of two guns to see what strength they were, and returned to the guide, who was in great alarm, and begged I would not distrust him because of the mistake, as it was caused by his anxiety to take me away from the piquets of the enemy. I bade him not to be frightened of me, for I was not annoyed, as such accidents were not unfrequent even when there was no danger to be avoided. It was now about midnight. We endeavoured to persuade a cultivator who was watching his crop to show us the way for a short distance, but he urged old age and lameness, and another whom I peremptorily told to come with us ran off screaming, and alarmed the whole village. We next walked quickly away into the canal, running under the Charbagh, in which I fell several times, owing to my shoes being wet and slippery and my feet sore. The shoes were hard and tight, and had rubbed the skin off my toes, and cut into the flesh above the heels.

"In two hours more we were again on the right direction, two women in a village we passed having kindly helped us to find it; about two o'clock we reached an advanced piquet of sepoys, who told us the way, after asking where we had come from and whither we were going. I thought it safer to go up to the piquet than to try to pass them unobserved.

"Kunoujee Lal now begged I would not press him to take me into Alumbagh, as he did not know the way in, and the enemy were strongly posted around the place. I was tired and in pain from the shoes, and would therefore have preferred going into Alumbagh; but as the guide feared attempting it, I desired him to go on to the camp of the Commander-in-Chief, which he said was near Bunnee (a village eighteen miles from Lucknow), upon the Cawnpore road. The moon had risen by this time, and we could see well ahead.

"By three o'clock we arrived at a grove of mango trees, situated on a plain, in which a man was singing at the top of his voice. I thought he was a villager, but he got alarmed on hearing us approach, and astonished us too by calling out a guard of twenty-five sepoys, all of whom asked questions. Kunoujee Lal here lost heart for the first time, and threw away the letter entrusted to him for Sir Colin Campbell. I kept mine safe in my turban. We satisfied the guard that we were poor men travelling to Umroula, a village two miles this side of the chief's camp, to inform a friend of the death of his brother by a shot from the British entrenchment at Lucknow, and they told us the road. They appeared to be greatly relieved on discovering that it was not their terrible foe, who was only a few miles in advance of them. We went in the direction indicated by them, and after walking for half an hour we got into a jheel or swamp, which are numerous and large in Oude. We had to wade through it for two hours up to our waists in water, and through weeds; but before we found out that we were in a jheel, we had gone too far to recede. I was nearly exhausted on getting out of the water, having made great exertions to force our way through the weeds, and to prevent the colour being washed off my face. It was nearly gone from my hands.

"I now rested for fifteen minutes, despite of the remonstrances of the guide, and went forward, passing between two piquets of the enemy, who had no sentries thrown out. It was near four o'clock in the morning when I stopped at the corner of a tope or grove of trees to sleep for an hour, which Kunoujee Lal entreated I would not do; but I thought he overrated the danger, and, lying down, I told him to see if there was any one in the grove who would tell him where we then were.

"We had not gone far when I heard the English challenge, 'Who comes there,' with a native accent. We had reached a British cavalry outpost; my eyes filled with joyful tears, and I shook the Sikh officer in charge of the piquet heartily by the hand. The old soldier was as pleased as myself when he heard from whence I had come, and he was good enough to send two of his men to conduct me to the camp of the advanced guard. An officer of H. M. 9th Lancers, who was visiting his piquets, met me on the way, and took me to his tent, where I got dry stockings and trousers, and, what I much needed, a glass of brandy, a liquor I had not tasted for nearly two months.

"I thanked God for having safely conducted me through this dangerous enterprise, and Kunoujee Lal for the courage and intelligence with which he had conducted himself during this trying night. When we were questioned he let me speak as little as possible. He always had a ready answer; and I feel that I am indebted to him in a great measure more than to myself for my escape. It will give me great satisfaction to hear that he has been suitably rewarded.

"In undertaking this enterprise, I was actuated by a sense of duty, believing that I could be of use to his Excellency, the Commander-in-Chief, when approaching, for its relief, the besieged garrison, which had heroically resisted the attack of thirty times its own number for nearly five months, within a weak and irregular entrenchment; and secondly, because I was anxious to perform some service which would ensure to me the honour of wearing our most gracious Majesty's cross.

"My reception by Sir Colin Campbell and his staff was cordial and kind to the utmost degree; and if I never have more than the remembrance of their condescension and of the heartfelt congratulations of Sir James Outram and of all the officers of his garrison, on my safe return to them, I shall not repine; though, to be sure, having the Victoria Cross would make me a prouder and a happier man.

"JAMES KAVANAGH.

"Camp, Alumbagh, 24th November, 1857."

The flag hoisted next day at twelve o'clock on the top of the Alumbagh building apprised us of Kavanagh's safe arrival. Every one was delighted at this, and none more so than Sir James Outram. I visited Mrs. Kavanagh, and congratulated her on the success which had attended her husband's dangerous expedition. I found her vexed and annoyed, and yet delighted; and she had reason to be so. No reward, indeed, would be too great for this brave man; and as neither Sir Colin nor Sir James has forgotten his services, he will doubtless not have reason to regret having exposed his life for the public good. Every civilian in the garrison felt proud that this enterprise had been undertaken by a non-military man; but at the same time there was no officer or soldier who envied him the honour he had earned for himself, and the good fortune which is of course in store for him.

Lieutenant Hutchinson meanwhile continued mining and countermining from Lockhart's post, erecting cannon-proof barricades, and making loopholes along the walls, so as to command the Khas bazaar. This officer showed the most consummate skill and the most unflinching courage throughout the very dangerous and difficult operations he was carrying on against the enemy. Even when the insurgents succeeded in exploding their mines, Lieutenant Hutchinson's measures were so well taken that they gained nothing by them. Being prepared against all contingencies, barricades, where breaches had been effected, were erected, expeditiously, carefully, and silently. On several occasions he had reasons to congratulate himself on the eminent success which attended him in these difficult undertakings. The enemy's shafts were destroyed in all directions, their miners killed, and listening galleries everywhere prepared. In these operations Lieutenant Hutchinson was aided by

Lieutenant Tulloch; Sergeant Day, 32nd; Lieutenant Hay, 78th Highlanders; and Corporal Thompson, of the same corps.

As Sir Colin approached the city, our offensive operations to assist the Commander-in-Chief in his movements were carried on with vigour. Opposite the Cavalier battery were the buildings of the Moty Mahal palaces, called the Hirn Khana (or "deer-house"); the Kal Khana (or "engine-room"), the king's stable, and the house next to the observatory, formerly the residence of Captain Bunbury, and now known as the mess-house, where the officers of the 32nd used to dine before the outbreak. These mines had been prepared by Captain Crommelin to effect breaches in the Hirn Khana. Unfortunately they had been charged for the 14th Nov., and the attack was delayed till the 16th. The powder, consequently, had become damped, and when they were fired did not explode with the expected force. This occurred on the afternoon of the 16th.

The one at the north corner of the advanced garden effected a breach; the centre mine failed, and the third, owing to its having already reached 290 feet without air-pipes, and not being able to be examined, nor the distance to the wall of the Hirn Khana surveyed, exploded a few feet short. The guns of our batteries were therefore required to batter down the walls.

Lieut. Hutchinson, with a party of the 64th under Captain Adolphe Orr, then sortied out, and took possession of the house where the latter had resided. Lieutenant Hall, with the 84th under Captain Willis, stormed the Hirn Khana, and loopholed the walls dividing it from the Kaiserbagh. Lieutenants Simond and Chalmers, accompanied by a detachment of the 90th under Colonel Purnell, advanced to the engine-house, drove the enemy out of it, and took possession of the most advanced building of that post. The enemy opening their guns on it from the Kaiserbagh, however, compelled its abandonment, and Colonel Purnell ordered it to be burnt. The east wall of its baradurree, or great gateway, was loopholed by the engineer officers, and during the night a battery erected and a trench-way made to our advanced gardens.

Captains Russell and Oakes at the same time advanced upon the king's stables, with a detachment of the 78th Highlanders, commanded by Captain Lockhart. They found the enemy hard pressed by our soldiers, from the Hirn Khana, and retreating. Many of the 78th, unable to restrain themselves, rushed forward to follow up the flying rebels, and were with difficulty made to give over the pursuit.

The position was then secured, and made over to the charge of Colonel Purnell and the 90th. Lieutenant Meara and a detachment of the 5th Fusiliers, and 100 men of the Sikh regiment of Ferozepore commanded by Lieutenant Cross, at the same time issued from other parts into the Hirn Khana, engine house and king's stables. Major Eyre from one battery, Captain Olpherts from another, and Captain Maude from a battery of three mortars, firing simultaneously, did great damage in the enemy's ranks. Our troops, so long inactive, had rushed on, determined to conquer or fall, and they were successful in every point.

These operations had been undertaken under the immediate orders and eye of Major-General Havelock, and were intended to aid Sir Colin Campbell while operating from the Secundrabagh. Lieutenant C. W. Havelock, 12th Irregular Cavalry, the General's nephew, and Lieutenants Moorsome, Hudson, and Hargood, on his staff, were conspicuous in effectively carrying out the General's aid. In these operations our loss was, two officers wounded; seven non-commissioned officers and men killed, and twenty-three wounded — many, I regret to say, mortally and dangerously.

CHAP. XIX.

SIR COLIN CAMPBELL'S OPERATIONS.

Sir Colin Campbell advances upon Lucknow.— His Force. — Lieutenant Gough's brilliant Charge. — Capture of the Delkusha. — Attack upon the Martinière College.—Captain Bourchier repulses the Enemy. —Advance upon the Secundrabagh.—Brigadier Hope's Charge.—Storming of the Secundrabagh Buildings.—The Enemy's desperate Resistance.—Emulation between Europeans and Sikhs. — Immense Slaughter of the Rebels.—Brigadier-General Grant's and Captain Peel's Naval Brigade. — Assault on the Shah Nudguff. — Attack upon the Mess House. — Capture of the Observatory. — Enemy's Attack repulsed. — Meeting between Sir Colin Campbell and Generals Outram and Havelock. — Havelock's Harangue.—His wonderful Self-command. — Officers who distinguished themselves. — Mr. Kavanagh's and Lord Seymour's Services.—Sir Colin Campbell's Despatch.—Sir Colin's Losses. — List of Officers killed.

SIR COLIN CAMPBELL had meanwhile left Cawnpore on the 9th November, and joining the troops under the command of Brigadier Hope Grant, pitched his tents at Bunnee about seven miles from Alumbagh. The force consisted of eight guns of Captain Peel's Naval Brigade, ten guns of Horse Artillery, six light field guns, and the heavy field battery of the Royal Artillery, Her Majesty's 9th Lancers, detachments of Sikh Cavalry and Hudson's Horse, and Her Majesty's 8th, 53rd, 75th, and 93rd regiments of Foot, two regiments of Punjab Infantry, and a small body of Native Sappers and Miners; altogether about 2700 infantry, and 700 cavalry.

After a brilliant charge by Lieutenant Gough, commanding Hodson's Irregular Horse, in which the enemy who had attacked the advanced guard had been beaten and despatched, the force moved on to the Alumbagh. Leaving his baggage there under the charge of the gallant 75th, Sir Colin, reinforced by about 700 more men, consisting of a detachment of Her Majesty's 23rd Royal Welsh Fusiliers and the 82nd Foot, together with two guns of Madras Artillery, some Royal Artillerymen, military train, and Royal Engineers, proceeded to the Delkusha ("Heart's delight"), a hunting castle of the former Kings of Oude, situated in a splendid and very extensive park, on an eminence of natural formation.

The advanced guard, which had been reinforced by companies of the 5th, 64th, and 78th, under Colonel Hamilton of the latter corps, were attacked by a heavy musketry fire from the enemy. The enemy were defeated, driven across the canal which intersects the park, and pursued past the Martinière College, which the enemy also were compelled to abandon. This building, known as Constantia House, is also in the centre of an extensive wood of mango trees, and capitally adapted for defence. It is only half a mile from Delkusha. Such terror did our men, however, inspire in the insurgents, that, after a desultory fight of short duration, they finally abandoned it, and left it in possession of our men. The Commander-in-Chief then made the Delkusha park his head-quarters, being provided with a fortnight's provisions for his own and our force.

An attack of the enemy on his advanced guard was quickly repulsed by Captain Bourchier's field battery, Captain Peel's heavy guns, 68-pounders, the 53rd, 93rd, and the 4th Sikhs, and pursued by the 9th Lancers. This happened on the 12th; and on the 14th the rear-guard, commanded by Lieutenant-Colonel Ewart, Her Majesty's 93rd, with Captain Blunt's Horse Artillery, and Colonel Crawford, Royal Artillery, joined him, having been much molested by the enemy's skirmishers, who hovered about him.

On the 16th, according to preconcerted arrangements, and in conjunction with General Havelock's movements, Sir Colin advanced towards us, through Secundrabagh, with his whole force, leaving the 8th to protect his camp at the Delkusha. The Secundrabagh ("Alexander's Garden") is a very extensive building, of strong masonry, in the midst of a large garden, encircled by a high wall,—now loop-holed in all directions,—and having barred windows all round.

Its natural advantages for defence were made the most of by a now desperate enemy, who evidently had determined to defend it to the last. It had been strongly garrisoned by the insurgents, a great number of whom occupied a village also, through which our force had to march to reach their destination.

Brigadier the Honourable Adrian Hope first led up his column. As they advanced, a fire was opened upon our troops, who were consequently ordered to move on in skirmishing order. Captain Blunt's Horse Artillery, and Captain Travers Royal Artillery heavy field guns were quickly brought up to answer the enemy's fire, which they did most effectively, in spite of a galling musketry fire with which the insurgents welcomed them from Secundrabagh as well as the village. Brigadier Hope now gallantly dashed onwards with his advanced guard, and after a well-sustained resistance, drove the enemy out of the latter position into the main building.

To the left of the village the enemy held a line of barracks outside of the Secundrabagh. This point a party of the 93rd Highlanders, under Lieutenant-Colonel Hay, and a detachment of the 53rd, under Captain Walton, attacked in the most daring manner, and, aided by Captain Blunt's gun, they dislodged the enemy. The Highlanders, who were the first in, then occupied the barracks, while the 53rd advanced in skirmishing order on the plain, and drove the insurgents before them as they advanced.

The Secundrabagh itself was then stormed. I believe — and this opinion is shared, I am confident, by every one who has been at Lucknow — that the assault upon Secundrabagh is not surpassed by any action we read of in the annals of warfare. Our men were harassed and fatigued to a degree; the forced marches they had had to make, the continued hardships they had had to go through (owing to the smallness of their numbers, the same men had to perform the same duties over and over again), the want of shelter, the unceasing marches and counter-marches, the necessity of being constantly on piquet duty and on the *qui vive*, — all this had prevented sleep or repose: but a fixed determination on their part to avenge their murdered countrymen, to do their duty, and to brave all obstacles in the attainment of their object, had spurred them on to unusual exertions.

The enemy, on the other hand, hopeless of obtaining mercy, and each individually certain of meeting an ignominious death, should they fall into our hands, were rendered desperate by their situation. Fanaticism and bigotry, and the very fear of us, nerved them on to resist to the death; and the manner in which they defended their stronghold proves that they were able to keep their resolution.

But nothing could daunt our men. The 4th Sikhs had been ordered to lead the attack, under the gallant Lieutenant Paul, who fell while heading his men, and the 93rd Highlanders, under Lieutenant-Colonel Gordon, the 53rd, under Captain Walton, and a battalion of detachments, under Major Barnston (H. M. 90th), were to cover the attack of their sable brethren in arms. The Europeans, however, had not patience enough for this, and jealous and fearful lest the Sikhs should gain the greatest honour, they rushed madly on, vying with each other who should be first in.

A small breach had been effected in one of the walls, and only a small body could rush in at once. Fortunately, the enemy had expected to be attacked from quite a different quarter, and the breach was in one of the most weakly guarded points. Our men could, therefore, come in in considerable numbers, before the insurgent guard could be reinforced. Still heaps fell. Yet our men dashed in as quickly as the narrow breach permitted, but that was not fast enough for their ardour. They went under the very loopholes of the enemy, and cunningly lying down while the insurgents let fly a volley at the caps fixed on their bayonets, which our men put up as a target for the time being, they, as soon as the enemy's fire was exhausted, and before they could load again, tore down the iron bars, broke up the barricades, and jumped down from the windows in the walls.

The enemy resisted desperately, but vainly, against their fury. Not less than 2000 dead bodies were counted next day. The slaughter had been terrific, and the gateway, the principal room, and the side chamber were literally inundated with blood, and piled with the dead and dying. No mercy was shown; and if some wretch had, as, however, was rarely the case, cowardice enough to throw down his arms and sue for pardon, none was given him. " Cawnpore " was hissed into the ear of every one of the rebels before a thrust of the bayonet put an end to his existence.

These operations had now gone on for nearly three hours, but more work was yet in store for our gallant troops. Sir Colin Campbell had other laurels to gain for Brigadier-General Grant, who commanded a division, the Naval brigade of Captain Peel, that had covered itself with glory in every engagement with the enemy, and, in short, all the other brave men of his army. While our attack was proceeding on the Secundrabagh, they had been molested by a most murderous fire directed on them from an extensive building, from which it was absolutely necessary for Sir Colin to dislodge the enemy. It was known as the Shah Nudjuff, and consisted of a large mosque, having in the centre a domed roof, with a parapet loopholed, and four minarets overtopping the whole, and filled with sharpshooters. It was situated in a fine garden of fruit trees, surrounded by loopholed high walls, and likewise defended by hosts of insurgents. The entrance had been blocked up with masonry, and in every point had been most carefully barricaded, loopholed, and fortified.

Against these buildings Captain Peel advanced with his heavy 68-pounders within a few yards of them, and, aided by a mortar battery and a field battery of Bengal Artillery, commenced a very heavy cannonade, which was answered by a murderous fire of the enemy's guns, who kept it up for three hours with tolerable effect. Captain Peel's gallant sailors were, however, covered by the 93rd, who kept up an incessant and galling musketry fire on the enemy. Brigadier Hope then led on his Highlanders, and Major Barnston his battalion to the assault. They stormed it in the most brilliant manner, entered, and filled the Shah Nudjuff with the corpses of the enemy. Our troops then ceased operations for the day, and reposed on the scene of action as much as a continual fire kept up by the enemy in the adjacent buildings permitted.

On the next day, the 17th, the place known as the Mess-house was cannonaded by Captain Peel's heavy guns. This building, defended by a deep ditch and loop-holed mud wall beyond, is on a considerable eminence, and consists of a large two-storied, flat terraced house, flanked by two square turrets. After Captain Peel's 68-pounders, aided by shells from the mortar battery in the Feradbuksh, had done considerable damage to this position, Captain Hopkins's detachment of the 53rd, a company of Captain Wolseley's 90th Regiment, Major Barnston's battalion under Captain Guise (90th Regiment), and a portion of Sikhs under Lieutenant Powlett, stormed it, surmounted all obstacles, effected an entrance, and carried it with a loud shout and a rush.

The Observatory, or Bank's house, to the rear of the Mess-house, was next attacked by a party of Sikhs, and taken. On that and the following day, Sir Colin Campbell from one side, and General Havelock from ours, occupied all the houses between our new entrenchments, the Mess-house, and the Motymahal.

To keep up a continued line of communication with the Dilkusha, was the next object, and a long chain of posts was after some tedious and difficult operations successfully made. In effecting this purpose, the brave Brigadier Russell was severely wounded, and his successor Colonel Biddulph, almost immediately after, killed. Lieutenant-Colonel Hall (82nd) succeeded to the command, and aided by Captain Bourchier's guns, finally effected his object.

Scarcely had they done so, however, when the enemy made a fierce attack on our piquets at the Mess-house, and the party of Highlanders under Colonel Ewart in the barracks taken on the 16th. Sir Colin himself advanced with bodies of H. M. 23rd and 53rd Foot, and reinforced the piquets, supported by the gallant Captain Remmington and his troop of Horse Artillery, who played on the enemy with great rapidity and beautiful precision.

The relief of Lucknow had been effected, and we were soon to be free. Sir Colin, while the fire was still very heavy on the afternoon of the 17th, was met by Sir James Outram and General Havelock. A loud long shout greeted the generals and their staff as they shook hands, amidst heartfelt cordiality, with Sir Colin Campbell. Proud indeed must Sir Colin have been at the success which had crowned all his measures, and which stamped him as one of the first generals of the age. The enemy had been foiled in every instance, and, notwithstanding his desperation, vigilance, and unquestionably excellent manœuvres, had succumbed to the Commander-in-Chief's superior generalship, and the indomitable valour and undaunted courage of our troops.

Sir Colin Campbell received the hearty thanks and congratulations of Sir James with evident satisfaction; and General Havelock, not less delighted and proud, harangued the troops who had so gallantly carried out all the Commander-in-Chief's brilliant manœuvres, in that concise and yet soul-stirring language for which he was so well known by his soldiers. While yet speaking, his attention was drawn to the place where his only son had just fallen, wounded by a musket ball from the enemy. Though his father's heart must have been then bleeding with anguish, and beating with curiosity to know the nature of the wound, the General, with wonderful self-command, continued his discourse without interruption, and then only amidst the cheers of the men, who were unacquainted with the sad event which had just happened, left to visit his wounded son. Fortunately it was only a slight wound, and he soon recovered from the effects of it.

The Commander-in-Chief's successful operations

had given all his officers and men opportunities to distinguish themselves, which none of them failed to seize. Major-General Mansfield, Chief of the Staff, Brigadier General Hope Grant, Capt. Peel, of the Naval Brigade, Brigadier Greathead, of Agra and Cawnpore celebrity, had earned fresh laurels, which they now shared with Brigadier Crawford, R.A., commanding the Artillery, Brigadier Little, commanding the Cavalry, Brigadier Russell, who unfortunately had been severely wounded, and Brigadier the Hon. Adrian Hope.

Sir Colin Campbell, in grateful acknowledgment of the intelligence, activity, skill, and courage of the Artillery in the field, honourably mentions, in his despatches of the 18th November, Major Turner, commanding the Bengal Artillery; Captains Remmington and Blunt, commanding troops of Horse Artillery of the same service; Captain Maxwell, B.A., attached to the Naval Brigade; Captain Travers, commanding Royal Artillery; Captains Middleton, R.A., and Bourchier, B.A., both commanding horse field batteries; Captain Longden, R.A., commanding mortar battery; Lieutenant Vaughan, R.N., and Lieutenant Walker, B.A., commanding a demi field battery; Lieutenants Ford and Brown, commanding the heavy field battery of Royal Artillery, after the death of the lamented Captain Handy; and Lieutenant Bridge, commanding two guns of Madras Horse Artillery.

Sir Colin particularly notices also the acting Chief Engineer, Lieutenant Lennox, R.E., and Lieutenant Scott, Madras Engineers, commanding sappers and miners, as well as Major Ouvry, commanding 9th Lancers; Major Robertson, commanding Military Train; Captain Hinde, H.M.'s 8th Regiment; Lieutenant-Colonel Wells, 23rd Fusiliers; Lieutenant-Colonel Gordon (93rd), commanding H.M.'s 53rd Regiment; Lieutenant-Colonel Hale, H.M.'s 82nd Regiment; Lieutenant-Colonel Leith Hay, 93rd Highlanders; Lieutenant-Colonel Hamilton, 78th Highlanders, commanding 1st battalion of detachments; Major Barnston, H.M.'s 90th Regiment, commanding 2nd battalion of detachments (dangerously wounded); and Captain Guise, H.M.'s 90th Regiment, who succeeded Major Barnston in his command.

Lieutenants Watson, Probyn, Younghusband, and Gough, respectively commanding detachments of the 1st, 2nd, and 5th Punjaub Cavalry and Hodson's Horse; Captain Green, commanding 2nd Punjaub Infantry; Lieutenant Willoughby, who succeeded to the command of the 4th Punjaub Infantry, on his three seniors in the corps being severely wounded;

Lieutenant Ryves, who commanded the 4th Punjaub Infantry from the evening of the 16th; Major Milman, 5th Fusiliers; and Lieutenant-Colonel M'Intyre, 78th Highlanders, in command of detachments employed in the advance on Dilkusha and the Martinière; Lieutenant-Colonel Ewart, 93rd Highlanders, who commanded at the barracks; Captains Dawson, 93rd Highlanders, Rolleston, H.M.'s 84th Regiment, and Hopkins, 53rd Regiment; and Lieutenants Fisher and Powlett, 2nd Punjaub Infantry, who commanded separate detachments or posts.

Captain Norman, the Assistant Adjutant-General; Colonel Berkeley, of H.M.'s 32nd; Major Alison, who unfortunately lost an arm, the Military Secretary; Captain Sir D. Baird, Bart., the Commander-in-Chief's principal aide-de-camp; Lieutenant Hope Johnstone, Deputy Assistant Adjutant-General to Major-General Mansfield, were the staff officers who particularly distinguished themselves. The following officers are also honourably mentioned:— Lieutenant G. Algood, Deputy Assistant Quarter-Master-General; Captains Maycock and Carey, Officiating Deputy Assistant Quarter-Master-General; Captain Rudman, Acting Assistant Adjutant-General, H. M.'s Forces; Captain Hatch, Deputy Judge-Advocate-General; Captains Alison and Forster, my Aides-de-Camp; Captain

Metcalfe, interpreter; and Lieutenant Murray, Aide-de-Camp to the Chief of the Staff.

Sir Colin Campbell thus speaks of the services rendered by Mr. Kavanagh, Lord Seymour, and the officers on the staff of Brigadier Hope Grant and other commanding officers:—

" Mr. Kavanagh, of the Uncovenanted Civil Service, who came out from Lucknow in disguise to afford me information at the imminent risk of his life, has won my most especial thanks, and I recommend him most cordially to the notice of your Lordship.

" Lord Seymour was present throughout these operations, and displayed a daring gallantry at a most critical moment.

" I concur most fully in the commendations that have been bestowed by General Grant and Officers Commanding Brigades on their respective Staffs as named below; but I would especially draw attention to the services of Captain Cox, H.M.'s 75th Regiment, Brigade Major of the 4th Brigade; and Lieutenant Roberts, Bengal Artillery, Deputy Assistant Quarter-Master-General; Captain W. Hamilton, H.M.'s 9th Lancers, Deputy Assistant Adjutant-General; Captain the Honourable A. H. Anson, H.M.'s 84th Regiment, Aide-de-Camp; and Lieutenant Salmond, 7th Light Cavalry, Acting Aide-de-Camp to Brigadier-General Grant.

" Captain H. Hammond, Bengal Artillery, Brigade-Major of Artillery (severely wounded); Captain H. Le G. Bruce, Bengal Artillery, who succeeded Captain

Hammond; Brevet-Major W. Barry and Lieutenant A. Bunny, Staff Officers of Royal and Bengal Artillery respectively: Lieutenant G. E. Watson, Bengal Engineers, Brigade-Major of Engineers; Captain H. A. Sarel, 17th Lancers, Brigade-Major of Cavalry; and Captains Bannatyne, H. M.'s 8th Foot, and Lightfoot, 84th Foot, Brigade-Majors of the 3rd and 5th Brigade; also Lieutenant P. Stewart, Bengal Engineers, Superintendent of the Electric Telegraph, who accompanied the force, and made himself particularly useful throughout.

"I must not omit to name, in the most marked manner, Soubadar Gokul Sing, 4th Punjaub Rifles, who, in conjunction with the British Officers, led the 4th Punjaub Rifles at the storming of Secundrabagh, in the most daring manner.

"Captain A. D. Dickens, Deputy Assistant Commissary-General, and Lieutenant W. Tod Brown, Deputy Commissary of Ordnance, have both distinguished themselves exceedingly in carrying on the intricate duties of their departments, with very scanty establishments, to meet the great demands upon them.

"Brigadier General Grant has made favourable mention of Surgeon J. C. Brown, M.D., Bengal Horse Artillery, whose great exertions have been deserving of all praise. He has since become Superintending Surgeon of the force."

Sir Colin thus concludes his despatch:—

"The number of Officers mentioned in this despatch may appear large; but the force employed was composed of many detachments, and the particular service was calculated to draw forth the individual qualities of the officers engaged."

The Commander-in-Chief's successes had not been won without heavy loss on his side: 122 officers and men were killed, and 345 wounded, of whom many subsequently died of their wounds; in all, 467 killed and wounded. Of these, 10 officers were killed, and 33 officers wounded. Sir Colin Campbell himself was wounded, but fortunately only slightly. The list of casualties contains the names of many gallant and brave officers who had covered themselves with glory; and among the wounded (of whom I trust most will live to have other opportunities of distinguishing themselves), I regret that I have not a list of the gallant non-commissioned officers and men, who had performed deeds of heroism even where all were brave.

The following is the nominal list of the officers who fell between the 16th and 18th of November, in the attacks on Secundrabagh, Shah Nudjuff, Messhouse, Observatory, and the adjacent buildings:—

KILLED.

"*General Staff.*—Lieutenant-Colonel G. Biddulph, Head of Intelligence Department, and Lieutenant A. O. Mayne, Deputy Assistant Quarter-Master-General.

"*Naval Brigade.*—Midshipman M. A. Daniel.

"*Artillery Brigade.*—Captain W. N. Hardy, Royal Artillery.

"*Cavalry Brigade.*—Captain G. Wheatcroft, 6th Dragoon Guards, doing duty with Military Train.

"*3rd Infantry Brigade.*—Lieutenant T. Frankland, 2nd Punjaub Infantry.

"*4th Ditto.*—Captain J. Dalzell, H. M.'s 93rd Highlanders; Captain J. T. Lumsden, 30th Native Infantry, Interpreter to H. M.'s 93rd Highlanders, and Lieutenant Dobbs, 1st Madras Fusiliers.

"*5th Ditto.*—Ensign W. T. Thompson, H. M.'s 82nd Regiment."

WOUNDED.

"*Staff.*—General Sir C. Campbell, G. C. B., Commander-in-Chief, slightly: Brigadier D. Russell, commanding 5th Brigade, severely; Major A. Alison, Military Secretary, severely; Captain F. M. Alison, A. D. C. to Commander-in-Chief, slightly; Captain the Honourable A. Anson, A. D. C., to General Grant, C. B., slightly; and Lieutenant C. J. Salmond, Orderly Officer to General Grant, C. B., slightly.

"*Naval Brigade.*—Captain J. C. Grant, Royal Marines, slightly; Lieutenant M. Salmon, Royal Navy, severely; and Midshipman Lord A. P. Clinton, Royal Navy, slightly.

"*Artillery Brigade.*—Major F. F. Pennycuick, Royal Artillery, slightly; Captain H. Hammond, Bengal Artillery, severely; Captain F. Travers, Royal Artillery, slightly; Lieutenants W. G. Milman and A. Ford, Royal

Artillery, slightly, and Assistant Surgeon H. R. Veale, Royal Artillery, severely.

"*Cavalry Brigade.*—Lieutenant R. Halkett, Hodson's Horse, severely.

"*3rd Infantry Brigade.*—Ensign J. Watson, 2nd Punjaub Infantry, dangerously.

"*4th Infantry Brigade.*—Captain B. Walton, H. M.'s 53rd Regiment, severely; Lieutenants A. K. Munro, H. M.'s 53rd Regiment, dangerously, and F. C. French, ditto, ditto, slightly; Major R. Barnston, H. M.'s 90th Regiment, dangerously; Lieutenant E. C. Wynne, H. M.'s 90th Regiment, severely; Ensign H. Powell, H. M.'s 90th Regiment, severely; Lieutenant-Colonel J. A. Ewart, H. M.'s 93rd Highlanders, slightly; Captain F. W. Burroughs, H. M.'s 93rd Highlanders, slightly; Lieutenants R. A. Cooper, H. M.'s 93rd Highlanders, severely; E. Welch, ditto, ditto, severely; O. Goldsmith, ditto, ditto, severely, and S. E. Wood, ditto, ditto, severely; Ensign F. R. M'Namara, ditto, ditto, slightly; Lieutenants W. Paul, 4th Punjaub Infantry, dangerously (since dead), J. W. M'Queen, ditto, ditto, severely, and F. F. Oldfield, ditto, ditto, dangerously (since dead).

"*5th Infantry Brigade.*—Lieutenant H. Henderson, H. M.'s 23rd Fusiliers, slightly, and Lieutenant-Colonel C. B. Hale, H. M.'s 82nd Regiment, slightly."

CHAP. XX.

THE RELIEF OF LUCKNOW.—EVACUATION OF THE RESIDENCY.

Lucknow relieved. — The Sweets of Liberty. — New Delights. — The Letter-bag. — Anxiety of my Friends. — Death of Mr. Cameron. — Mr. M'Rae. — Lieutenant Dashwood's sad End. — Brigadier Inglis. — Mr. Gubbins and Sir Colin Campbell. — Kindness of Mr. Gubbins to wounded Officers. — Mr. Gubbins at the Council of War. — Bursting of useless Guns. — Narrow Escape. — The Ladies, Children, and Wounded leave the Residency. — Mrs. Inglis's noble Act. — Her Description of the Ladies' Exodus. — Move upon the Kaiserbagh. — Strategic Manœuvre of Sir Colin Campbell. — Evacuation of Lucknow. — Freedom. — Manœuvres. — Services of the 9th Lancers. — The Commander-in-Chief's General Order. — His Acknowledgment of the Services of Non-military Men.

THE delight with which we hailed Sir Colin Campbell's army, was only equalled by that which we experienced on the arrival of General Havelock's gallant soldiers.

We were soon to be free — we were soon to taste the sweets of liberty again — we were to know what pleasures life had yet in store for us. An orange was brought in; it tasted deliciously. A loaf of bread and some fresh butter was given us. No epicure ever enjoyed a meal with greater relish than we did this simple food. Some rum was handed to us. The most exquisite liquor was never drunk with such real enjoyment.

But a still greater pleasure was yet to come. Several cart-loads of letters and newspapers had arrived. So long debarred from all intercourse with the rest of the world, we looked forward to news from our friends with the most painful anxiety. I was fortunate enough to receive about a dozen letters, and more were yet in the post office, which was crowded with anxious inquirers for letters to their address.

My poor brother had long thought me dead. He had written to half a dozen people at Lucknow to know what had become of me, and implored me, should I be still alive, to come down to Calcutta at once. There were letters from Europe, too;—from my parents, from my sister, from other friends, forwarded last July, and detained in the army post office for five months. They were anxious enough at home, but they had no idea of my being in the very midst of the dangers which had threatened India. The letters had been forwarded by my brother at Calcutta, and a letter of credit on a friend then at Cawnpore, was enclosed. This was fortunate, for I had no money, having been robbed, *by a friend,* of a bag containing a hundred rupees. I had no evidence to prove the theft, but I was convinced it was ——— who stole it.

Lady Inglis, in her journal, describes this period in simple but graphic terms:—

"To-day (18th Nov.) we have had a quantity of English letters, the first we have had for six months. The very sight of them made me feel quite bewildered, and I have not yet been able to read more than one. I need not say how much I have thought of you all—how many, many sad hearts and homes there must be in England just now; and really at present one cannot see an end to our troubles. The whole of Bengal is in such an unsettled state that no one can tell when or where a fresh disturbance may break out. Sir Colin is much liked; he is living now exactly as a private soldier, takes his rations, and lies down whenever he can to rest. This the men like, and he is a fine soldier. A Commander-in-Chief just now has indeed no enviable position."

Several of our companions in misfortune, however, who had survived the greatest dangers, and had even joined in the welcome to General Havelock's force, never shared these pleasures. Among these I must name Mr. R. Cameron, a gentleman of considerable means and great information, who died of dysentery, brought on by fatigue and bad living. He had visited Oude to inquire into the resources of the country, and had entered into some commercial speculations in conjunction with Captain W. W. Need, who had been killed in the beginning of the siege. During the siege he had been attached to the Post Office garrison, and had made himself particularly useful in volunteering for all sorts of fatigue parties and expeditions of danger. He had also, without any previously acquired knowledge of mortar practice, become an excellent artillery officer; and owing to the officers of that branch having been almost all killed or wounded, his services became very valuable. The shells thrown by both himself and Mr. Ward of the 48th Regiment were fired with beautiful precision.

Mr. M'Rae also, a civil engineer, was very useful as such, and as an officer of a mortar battery. He, too, was wounded no less than three times. A bullet at last shattered his arm, and amputation was recommended; but he refused to permit the operation, and he still lives, let us hope to live yet many years.

Another unfortunate was Lieutenant Dashwood of the 18th Native Infantry, whose brother had died in the beginning of the siege. He was taking a sketch of the shattered building of the Residency, when a round shot fired from across the river fractured both his legs. He lived long enough to hear of our relief, but died shortly after at Alumbagh.

Brigadier Inglis' activity, vigilance and skill had been unceasing throughout these long five months. His presence had animated the men, and every important operation was carried out under his very eye. His services were amply acknowledged by the generals who relieved us, but his deeds speak more eloquently than even the powerful language of General Outram and Sir Colin Campbell. England will not allow him to go unrewarded.*

Sir Colin Campbell's army remained in occupation of the positions they had taken outside, and we received orders to prepare for leaving,—orders which took many of us by surprise, for we hoped that the Government would not allow the city of Lucknow to remain in possession of the rebels, after all the difficulties and blood expended to enter it. Our noble deliverers had made immense sacrifices to relieve us, and it had cost as many lives as had been saved. The knowledge, however, of Sir Colin's move into Oude having been undertaken with no other view than to aid the beleaguered garrison, still further enhanced our gratitude.

The Commander-in-Chief visited us within our

* Since the above was written, Brigadier Inglis has been promoted to the well-merited honour of a K.C.B., and the rank of a Major-General.

entrenchments, and was welcomed by the authorities with due honour. Mr. Gubbins, among others, pressed forward to meet the General, who, according to what we then heard, was invited by him to a dinner, which was accepted. It is said there were champagne and claret, *saucisses aux truffes*, hermetically sealed, and truffled provisions of all kinds, vegetables and meat in plenty, provided for his excellency's palate; but Sir Colin, far from feeling pleased at the splendid repast spread out for him, refused to partake of it. "How is it, Mr. Gubbins, that these things were not given to the starving garrison?" were his words.

To do Mr. Gubbins justice, however, I must confess that he was not devoid of generosity. I have heard that, on one or two occasions, he had sent wine to the hospital, and it is undoubtedly a fact that several wounded officers received shelter and care at his quarters. Mr. Cameron died at his house; and Lieutenant Lester, Mr. Lucas, and many others, were tended with great solicitude and kindness by Mrs. Gubbins and other ladies in the house.

If a widely believed report is true, it was owing to his advice, and that of the late Mr. Ommaney, that the expedition to Chinhutt, whence all our subsequent misfortunes arose, was undertaken. Brigadier Inglis, at the council of war, where this move was proposed and finally determined upon, most strongly objected to it, and it was only on the distinct assurance of Mr. Gubbins, that the intelligence which he had received made such a manœuvre not only advisable but necessary, that the late Sir Henry Lawrence at last consented to it.

One of the greatest insults we received at the hands of the enemy was their playing, on the opposite banks of the Goomtee, regularly every morning, and sometimes of an evening, all our popular English airs. We listened to the "Standard Bearer's March," the "Girl I left behind me," and "See the Conquering Hero comes," with any but pleasant feelings. The disloyal rascals had even the impudence to finish their music with the loyal hymn "God save the Queen."

The women and children, and the sick were ordered to the Dilkusha encampment, where tents were pitched for them; while the men were obliged to stay behind for several days, to continue in guard of the various garrisons. Only a small amount of baggage was allowed for each person, and most of our things were, therefore, obliged to be left behind. Such a scene as the Residency then presented was really sad to behold. Women's apparel, children's clothes, rich dresses, men's waistcoats and coats, cooking utensils, plate, plated and china ware, all sorts of merchandise and household furniture, coverings, beddings:—each and everything was left behind. Anything might be had merely for the taking of it: and everywhere were seen, soldiers and civilians, helping themselves to what, but the day before, they would have paid large sums for. It was really annoying to think that the insurgents would, after all, obtain what we could not take away. Fortunately, our European articles of dress could have been of little use to them.

The guns had been removed from most of the batteries; and we were, therefore, to be particularly vigilant. Other guns, without carriages, formerly the property of the King of Oude, were burst. I had a narrow escape from the debris of one of them, a piece falling right between a friend and myself, making a large hole in the roof of the shed in which we were standing at the time.

The ordnance stores and the treasure were removed at the same time as the state prisoners and the families. Many delicate ladies had to walk over very rough ground, a distance of about six miles, but exposed at one place only to the fire of the enemy's musketry. Only one old lady was wounded in the leg. The rest all reached in safety. Mrs. Inglis, on this occasion, acted in a most noble manner. A dooly, or hospital litter, being prepared for her, she unhesitatingly refused it, saying that she was well able to walk, while so many wounded men and sick women were so much in want of a conveyance.

In her journal, Lady Inglis does not speak of this fact. She thus narrates the exodus of the weaker members of the garrison:—

"That evening (17th Nov.) the Commander-in-Chief sent an order for all the sick and wounded, women, and children to be moved out of the Residency to the Dilkoosha Park the next night, and for the force to abandon the place altogether, blow up the guns, destroy the ammunition, &c. The next day a change was made in the arrangements, and only the sick were sent away. We were detained till yesterday, when a general exodus took place of all the incumbrances in the garrison. In the meantime good news had arrived of fresh troops being in Oude, and a rumour went abroad that Lucknow was not to be abandoned. At about four o'clock P.M. we made a start, and left the place where we had passed so many anxious hours. John * could not accompany us, but sent his aide-de-camp, Captain Birch, a very nice creature, and a most gallant young officer; he is a great comfort to John, and they get on capitally together. We were obliged to walk, having no carriage horse, five of our horses were turned loose at the commencement of the siege; the road was quite safe, ex-

* Her husband, Brigadier Inglis.

cept in three places, where it was overlooked by the enemy's position, and we had to run; one poor woman was wounded in one of these places; we arrived at Secunde Bagh about six, and found everyone assembled there, awaiting an escort and doolies to carry us on. When I tell you that upwards of 2000 men had been hastily buried there the day before, you can fancy what a place it was; however, we met many friends, General Grant and several officers of the 9th Lancers, whom we knew; Captain Rudman, the old Adjutant of the 32nd, and Deighton Probyn came up and introduced himself to me; he is looking very well and handsome, we were regaled with tea and plenty of milk, and bread and butter —luxuries we had not enjoyed since the commencement of our troubles. At ten o'clock we recommenced our journey; most of the ladies were in palanquins, but we had a covered cart, drawn by two obstinate bullocks; we had a force of infantry and cavalry with us, but had not proceeded half a mile when the column was halted, and an order sent back for reinforcements; some noise was heard, and it was feared we might be attacked; however, it proved a false alarm, and after two disagreeable and rather anxious hours, we arrived safely at this place, and were quartered in some tents pitched for our reception; Colonel Little, 9th Lancers, took care of us. To-day we have pitched our own tent, and Mrs. Case, her sister, I, and the children occupy the half, having given the other to a poor sick lady. We are very comfortable, though rather pressed for room, and most thankful to breathe the fresh air once again; but I feel very lonely without my darling husband, and most anxious to know whether he will remain here, or go on with us to Cawnpore. A separation is inevitable, and my heart is very sad at the idea; for six months I have never spent a quiet day — hardly an hour in the day with him; still I saw him occasionally, and knew he was safe, which was an unspeakable comfort; now, I fear, I have many months of intense anxiety before me; but God has preserved him hitherto where dangers met him at every step, and I trust He will hear my prayers and spare us yet to live happily together."

We will now return to Sir Colin Campbell's movements.

On the 20th and 21st, Captain Peel, aided by Havelock's batteries in the palaces, breached the Kaiserbagh. The enemy, judging from our previous manœuvres, expected an immediate attack as soon as our bombardment should have ceased. Our shells continued to be thrown into the king's palace, however, the whole of that day. The firing was begun again next day, and lessened only on the 22nd, the day fixed upon for our evacuation. Our bombardment had evidently done a great deal of damage, and their fire, at first very lively, gradually slackened.

Piquets were thrown all around our positions, the men comprising them being constantly subject to annoyance from the enemy's fire, but all responded heartily to what was expected from them, and every man did his duty. We were thus enabled to effect the evacuation of Lucknow, according to the plan proposed by Sir Colin Campbell and Sir James Outram.

Nothing was left to chance, all was scientifically arranged and ably carried out. The evacuation of Lucknow in the face of an innumerable enemy, rendered desperate with rage and vexation, and burning for revenge at the numberless defeats he sustained, was a strategic manœuvre of which Sir Colin Campbell might well be proud. But that this should have been effected without the loss of a man, proves beyond a doubt that the present Commander-in-Chief of the Indian army may lay claims to rank in genius with generals of the highest celebrity.

It was twelve o'clock at night, on the 22nd of November, when we finally prepared to evacuate. I had gone to sleep for a couple of hours, and was woke up by a friend shaking me by my shoulder, and calling me by name. With a havresack by my side, my pouch and belt over my shoulders, and my musket in my hand, I was soon by the side of the other members of our garrison. The lights were left burning, and we stole out as quietly and silently as possible, the enemy keeping up the usual desultory fire of matchlocks and musketry.

There was one man left behind. Captain Waterman having gone to his bed in a retired corner of the Brigade mess-house, overslept himself. He had been forgotten. At two o'clock at night he got up, and found to his horror that we had already left. He hoped against hope, and visited every outpost. All was deserted and silent. To be the only man in an open entrenchment, and 50,000 furious barbarians outside! It was horrible to contemplate! His situation frightened him. He took to his heels, and he ran, ran, ran through the Feradbuksh and the Tehree Kothee till he could scarcely breathe. Still the same silence, the same stillness, interrupted but by the occasional report of the enemy's gun or musketry. At last he came up with the retiring rear guard, mad with excitement, breathless with fatigue. The horror of his position had been too much for his nerves, and affected his intellect for the time.

I must confess that there was a feeling of regret mixed up with the joy of at last being free. To leave the position which we had so long defended at last in the hands of the enemy, who was to have our batteries, and trenches, and mines, and who would rummage our chambers and residences, was a thought which none of us liked.

But we were in excellent spirits for all that, though it was a bitterly cold night. We had to pass through a narrow lane, and much out of the usual way, through a village and Secundrabagh, the scenes of the late glorious achievements of Sir Colin Campbell. When going past these buildings we had to hold our noses, the effluvium arising from the interior being anything but agreeable.

The old garrison was the first to pass through, " each exterior line retiring through its supports," and "the extreme posts on the left under Lieutenant-Colonel Hale, H.M.'s 82nd, Lieutenant-Colonel Wells, H.M.'s 23rd foot, and Lieutenant-Colonel Ewart, H.M.'s 93rd Highlanders, made their way by a road which had been explored for them, after the Commander-in-Chief considered that the time had arrived, with due regard to the security of the whole, that their posts should be evacuated."

Had the insurgents attacked us, they would have been met by the brigade of the Honourable Adrian Hope; but so far from this being necessary, the enemy continued firing into our old positions long after we had left them. The Commander-in-Chief himself accompanied the last line of infantry and guns, and thus ensured the safe retreat of the troops that had gone before.

Brigadier Little, commanding the Cavalry, and Major Ouvry, 9th Lancers, were indefatigable in keeping up the line of communication with Dilkusha; and "the officers commanding the Irregular Cavalry," says Sir Colin Campbell, "Lieutenants Watson, Younghusband, Probyn, and Gough, as well as all the officers of the 9th Lancers, were never out of the saddle all this time, and well maintained the character they have won throughout this war."

The Commander-in-Chief allowed us one day's rest at Dilkusha, and we encamped on the 23rd in a large park, where we had for the first time a dinner of which the gods might have envied us the enjoyment. The following General Orders by the Commander-in-Chief were circulated about this time. I copy them entire:—

"GENERAL ORDERS BY HIS EXCELLENCY THE COMMANDER-IN-CHIEF.

"*Head Quarters, Shah Nujeef, Lucknow, 21st November,* 1857.

"Although the Commander-in-Chief has not yet had time to peruse the detailed Report of Brigadier Inglis respecting the defence made by the slender garrison under his Command, His Excellency desires to lose no time in recording his opinion of the magnificent defence made by the remnant of a British Regiment, Her Majesty's 32nd, a Company of British Artillery, and a few hundred sepoys, whose very presence was a subject of distrust, against all the force of Oude, until the arrival of the reinforcement under Major-General Sir J. Outram, G. C. B., and Sir H. Havelock, K. C. B.

"2. The persevering constancy of this small garrison, under the watchful command of the Brigadier, has, under Providence, been the means of adding to the prestige of the British Army and of preserving the honour and lives of our country-women.

"There can be no greater reward than such a reflection; and the Commander-in-Chief heartily congratulates Brigadier Inglis and his devoted garrison on that reflection belonging to them.

"3. The position occupied by the garrison was an open entrenchment, the numbers were not sufficient to man the defences, and the supply of artillery-men for the guns was most inadequate. In spite of these difficult circumstances, the Brigadier and his garrison held on; and it will be a great pleasure to the Commander-in-Chief to bring to the notice of the Government of India the names of all the officers and soldiers who have distinguished themselves during the great trial to which they have been exposed.

"4. The Commander-in-Chief congratulates Sir James Outram and Sir Henry Havelock on having been the first to aid Brigadier Inglis.

"The Governor-General in Council has already expressed his opinion on the splendid feat of arms by which that aid was accomplished."

"*Head Quarters, Shah Nujeef, 22nd November,* 1857.

" When the Commander-in-Chief issued his Order of yesterday with regard to the old garrison of Lucknow, His Excellency was unaware of the important part taken in aid of the soldiers by the civil functionaries who happened to be at the Residency when it was shut in by the enemy.

" 2. His Excellency congratulates them very heartily on the honour they have won in conjunction with their military comrades. This is only another instance that in danger and difficulty all Englishmen behave alike, whatever their profession."

" *Head Quarters, La Martinière Lucknow, 23rd November,* 1857.

" The Commander-in-Chief has reason to be thankful to the force he conducted for the relief of the garrison of Lucknow.

" 2. Hastily assembled, fatigued by forced marches, but animated by a common feeling of determination to accomplish the duty before them, all ranks of this force have compensated for their small number, in the execution of a most difficult duty, by unceasing exertions.

" 3. From the morning of the 16th till last night, the whole force has been one outlying piquet, never out of fire, and covering an immense extent of ground, to permit the garrison to retire scatheless and in safety, covered by the whole of the relieving force.

" 4. That ground was won by fighting as hard as it ever fell to the lot of the Commander-in-Chief to witness, it being necessary to bring up the same men over and over again to fresh attacks; and it is with the greatest gratification that His Excellency declares he never saw men behave better.

"5. The storming of the Secundrabagh and the Shah Nujeef has never been surpassed in daring, and the success of it was most brilliant and complete.

"6. The movement of retreat of last night, by which the final rescue of the garrison was effected, was a model of discipline and exactness. The consequence was, that the enemy was completely deceived, and the force retired by a narrow, tortuous lane, the only line of retreat open, in the face of 50,000 enemies, without molestation.

"7. The Commander-in-Chief offers his sincere thanks to Major-General Sir James Outram, G. C. B., for the happy manner in which he planned and carried out his arrangements for the evacuation of the Residency of Lucknow.

"By Order of His Excellency the Commander-in-Chief.

"W. MAYHEW, *Major.*
"*Deputy Adjutant-General of the Army.*"

CHAP. XXI.

CONCLUSION.

Civilian Guard on the State Prisoners. — Our Escort. — Sir James Outram's Column remains at Alumbagh. — Mournful Death of General Havelock. — Gratitude and Sorrow of the British Nation. — Captain Havelock. — March from the Alumbagh. — A weary Journey. — Fatigue and Anxiety. — Wyndham's Defeat. — Sir Colin's opportune Arrival saves our Cawnpore Entrenchment. — The Gwalior Rebels occupy the Station of Cawnpore. — The Late General Wheeler's Entrenchments. — Sad Mementos of Sufferings. — Recollections of Sir Hugh Wheeler. — Our Communications with the Town cut off. — Our Entrenchment on the Ganges. — A Friend's Escape from the Scenes of Rebellion. — The only Survivor of the Futtygurh Massacre. — Warm Reception at Allahabad. — My Arrival at Calcutta.

OUR military duties did not yet cease. A number of civilians, among whom I was one, were told off as a guard on the state prisoners. One of them, Rooknaood-Dowlah, had died previous to the Commander-in-Chief's arrival; and another, the Rajah of Toolseepore, expired on the way to the Alumbagh. The whole of Brigadier-General Hope Grant's division served us as an escort to Alumbagh, Sir Colin himself heading it, while Sir James Outram was left with his division at Dilkusha, to prevent any possible molestation from the enemy.

On the 25th an event happened which detracted not a little from the joy we were then experiencing. The gallant, the noble, the undaunted Havelock died at Dilkusha, of dysentery, caused by over-exertion and fatigue. It appeared as if he had strained every nerve to accomplish one object, and, having seen its accomplishment, succumbed to the prostration which the exertion had entailed. Havelock expired at the very time when the people of England with one voice proclaimed him entitled to the highest honour a nation can bestow, when his name was in every one's mouth, and when we of the old Lucknow garrison— grateful as we felt towards the gallant old commander who had rescued us from immediate peril, and who afterwards shared our privations, dangers, and discomforts for two months longer— should have been still more happy had we seen him able to enjoy the honours in store for him. Yet the knowledge of having a place in the affections of the British nation, and the gratitude of every European in India, must have been, even on his deathbed, a sufficient reward. His brevet of K. C. B. reached him only a very few days before his death.

Havelock had been a good and a religious man. He had always family worship, and never undertook an expedition without having previously implored the Divine aid. It was this confidence in Providence which made him go on to assured victory, and to conquer every difficulty in his way.

The British nation will not fail to confer on the son some of the well-earned honours of the father, so that the name may be transmitted to the latest posterity.* Captain Henry Marshman Havelock inherits not a few of the General's virtues and abilities.

We left Alumbagh suddenly, on the receipt by Sir Colin of some important message from Cawnpore. And never shall I forget that long, long, weary, weary march. To walk fifteen miles continuously, scarcely interrupted by a short ride on the back of a camel, or on the top of a primitive hackery, to arrive at an encamping ground tired to exhaustion (for, after our long sojourn in Lucknow, none of us could boast of a strong constitution), without knowing

---

* This hope has been fulfilled. Capt. Havelock has been advanced to the dignity of a Baronet, with a pension of 1000*l.* a year and the rank of a major in the army. His mother, Lady Havelock, has also received a pension of 1000*l.* a year.

where to lay one's head, was bad enough for a man, but for a delicate lady it must have been terrible indeed.

But we were not long allowed to remain at our second encamping ground. A few hours, and another still longer march was begun. On, on we went, in one long, long line,— certainly not less than seven or eight miles in length, and over a distance of more than thirty miles, till we arrived a very short way from the Cawnpore bridge of boats. Some bad news had gone before, and we heard the booming of cannon at a distance. What could it mean? A large fire, too, was visible, and, as we approached, we found ourselves in the midst of war again.

Brigadier Wyndham had been defeated, and the station of Cawnpore, on the other side of the canal, was in entire possession of a large army of Gwalior rebels, headed by Nana Sahib, Koer Sing, and other insurgent chiefs.

But for the rapidity of Sir Colin Campbell's movements and his superior generalship, the bridge of boats would have been lost, and we should have been cut off from all communication with the other side, with an enemy in our front and another in our rear. The rebel Mahrattas had actually brought some guns to bear upon our troops, but our artillery silenced them before others could be conveyed to the river's edge. Sir Colin Campbell had saved the Cawnpore entrenchments. He remedied the mistakes of the "hero of the Redan." Still the enemy held the station; and in our encamping ground near the Artillery Barracks, where we remained for five days, a few shells occasionally favoured us with a visit.

The house where the Nana's ruffians had slaughtered our women was in the hands of the enemy, but all the ground this side of the canal remained in our hands.

I went to see the position occupied by the late General Sir Hugh Wheeler. A more mournful sight can scarcely be imagined. The barracks which he had so gallantly defended, dignified with the name, but not the strength of "entrenchments," were even more battered to pieces than our own at Lucknow had been.

The walls were scribbled over in many places by the unfortunate sufferers. In one place was written, "Here a round shot came and killed young Wheeler. His brains and hair are scattered on the wall."

At another place were the words, "This is worse than the siege of Jerusalem — My God, my God, when wilt thou deliver us?" At another, again, "Countrymen, revenge our deaths!"

One sentence, scarcely legible, written by one of my friends, the late Post-Master of Cawnpore, ran thus:--

> "4th June, wounded in the thigh.
> 6th „   ditto leg, bullet.
> —   —   ——   — fractured.
> — shell — — all this and still alive."   "L. ROCHE."

What misery the Cawnpore martyrs must have endured. Poor Sir Hugh Wheeler, too! He, two of his sons, his wife, and his daughters, had been fellow passengers of mine in the Bentinck, when I returned from a voyage to Europe three years ago. I thought of the good old gentleman, who had shown me particular kindness, and pictured to myself the horrible scenes in which he and his devoted band fell victims. I left the place sad and melancholy.

All communications with the town were cut off, and it was difficult for us to obtain provisions; but our force evidently held the enemy in check, and neither in the camp which we occupied, nor in the fortified entrenchment on the banks of the Ganges, were we seriously molested.

Indeed, I visited the latter frequently, and had the pleasure of meeting an old friend there, a Mr. Briant, who had been saved from all the dangers of the first outbreaks by the greatest good fortune in the world. He had run before the storm which had threatened to overtake him. From Bareilly, two days before the murder of Messrs. Robertson, Orr, and others, he escaped with his family to Futtygurh, arrived there a couple of days before the mutiny of the 10th Native Infantry, and reached Cawnpore thirty-six hours before the outbreak, succeeded in persuading his wife's family to quit that devoted place, and was just in time — within a few minutes — to make his escape in a steamer to Calcutta from Allahabad, when the outrages there commenced, by which so many Europeans lost their lives.

I had also the pleasure of meeting another old acquaintance, Mr. Gavin Jones, the only survivor of all the defenders of the Futtygurh station. On the abandonment of the fort by the Europeans, Mr. Jones found himself in the boat which was attacked by the natives. He was the only one saved, and escaped, with a bullet-wound, to the other boats, where he met with the greatest kindness, had fresh linen given to him, and a meal prepared. Instead, however, of accompanying the sixty persons who were passengers in the boats to Cawnpore, where they were eventually all slaughtered, Mr. Jones, rendered reckless by despair at his and his companions' condition, and the death by a wound, of his brother, who had fallen at his very feet, walked into a village alone, with a view of being killed. But instead of meeting death, the zemindar owning the estate protected him, and, on the recapture of Cawnpore, sent him to that station. I spent two or three happy days in the company of these friends, notwithstanding the fire of the enemy.

At last, however, we left, only a couple of hours' notice being given us. Our escort consisted of but 500 men of the 34th; but, making long forced marches, we escaped all the dangers of the road, which were not a few, and arrived at Allahabad by railway from Chimmey. There we met with the most enthusiastic reception. I had friends, and was kindly received by them. Collector Jones, Vincent, and others, could not have been kinder. My uncovenanted Lucknow companions, however, did not fare half so well. The authorities obliged them to leave the comfortable barracks at first assigned for them, and then made them remove into cold, small cooking tents, pitched outside the fort.

Of my Agent Archer's fate, no doubt remained. Our property could no longer be traced; and of what I had possessed there, a few broken articles and empty cases were all that remained.

Before leaving, I had the satisfaction, however, of

hearing of Sir Colin Campbell's victories over the Nana's army. He had only waited for our departure to attack and rout them.

Notwithstanding the persuasions of my friends to the contrary, I ventured, in company with my friend Briant, to leave for Calcutta by dak (post), in a carriage by ourselves, meeting at Benares with an equally kind reception.

My adventures closed on my arrival at Calcutta, where I had the unspeakable pleasure of again shaking my dear brother by the hand.

POSTSCRIPT.

I am enabled, before going to press, to add that the last mail (25th January) brought the news, supplied by the *Calcutta Englishman*, of the murder of the prisoners, Sir Mountstuard Jackson, Captain Patrick Orr, Lieutenant Burnes, and Sergeant Norton, and the death of little Miss Christian. Mrs. Orr and Miss Madeleine Jackson are still alive.

APPENDIX.

List

OF

OFFICERS AND NON-MILITARY MEN
AND THEIR FAMILIES

PRESENT BEFORE AND DURING THE WHOLE OF THE

SIEGE OF LUCKNOW.

Abbott, Mrs., and child (*child dead*).

Aitkin, Lieut. and Quartermaster, 13th Native Infantry, and wife.

Alexander, Clare, 1st Lieut. Artillery (*killed*).

Alexander, J., 2nd Lieut. Artillery (*wounded*).

Allnut, Clerk in Bank, wife (*dead*), and four children (*one dead*).

Alone, A., Mr. (*wounded*), Innes' Outpost, and sister.

Alone, B., Uncovenanted Service, Innes' Outpost, and mother (*wounded*).

Anderson, Major, Civil Engineers (*dead*).

Anderson, 25th Native Infantry, wife (*dead*), and two children (*one child dead*).

Anderson, J. C., Lieutenant Engineers.

Anderson, Mrs. Dr.

Anthony, David, Uncovenanted Service, Financial Garrison.

Apthorp, Major, 41st Native Infantry, wife, and child (*dead*).

APPENDIX.

Archer, Mr. (Martiniere), wife, and two children.
Arno, Miss.
Arthur, Lieutenant, 7th Light Cavalry (*killed*).

Bailey, G. (*wounded*).
Balley, Mrs., and two children.
Banks, Major, Provisional Chief Commissioner (*killed*), wife and child.
Barbor, Adjutant, 2nd Oude Cavalry (*killed*), and wife.
Barfoot, Mrs.
Barlow, Captain, Brigade Major Oude Irregular Force (*dead*), and wife.
Barnett, Mrs., and child.
Barrett, Uncovenanted Service (*dead*), wife and three children (*one child dead*).
Barry, Mr., Uncovenanted Service.
Barsotelli, Signor, of Calcutta.
Bartrum, Mrs., and child (*dead*).
Barwell, Lieutenant, Fort Adjutant, Major of Brigade, wife and child.
Bassano, Captain, Her Majesty's 32nd (*wounded*).
Bates, A., Uncovenanted Service, and wife.
Bax, Lieutenant, Second in Command, 1st Oude Cavalry (*killed* in district).
Baxter, Uncovenanted Service (*dead*); wife and three children (*one child dead*).
Beale, Uncovenanted Service (*killed*); wife and two children (*all dead*).
Bell, Overseer, mother-in-law (*killed*); wife and child.
Benson, Mr., Deputy Commissioner; wife and child (*child dead*).
Best, Uncovenanted Service, Judicial Garrison; wife and child (*child dead*).

LIST OF OFFICERS, ETC.

Bickers, Uncovenanted Service (*wounded*); wife and three children.
Birch, F. W., Lieutenant 71st, Aide-de-Camp (*slightly wounded*).
Birch, Mr. H. H., Uncovenanted Service, and Miss Birch.
Birch, Lieutenant, 59th Native Infantry (*killed*), and wife.
Bird, Dr., Assistant Surgeon.
Bird, Major, 48th Native Infantry.
Bird, Mrs., and two children (*one child dead*).
Blaney, P., Sagos Garrison (*wounded*).
Blaney, C., Bhoosa Garrison (*wounded*), Uncovenanted Service, wife and nephew.
Blenman, Uncovenanted Service (*wounded*), and mother.
Blunt, Clerk, Judicial Garrison, and wife.
Blythe, Uncovenanted Service, wife and child (*child dead*).
Boileau, Mrs., widow of Mr. Boileau of the Civil Service, and four children (*one dead*).
Boileau, Captain T. F., 7th Light Cavalry, 2nd in Command Volunteer Corps (*wounded*), wife and two children.
Bonham, 2nd Lieut Artillery (*wounded four times*).
Boulderson, Mr. Assistant Commissioner (*slightly wounded*).
Boulton, Lieutenant, 2nd Light Cavalry (*killed* in District).
Bowhear, Miss.
Boyd, Assistant-Surgeon, 32nd Regiment.
Brackenbury, Lieutenant, 32nd Regiment (*killed*).
Brandoff, Mrs.
Brett, Mrs., and child (*child dead*).
Brown, C., Clerk, Sagos' Garrison (*killed*).
Brown, J., Clerk, Anderson's Garrison (*killed*).
Brown, W., Uncovenanted Service, and wife.
Brown, Apothecary's Apprentice, Her Majesty's 32nd (*wounded*).

Browne, Oswin, Uncovenanted Service (*dead*), and wife.
Browne, G., Lieutenant, 32nd Regiment (*wounded*).
Browne, Miss.
Bruere, Major, 13th Native Infantry (*killed*), wife and four children.
Burmester, Captain, 48th Native Infantry (*killed* in District).
Bryce, 2nd Lieutenant Artillery (*wounded, dead*).
Brydon, Surgeon, 71st Native Infantry (*wounded*), wife and two children.
Bryson, Alexander, Uncovenanted Service, Sagos' Garrison (*killed*), wife and four children (*one child dead*).
Burnett, Mrs., and child.

Cameron, of Allahabad (*dead*).
Cameron, Mr. R., of Calcutta (*dead*).
Campagnac, C., Uncovenanted Service, wife and daughter.
Campagnac, Lieut., late King's Service, wife and daughter.
Campbell, W., Ensign, 71st Native Infantry.
Campbell, C. W., Lieut., 71st Native Infantry (*wounded*).
Campbell, W., Ensign, 71st Native Infantry.
Campbell, Surgeon, 7th Light Cavalry (*killed*).
Cane, Mrs., and three children.
Capper, Mr., Civil Service, Deputy Commissioner.
Carnegie, Capt., Provost-Marshal.
Case, Lieut.-Col., 32nd Regiment of Foot (*killed*), wife and sister.
Casey, Uncovenanted Service (*dead*); wife and five children, (*one child dead*).
Catania, C., Volunteer.
Catania, T., Uncovenanted Service, and mother.
Chambers, Lieut., Adjutant 13th Native Infantry (*wounded*).
Charlton, Ensign, 32nd Regiment (*wounded*).
Chrestien, Uncovenanted Service, and wife.
Clancey, Mrs., and two children.

LIST OF OFFICERS, ETC.

Chick, late Sub-Editor of "Central Star," Judicial Garrison, wife and two children (*one child dead*).
Clancey, Uncovenanted Service, Judicial Garrison (*killed*).
Clarke, Stanley, Lieut. First Oude Infantry, and wife.
Clarke, Mrs., and child (*both dead*).
Clarke, J. Longueville, Lieutenant, Second in Command, 2nd Oude Irregular Infantry (*killed in district*).
Clarke, Miss.
Clery, Lieutenant, Her Majesty's 32nd.
Collins, Mr. R. M., Uncovenanted Service, Civil Dispensary, wife and child (*both dead*).
Collins, W., Assistant to Mr. F. Deprat.
Connell, Mrs., and child.
Cook, Lieut. 32nd Regiment (*wounded*).
Cook, Mrs., and four children (*one child dead*).
Couper, Mr. G., Civil Service, Secretary to Commander-in-Chief, wife and three children.
Court, Mrs., (Sergt.) and two children.
Crabb, Uncovenanted Service (*killed*).
Crank, Mr., (Martiniere).
Cubitt, Lieut. 13th Native Infantry (*wounded*).
Cunliffe, 2nd Lieutenant Artillery (*killed*).
Cunliffe, Mr., Civil Service (*killed in district*).
Curtain, Mrs., and three children.
Curwan, Mrs., and child.

Dacosta, Mrs.
Dallicott, Hospital Apprentice, Her Majesty's 32nd (*killed*).
Darby, Assistant Surgeon, 10th Oude Infantry.
Darrah, Lieutenant, 41st Native Infantry, wife and two children.
Dashwood, Lieutenant, 48th Native Infantry (*dead*), wife and three children (*one child dead*).
Dashwood, Ensign, 18th Native Infantry (*killed*).

Deprat, Mr. F., Merchant (*killed*).
Derozario, Mrs.
De Verrine, Mr. (Martiniere).
Dias, Uncovenanted Service, and wife.
Dinning, Captain, 71st Native Infantry.
Dodd, Mr. (Martiniere).
Donnithorne, Uncovenanted Service, Financial Garrison, wife and two children (*one child dead*).
Dorin, Mrs. (*killed*).
Dorrett, R., Uncovenanted Service, Financial Garrison.
Dubois, Uncovenanted Service, and wife.
Dudman, E., Uncovenanted Service, mother, wife, and three children (*two children dead*).
Duffy, Mrs., and child.
Duhan, Mr., Volunteer.

Edgehill, Captain, Military Secretary, wife and one child.
Edmonstone, Lieutenant, 32nd Regiment (*wounded*).
Eldridge, Riding Master, 7th Light Cavalry (*killed*).
Ereth, Mr., Railway Contractor (*killed*), wife (*wounded*).
Evans, Mrs. (*dead*).
Ewart, Clerk, Judicial Garrison.

Farquhar, Lieutenant, 7th Light Cavalry (*wounded*).
Farquharson, Lieutenant, 48th Native Infantry (*killed*).
Fayrer, Mr., Volunteer, Oude Irregular Force (*killed*).
Fayrer, Assistant Surgeon, Residency Surgeon, wife and child.
Fernandes (Uncovenanted Service).
Fitzgerald, W. E., Uncovenanted Service, wife, mother, and three children (*one child dead*).
Fitzgerald, Mrs., and child.
Fletcher, Lieutenant, 48th Native Infantry (*wounded*).
Forbes, Captain 1st Oude Cavalry (*slight wound*), wife and three children (*two children dead*).
Forbes (Uncovenanted Service), and mother.

Forder, W., Mr., Postmaster, Post Office Garrison.
Forester, Clerk (*wounded*).
Foster, Lieutenant, 32nd Regiment (*wounded, recovered*).
Francis, Major R.B., Commanding Muchee Bhawn (*killed*).
French, (Uncovenanted Service).
Fullerton, Lieutenant, 44th Native Infantry (*dead*), wife and child (*child dead*).
Fulton Captain, Garrison Engineer (*killed*).

Gabriel, Uncovenanted Service, wife and three children.
Gall, Major, 2nd Oude Cavalry (*killed*), and wife.
Gamboa (*deserted*), and mother.
Gardner, Miss (*wounded*).
Garland, Mr. R., Uncovenanted Service, Extra Assistant Commissioner (*dead*), wife and child.
Garrett, Mrs. and two children.
Germon, Captain, 13th Native Infantry, and wife.
Giddings, Paymaster 32nd Regiment, and wife.
Gordon, Mr. J., Uncovenanted Service, Judicial Garrison, wife and two children.
Graham, Lieutenant, Adjutant 1st Oude Cavalry (*dead*), wife, two children (*one child dead*).
Graham, Lieutenant, 3rd Oude Irregular Cavalry (*wounded*).
Grant, Lieutenant, 71st Native Infantry (*killed*).
Grant, Lieutenant, Bombay Army, 2nd in command 5th Oude Infantry (*killed*); wife and child (*both dead*).
Grant, Mrs. (Sergeant).
Graves, Lieutenant, 41st Native Infantry (*dead*).
Gray, Brigadier, Oude Irregular Force.
Graydon, Lieutenant, Commanding 7th Oude Infantry (*killed*).
Green, Captain, 48th Native Infantry, and wife (*dead*).
Green, Ensign, 13th Native Infantry (*dead*).
Greenhow, Assistant-Surgeon Oude Irregular Force.

Griffiths, Mrs. (Sergeant), and three children.
Gubbins, Mr. M. R., Financial Commissioner, and wife.

Hadow, Surgeon, 5th Oude Infantry.
Hale, Mrs., and child (*both dead*).
Halford, Colonel, 71st Native Infantry (*dead*), wife and daughter.
Hamilton, W., wife and three children (*two children dead*).
Hampton, Miss.
Handscombe, Brigadier, Commanding Oude Brigade (*killed*).
Hardinge, Lieutenant, Oude Irregular Force, Deputy-Assistant-Quarter-Master-General (*wounded*).
Hardingham, F., Uncovenanted Service, and mother.
Harmer, Lieutenant, 32nd Regiment (*wounded*).
Harris, Rev. H. P., Assistant Chaplain, and wife.
Hawes, Captain, 5th Oude Infantry (*wounded*).
Hay, Lieutenant, 48th Native Infantry (*wounded*).
Hayes, Captain Fletcher, Military Secretary (*killed*), wife and child.
Hearsey, Captain W., Oude M. Pol.
Hely, Veterinary Surgeon, 7th Light Cavalry (*killed*).
Hembro, Uncovenanted Service, wife and three children.
Hernon, Mrs., and four children.
Hewitt, Ensign, 41st Native Infantry (*wounded*).
Higgins, Apothecary, Her Majesty's 32nd, wife (*dead*), and two sisters.
Hill, Mr. James, (Merchant).
Hilton, (Martiniere), wife and two children.
Hoff, Edward, Uncovenanted Service, Sagos' Garrison, wife and child (*child dead*).
Horan, Mrs. (*killed*), and three children (*one child dead*).
Horn, Mrs., and three children.
Howard, B.

Hughes, Capt., 4th Oude Infantry (*killed*).
Hutchinson, Lieut., attached to Engineers.
Hutton, Uncovenanted Service.
Huxham, Lieut., 48th Native Infantry (*wounded*); wife and two children (*one child dead*).
Hyde, Apothecary (*wounded*); wife and two children.

James, Lieutenant, Deputy-Assistant Commissary-General (*wounded*).
Jeoffroy, Mr., of Calcutta.
Inglis, Brigadier, Commanding Garrison, wife and three children.
Inglis, H., Lieutenant, 41st Native Infantry (*wounded*).
Inglis, Ensign, 63rd Native Infantry.
Innes, McLeod, Lieutenant, Engineers.
Johannes, Merchant, wife and child.
Johnson, Uncovenanted Service.
Jones, Uncovenanted Service, and wife.
Jones, T. E. (*deserted*).
Joseph, Mrs., and three children.
Joyce, W., Uncovenanted Service, Judicial Garrison, wife and child.
Joyce, R., Uncovenanted Service, Judicial Garrison.
Ireland, G., Uncovenanted Service, wife and child.
Ireland, W.

Kavanagh, H., Uncovenanted Service, wife and four children (*one child dead*).
Keir, Lieutenant, 41st Native Infantry.
Kemble, Captain, 41st Native Infantry (*wounded*).
Kendall, Mrs., and child (*child dead*).
Kennedy, Mrs. and Miss.
Keogh, Mrs., (Sergt.) and five children (*three children dead*).

Kight, Mr. Fitz-Herbert, Editor of "Central Star;" Local Serjeant Financial Garrison.
Kingsley, wife of Sergeant Kingsley, and four children.

Langmore, Lieutenant, Adjutant 71st Native Infantry.
Lawrence, Sir H. M., Chief Commissioner of Oude, K.C.B. (*killed*).
Lawrence, Mr., Civil Service, Deputy Commissioner (*wounded*).
Lawrence, Lieutenant, H. M. 32nd.
Lawrence, John, Uncovenanted Service, wife and two children (*one child dead*).
Leach, Mr. F., Civil Apothecary, Civil Dispensary.
Leslie, Uncovenanted Service, and wife.
Lester, Lieutenant, 32nd Native Infantry (*killed*).
Lewin, 2nd Lieutenant (*killed*); wife and two children.
Lincoln, Uncovenanted Service, wife and child.
Longden, Mrs. (Sergeant).
Longton, Mrs. and child.
Loughnan, Lieutenant, 13th Native Infantry.
Lowe, Major, Commanding 32nd Regiment (*wounded*).
Luxted, Pensioner, Uncovenanted Service, wife and daughter.
Lynch, Mrs. (Sergeant), and child.

Mahar, Mrs. (Sergeant), and two children.
Mansfield, Captain, Her Majesty's 32nd (*dead*).
Manton, Mrs. (Sergeant).
Marley, Mrs. and child.
Marriott, Major, Pension Paymaster, and wife.
Marshall, W., Opium Contractor (*killed*), and wife.
Marshall, Miss.
Marshall, J., Mr., Supervisor, Post Office, wife and child.

LIST OF OFFICERS, ETC.

Martin, Lieutenant, 7th Light Cavalry (*killed*).
Martin, Mr., Deputy Commissioner, wife and two children (*dead*).
Martin, Bandmaster, P. O., and wife.
Martiniere College, about fifty boys (*a few wounded and dead*).
Master, Lieutenant-Colonel, 7th Light Cavalry.
May, W., Uncovenanted Service, Engineers, P. O.
McAuliff, Uncovenanted Service (*killed*).
McCabe, Captain, Her Majesty's 32nd Foot (*killed*).
McDonald, Surgeon, 4th Native Infantry (*dead*).
McDonnough, Mrs., and two children.
McFarlane, 2nd Lieutenant Artillery (*wounded*).
McGrath, Ensign, Her Majesty's 84th Regiment.
McGregor, Ensign, 41st Native Infantry (*dead*).
McGrennan, Uncovenanted Service, Civil Dispensary, and wife.
McLean, Captain, 71st Native Infantry (*killed*).
Macmanus, Uncovenanted Service (*killed*).
Mecham, Lieutenant, Adjutant 7th Oude Infantry.
Mendes, Uncovenanted Service (*killed*), and wife (*dead*).
Miller, Mrs., and four children.
Mitchell, Uncovenanted Service.
Molloy, Mrs., and five children.
Morgan, J. J., Uncovenanted Service, Artillery (*wounded*), and wife.
Morton, Mrs., and child (*child dead*).
Morton, Mrs., and two children (*both children dead*).

Nazareth, Uncovenanted Service, wife (*dead*) and two children.
Need, Captain W. W., merchant, (*killed*), wife and three children.
Nepean, Miss.

Nugent, Mrs., Senior.
Nugent, Mrs., Jun., and three children.

O'Brien, Lieutenant, Her Majesty's 84th (*wounded*).
O'Dowda, Ensign, 48th Native Infantry (*wounded*).
Ogilvy, Surgeon, Sanitary Commissioner, and wife.
Oliver, Overseer, Magazine (*wounded*), wife and two children.
Ommaney, Mr., Judicial Commissioner (*killed*), and wife.
Ommaney, two Misses.
Orr, Adolphe, Captain, Oude Military Police, wife and child.
Ouseley, Lieutenant, 48th Native Infantry, wife and three children (*two dead*).
Overitt, Apothecary, 32nd Regiment.
Overitt, R., Jun, Apothecary's Apprentice, Hospital 32nd Regiment.
Owen, ——, Uncovenanted Service.
Owen, Alfred.

Palmer, Lieut.-Colonel, 48th Native Infantry, and daughter (*killed*).
Parry, Secretary of the Delhi Bank, wife and four children.
Partridge, Assistant Surgeon, Oude Irregular Force.
Pearce, Uncovenanted Service, Artillery, wife and two children.
Pedron, Mrs.
Pelling, Mrs.
Peters, Mrs.
Peuder, Mrs., and four children.
Pew, Senior, Uncovenanted Service, and wife.
Pew, A., Junior, Uncovenanted Service, wife and two children (*one child dead*).
Phillips, Uncovenanted Service, Judicial Garrison, and wife.
Phillips, W., Uncovenanted Service, wife and child.
Pidgeon, Uncovenanted Service, Judicial Garrison (*killed*), and wife.

LIST OF OFFICERS, ETC.

Pitt, Surgeon, 13th Native Infantry, and wife.
Polehampton, Rev. H. S., Assistant Chaplain (*dead*), and wife.
Potter, Clerk, Judicial Garrison.
Power, Captain, Her Majesty's 32nd Regiment (*killed*).
Purcell, Mrs., and child.

Queiros, F., Uncovenanted Service, wife and child.
Queiros, E., Junior, Uncovenanted Service.
Queiros, A.

Radcliffe, Captain, 7th Light Cavalry, commanding Volunteer Corps (*killed*), wife and three children (*one child dead*).
Rae (Pleader), (*wounded*), and wife.
Raleigh, Cornet, 7th Light Cavalry (*killed*).
Ramsay, Telegraph Office (*killed*), and wife.
Rees, L. E., Mr., of Calcutta, Innes' Outpost.
Reilly, Mrs., and child (*child dead*).
Rennick, Mrs.
Roberts, Miss.
Robinson, Miss.
Rodgers, Miss.
Ruggles, Lieutenant, 41st Native Infantry, and wife.
Rutledge, Uncovenanted Service (*wounded*), wife and two children.
Ryder, Mrs. (Sergt.)

Sago, Mrs.
Samson, Mrs.
Sanders, Capt., 41st Native Infantry.
Sangster, Uncovenanted Service, sister, wife, and two children.
Savaille, Miss.
Schilling, Mr., (Principal, Martiniere,) and sister.
Schmidt, R. (*wounded, since dead*).
Scott, Surgeon, 32nd Regiment.

Scott, Mrs., and child (*child dead*).
Sewell, Lieut., 71st Native Infantry.
Sequera, J., Senior, Uncovenanted Service, Invalids, and wife (*killed*).
Sequera, Edwin, Uncovenanted Service (*killed*), and sister.
Sequera, H., Uncovenanted Service.
Sequera, C., Bhoosa Garrison (*wounded*).
Sexton, Mrs.
Sheppard, Lieut., 2nd in command 2nd Oude Cavalry (*killed*).
Simons, Capt., Artillery (*killed*).
Sinclair, J., Merchant (*wounded*), and mother.
Sinclair, pensioner.
Smith, Adjutant, 48th Native Infantry (*wounded*).
Smith, Mrs., and three children.
Soppitt, Lieut., 4th Oude Infantry, and wife.
Soule, J.
Staples, Capt., 7th Light Cavalry (*killed*), and wife.
Stevens, Capt., Her Majesty's 32nd Regiment (*killed*), wife and daughter.
Strangways, Capt., 71st (*wounded slightly*), wife and four children (*one child dead*).
Stribling, Quarter-Master, 32nd Regiment.
Stuart, Capt., 3rd Native Infantry, wife and child.
Studdy, Ensign, 32nd Regiment (*killed*).
Sullivan, Hospital Steward, Her Majesty's 32nd Regiment.
Swaries (*wounded*), wife and three children.
Symes, Mr. W., Anderson's Garrison.

Thaine, Lieutenant, 13th Native Infantry.
Thomas, 1st Lieutenant, Artillery, Madras, wife (*dead*), and child.
Thompson, Apothecary, Acting Assistant Surgeon, Oude Irregular Force, wife and three children.

Thornhill, Mr., Assistant Commissioner (*killed*), wife and child (*child dead*).
Thriepland, Clerk, Judicial Garrison (*wounded*).
Todd, Clerk, Judicial Garrison, wife and child.
Tulloch, Lieutenant, 58th Native Infantry, Engineers Department.
Twitchem, Mrs.

Vanrenen, Lieutenant, 2nd in command 9th Oude Infantry.
Velozo, Clerk, Uncovenanted Service, wife and sister.
Vaughan, Uncovenanted Service (*wounded, since dead*), wife and child.
Virtue, Mrs. and Miss.

Wall, Mr. (Martiniere).
Ward, Ensign, 48th Native Infantry.
Ward, Uncovenanted Service.
Warner, Lieutenant, 7th Light Cavalry.
Waterman, Captain, 13th Native Infantry (*wounded*).
Watson, widow of Sergeant Watson, and child.
Watson, Lieutenant, 2nd in command 7th Oude Irregular Infantry, wife and child.
Webb, P. C., Lieutenant, 32nd Regiment (*killed*).
Wells, Surgeon, 48th Native Infantry (*wounded slightly*), wife and child.
Wells, Uncovenanted Service (*killed*), Artillery, wife and child.
Weston, Captain, 65th Native Infantry, Oude Military Police.
Wharton, J., Clerk, Sagos' Garrison.
Wilkinson, Mrs. (*dead*).
Williams, F., Clerk, Sagos' Garrison, wife and two children.
Williams, St. Clare, Extra Assistant-Commissioner, Sagos' Garrison.
Wilson, T. F., Captain, Deputy-Assistant-Adjutant-General (*wounded slightly*).

Wiltshire, Uncovenanted Service (*dead*).

Wittenbaker, Senior, Uncovenanted Service, Financial Garrison, wife and eight children.

Wittenbaker, Junior (*killed*), Financial Garrison.

Woods, widow of Serjeant Woods, and three children (*one child dead*).

Worsley, Ensign, 71st Native Infantry.

Yerbury, Commissariat Dept., wife and two children.

THE END.

Printed in Dunstable, United Kingdom